D0219112

RAP
AND HIP HOP
CULTURE

RAP AND HIP HOP CULTURE

FERNANDO OREJUELA

New York | Oxford

OXFORD UNIVERSITY PRESS

Oxford University Press is a department of the University of Oxford.
It furthers the University's objective of excellence in research,
scholarship, and education by publishing worldwide.

Oxford   New York
Auckland   Cape Town   Dar es Salaam   Hong Kong   Karachi
Kuala Lumpur   Madrid   Melbourne   Mexico City   Nairobi
New Delhi   Shanghai   Taipei   Toronto

With offices in
Argentina   Austria   Brazil   Chile   Czech Republic   France   Greece
Guatemala   Hungary   Italy   Japan   Poland   Portugal   Singapore
South Korea   Switzerland   Thailand   Turkey   Ukraine   Vietnam

Copyright © 2015 by Oxford University Press.

For titles covered by Section 112 of the US Higher Education
Opportunity Act, please visit www.oup.com/us/he for the
latest information about pricing and alternate formats.

Published in the United States of America by
Oxford University Press
198 Madison Avenue, New York, NY 10016
http://www.oup.com

Oxford is a registered trade mark of Oxford University Press.

All rights reserved. No part of this publication may be reproduced,
stored in a retrieval system, or transmitted, in any form or by any means,
electronic, mechanical, photocopying, recording, or otherwise,
without the prior permission of Oxford University Press.

Library of Congress Cataloging-in-Publication Data
Orejuela, Fernando.
  Rap and hip hop culture / Fernando Orejuela.
    pages cm
  Includes bibliographical references and index.
  ISBN 978-0-19-998773-3 (alk. paper)
1. Rap (Music)--History and criticism. 2. Music--Social aspects. I. Title.
  ML3531.O74 2014
  782.421649--dc23

                                                      2014003480

CONTENTS

Chapter 4 | Rap's African and African American Cultural Roots   **40**

Chapter 5 | **Old-School DJs and MCs** 57

Chapter 6 | **The Golden Era** 80

Chapter 7 | Hardcore: "Message Rap" and "Gangsta Rap"   **107**

Chapter 8 | Hardcore II: Gangsta in the '90s and Responses from Within the Rap Community

135

Chapter 9 | Hip Hop Culture and Rap Music in the Second Millennium

173

PREFACE

"The changing same": a quick, user-friendly definition for the concept of tradition penned by Amiri Baraka (a.k.a. LeRoi Jones) in 1968. It is a key expression that will guide the reader in the following pages just as it has guided the author. As a fan and student of hip hop culture, I have experienced and traced the changes since the days that I heard my first rap song play on the radio in 1979. Many sonic innovations and subcultural transmutations followed. Some of those changes I have felt in the actions of the artists from my generation, such as Snoop Dogg reinventing himself as Snoop Lion, or Jay-Z removing the hyphen from his name, or the maturation of the youngest generation, teenaged artists like Earl Sweatshirt dropping his sociopathic, absurdist rhymes for stories dealing with serious issues such as depression on his debut solo album, *Doris* (2013). Other changes, such as the ways artists have transformed the recording industry and modes of self-production, are more jarring. From a generational standpoint, it is hard not to miss and yearn for holding the vinyl in my hands, placing the needle on the record, studying the art on the 12x12 album cover, reading the liner notes, and letting the songs play until it was time to flip the record over to side 2. Fast-forward to the summer of 2013, and hip hop product is digital and sites for purchasing it are virtual. As a sign of this revolutionary change, Samsung made a $5 million deal with rapper Jay Z (as Jay-Z) to release his 2013 album *Magna Carta Holy Grail* for owners of Samsung Galaxy smartphones to download before the release date. As a result, the album went platinum even before it was formally made available to the public.

Those changes mostly reflect access to the musical product. The sameness is ever present, persisting in the structure and performance of the music, whether we are talking about *Magna Carta Holy Grail* by veteran Jay Z or the 2013 *Electric Highway* mixtape by Chicago newcomer Rockie Fresh. Through the flow of their lyrical narratives, the percussive musicality central to the soundscape, and the proud boastfulness of their rap personae, they maintain the cultural spirit of rap music since its inception. It is this dynamic aspect of hip hop culture and its most dominant element, rap music, that fascinates me and the students that I have taught. It is, in part, for those students and prospective students that I put together this book.

I began teaching hip hop studies in 1998 as an associate instructor for the rap music course created by my mentor Portia K. Maultsby and then became the professor of record for a large lecture in 2003. The course fully crossed over alongside the music, which has become *the* pop music of this generation at least since the late 1990s. While the genre's popularity grew, I was observing students distancing themselves from cultural components that created the hip hop forms and the music's core aesthetics. My students' love for "gangsta rap" and discussion of current trends and issues suffered from a general lack of historical and cultural awareness. The more we treated hip hop with color-blind lenses and the more homogenized the sound became, the more difficult it was to discuss what hip hop was, is, and is yet to be.

That became the inspiration for this survey study so that the students could have a foundation on which to build their discussions on the current state of hip hop. Basic knowledge of poetics and folk narrative opens the door to H. Samy Alim's treatment of linguistics and black vernacular. A general comprehension of abstract ideas like community, youth commingling, and gang life allows students to understand the ideas of subculture or underground hip hop communities discussed in the works of Anthony Kwame Harrison or Marcyliena Morgan.

Hip hop studies has grown and continues to grow in the academy, and courses being taught on college campuses are no longer isolated to programs in African American studies, minority studies, folklore, ethnomusicology, or culture studies. There are courses being taught nationwide in traditional departments of English, art, history, and music—even in music schools like the one here at Indiana University, where I was once told by a colleague that I could teach rap as poetry, but "don't call it music." Now that hip hop studies is a cross-disciplinary and interdisciplinary academic enterprise, let us, as students, discuss the current canon being created in print, on digital video, and on the Internet.

One problem that students of hip hop culture face is in defining the term "hip hop" itself. Fans, journalists, artists, scholars, and the like all use the term "hip hop" reductively in everyday conversations. We continue to focus on two hip hop brands of music that became dominant in the 1990s and continue to the present: hardcore rap and R&B–rap fusion. As an umbrella term to refer to music alone, it fails to describe the scope of the culture, its original four elements (DJing, MCing, breaking [b-boying], and graffiti), ideology, historical figures, and current population that remain relevant to hip hop's mission. Fans, hip hop heads, casual listeners of rap, industry moguls, music scholars, and average Janes and Joes all believe to be able to identify the "real" hip hop, yet the definitions are not in perfect sync with each other. There are no gatekeepers and that is not the purpose of this book. The purpose is rather to provide a few tools to discuss and debate definitions, histories, characteristics of the art forms, and movements that have taken place since this subculture arose. In the first chapter, we address some of these foundational questions and lay out the scope for the text that follows.

I also understand that contemporary students view books as an archaic relic of the past, the same way they question the rationale behind purchasing an entire album as opposed to just a couple of singles that are standouts or hits. While it might be cost-effective to download "Nuthin' but a 'G' Thang" for $1.29, the consumer misses the holistic intention of the artist, the comprehensive story of a particular time and place, the encapsulated cinematic vision of South-Central Los Angeles life that Dr. Dre created on the album *The Chronic*, which was the source for this song. It's as if we crop the singular image of the creation of Adam to represent the whole narrative of Michelangelo's Sistine Chapel fresco panels: iconic representation, perhaps, but not enough.

Rather than studying the history of hip hop as an entirety, it is more convenient to look for single items of interest on any Internet search vehicle, as we encounter them in our daily lives, haphazardly, on a whim, or while we are reading a volume such as this one. In fact, many of the songs and videos mentioned through these pages are readily available on a number of audio and video websites, and it would be beneficial to listen to them as you read. However, not all Internet resources are peer reviewed or edited for content. There are strong resources, such as Davey D's Hip Hop Corner (www.daveyd.com), which has been operating since the latter part of the 1990s. Davey D was an MC in the 1970s and has been actively engaged with historical figures in hip hop culture since even before the age of the World Wide Web. He maintains a rich archive of interviews that are excellent resources for any fan or student of hip hop culture.

When reading interviews and other unedited materials on websites, it's important to examine critically the accounts of hip hop's emergence and other information you may find. For example, at the 1989 New Music Seminar, Davey D interviews DJ Kool Herc and asks, "What year did the [hip hop culture] happen?" Herc replied at that time, "1970"—a date that is significantly different from all other accounts. Faulty memory? A generalization—as in, "the 1970s"? Or is Herc, in fact, referring to the seedling parties that led to the first party he and his sister threw at 1520 Sedgwick Avenue—a result of putting together his father's PA system? We as readers are left to critique and compare Herc's response with other interviews and historical accounts.

Similarly, *Wikipedia*, the collaboratively edited Internet encyclopedia, is typically the first place masses of Internet users around the world search for immediate information. While much of the information can be accurate, subtle inaccuracies can change the significance of artistic endeavors and the history of this culture. As a dynamic resource, *Wikipedia* can be updated and corrected over time, but that also means that inaccuracies or misinformation can be introduced that may go unchallenged. Informed students will always compare several sources and check any assertion in order to come up with their own interpretation of the claims and counterclaims made by various hip hop artists.

This book is broad in scope yet meant to be very concise. One of the purposes is to provide a survey of the music styles chronologically with some representative listening guides for the reader to follow. The second, and the one I am most committed to, is engaging the reader with hip hop culture and exploring the roles of music and art in human life: the social, cultural, subcultural, and historical. A text like this one is not meant to fossilize the music or the culture into just one thing; quite the contrary. As a gateway, this book opens up discussion about hip hop culture specifically but also American culture generally as those intersections and discoveries of new intricacies about human interaction, communication, and art come into question.

My students have been an important reason why I put this book together, but it is my goal to welcome any "student" of hip hop culture to analyze the relationship between music and culture. The other reason that I have invested my life studying hip hop scenes and youth subcultures has been personal. First, I am a fan. Of the four elements most commonly accepted—graffiti, breakdancing, DJing, and MCing—I fell in love with graffiti and dance first and listened to rap music recreationally until I heard my first Public Enemy song in the '80s. Rap music became something else. It was that introduction to lyrical activism that connected me to the "fifth" element of hip hop culture that has been most fervently articulated and advocated by Afrika Bambaataa, a godfather of hip hop, and KRS-One, a second-generation, conscious MC: knowledge.

"Knowledge" as a potential fifth element of hip hop speaks to the idea of self-awareness and self-sufficiency. While it is an ideal—maybe even idealistic—the earliest culture tends to be romanticized by members of the community, fans, and scholars alike. To a degree, I am probably guilty of that, too. I fear that I might be describing a utopia within the virtual walls of American ghettos. However, this youth music subculture did not create a utopia. Not everyone involved in the original hip hop community bought into the mission. To be clear, almost all the DJs had a security team of ex–gang members present to protect themselves and help control the crowd. Some of the DJs carried guns to protect their gear; some MCs used the parties to sell marijuana. These dichotomies perhaps reflected best the environment's balance of violence and peace, escapism and reality.

While the calls of "No violence!" might not have been universally accepted or practiced, they were heard. These calls were not about pacifism, but activism: a call to react to the social injustices and institutionalized racism through this party scene. Forty years since the historic hip hop parties began, fifty-plus years since antidiscrimination laws and affirmative action were implemented, black and Latino unemployment, poverty, and homelessness are about twice that of whites. In 2011, more than half of all prisoners still comprise blacks and Latinos despite the fact that these two only make up approximately one-quarter of the US population. Among inmates between the ages of 18 and 20, black males were imprisoned at more than nine times the rate of white males. African Americans are sent to prison for drug offenses at ten times the rate of whites. Youth-on-youth violence and homicide remain too high in American inner cities and are often based on grounds of territorialism or some code of masculinity. The fact that in 2013, Florida legislation supported the right of an armed neighbor to track, intimidate, and eventually kill 17-year-old Trayvon Martin because of his color, age, and the hoodie that he was wearing is emblematic of the continuing racism in America and reminiscent of the atrocious 1955 slaying of African American teenager Emmett Till. The ghettos of the 1960s, 1970s, 1980s, and 1990s mentioned in this book maintain today the same demographic, largely black and Latino. The current hip hop generation has a means to combat these perennial American problems through lyrical expression, music production, art, dance, and education, but the bigger problems need to be addressed by the rest of us.

Music and art can express a culture's concerns, needs, and ideas about beauty, but they can also edify and inspire their audience. Studying hip hop culture, whether in a classroom or independently, and reading an introductory book like this one or a scholarly culture critique, might breed a few more hip hop scholars, but, hopefully, more "students" interested in policy making, social action, city and state governance, journalism, and advocacy can come up with solutions to the inequality that continues to plague American society and bring to fruition what my generation has yet to do. Studying hip hop is just one way to begin.

Of course, every scholar studying culture wants to get it right, and it is my hope that I have offered a fair assessment for every kind of reader, whether you are an insider or outsider of this culture. Changes and challenges are to be expected, and I encourage the debate. Even in the time that I wrote this book, new challenges are appearing on the blogosphere with original, South Bronx party scenesters claiming that the "first parties" happened a couple of years before Kool Herc and Cindy's Back-to-School Jam. Other "originals" are stating the music of that earliest period was called "zugga zugga and cutting." Time will tell; I plan to follow through, and I welcome younger scholars to do the same.

ACKNOWLEDGMENTS

Although only one name appears on the cover of this book, it could not have been born without the assistance and guidance of many individuals. To the students of my hip hop courses, past and present, it is your active engagement that inspired me to create a book for people from diverse backgrounds and across disciplines. For the faculty and staff members in my home department of folklore and ethnomusicology, as well as my adjunct homes in African American and African diaspora studies and Latino studies, your backing and encouragement made all the difference in my teaching and scholarly practice. I am grateful to the reviewers who participated in this project, Anthony Ratcliff, William E. Smith, and Glenn Pillsbury, for their constructive suggestions on early drafts of this book. I am also indebted to the anonymous readers whose comments and suggestions were extremely helpful, especially as I tried to speak across disciplinary lines. There is a select group of graduate students and former undergraduate students that helped me overcome discursive obstacles when concepts were not always clear. They include Alex Goulet, Ben Jackson, Eric Morales, Marsha Horsely, Mark Miyake, Caralee Jones, Malaika Baxa, Josephine McRobbie, Eric Bindler, Julián Carrillo, Walter Tucker, Dorothy Berry, Maria Trogolo, Floyd Hobson, and June Evans. More thanks than I can express in this short paragraph must go to Langston Collin Wilkins for our regular discussion on hip hop culture and your own ethnographic project on the Houston hip hop scene, and to Matt Alley for your musicianship and assistance putting together the Listening Guides in this text. Portia K. Maultby's immeasurable love, support, and mentorship for this project and all the projects that led me here cannot be repaid, but I hope you see your influence in the pages that follow. Jerry Stasny, for your love and support, especially with the number of iTune gift cards you sent my way when research funds came short, I thank you from the bottom of my heart. I am lucky to have worked with the team at Oxford University Press, Emily Schmid, Theresa Stockton, and Teresa Nemeth, whose commitment to precision in writing and book design helped make *Rap and Hip Hop Culture* sharper and clearer. Lastly, Richard Carlin for introducing me to a new way of writing, one that was very different from the ethnographic training I had. I hope that your patience, support, tutelage, and friendship are reflected on every page of this book. You are a most exceptional editor and guide.

The author gratefully acknowledges permission from the following sources to reprint material:

"Accordian." Words & Music by Otis Jr. Jackson & Daniel Dumile Thompson. © Copyright 2004 Lord Dihoo Music. Nettwerk One Music Limited. This Arrangement © Copyright 2014 Nettwerk One Music Limited. All Rights Reserved. International Copyright Secured. Used by Permission of Music Sales Limited.

"Before Redemption." Lyrics recorded by Gospel Gangstaz. By Charles Washington, Ed Valenciano © 1994 Broken Songs, Italy Tevra Music (admin Broken Songs, division of Meis Music Group).

"Bird In The Hand." Words and Music by O'Shea Jackson, Mark Jordan, George Clinton, William Collins, Ronald Dunbar, Garry Shider and Donnie Sterling. © 1991 UNIVERSAL MUSIC CORP., GANGSTA BOOGIE MUSIC, STREET KNOWLEDGE PRODUCTIONS, INC., BRIDGEPORT MUSIC, INC., EMI BLACKWOOD MUSIC INC. and BRITTOLESE MUSIC. All Rights for GANGSTA BOOGIE MUSIC Controlled and Administered by UNIVERSAL MUSIC CORP. All Rights for BRITTOLESE MUSIC Administered by EMI APRIL MUSIC INC. All Rights Reserved Used by Permission - contains elements of "Big Bang Theory" Words and Music by George Clinton, Ronald Dunbar and Donnie Sterling and "Bop Gun" Words and Music by George Clinton, William Collins and Garry Shider. *Reprinted by Permission of Hal Leonard Corporation.*

"Earl." Written by: Thebe Kgositsile & Tyler Okonma. © 2010 Sony/ATV Music Publishing LLC, Randomblackdude Publishing, Golf Wang Steak Sauce. All rights on behalf Sony/ATV Music Publishing, LLC, Randomblackdude Publishing & Golf Wang Steak Sauce administered by Sony/ATV Music Publishing LLC, 8 Music Square West, Nashville, TN 37203. All rights reserved. Used by Permission.

"Excursions." Words and Music by Kamaal Ibn John Fareed, Ali Shaheed Jones-Muhammad and Malik Izaak Taylor. © 1991 by Universal Music–Z Tunes LLC and Jazz Merchant Music. All Rights Administered by Universal Music–Z Tunes LLC International Copyright Secured. All Rights Reserved. *Reprinted by Permission of Hal Leonard Corporation.*

"Forever." Words and Music by Aubrey Graham, Kanye West, Matthew Samuels, Dwayne Carter and Marshall Mathers. © 2009 EMI Blackwood Music Inc., Love Write LLC, Please Gimme My Publishing Inc., Sony/ATV Tunes LLC, 1damentional Publishing LLC, Songs Of Universal, Inc., Shroom Shady Music, Warner-Tamerlane Publishing Corp.and Young Money Publishing, Inc. All Rights on behalf of EMI Blackwood Music Inc., Love Write LLC, Please Gimme My Publishing Inc., Sony/ATV Tunes LLC and 1damentional Publishing LLC Administered by Sony/ATV Music Publishing LLC, 424 Church Street, Suite 1200, Nashville, TN 37219. All Rights on behalf of Shroom Shady Music Controlled and Administered by Songs Of Universal, Inc. All Rights on behalf of Young Money Publishing, Inc. Administered by Warner-Tamerlane Publishing Corp. International Copyright Secured. All Rights Reserved. *Reprinted by Permission of Hal Leonard Corporation.*

"I Need Love." Words and Music by James Todd Smith, Dwayne Simon, Bobby Ervin, Darryl Pierce and Steven Ettinger. © 1987, 1995 Sony/ATV Music Publishing LLC, LL Cool J Music and Universal Music Corp. All Rights on behalf of Sony/ATV Music Publishing LLC and LL Cool J Music Administered by Sony/ATV Music Publishing LLC, 8 Music Square West, Nashville, TN 37203. International Copyright Secured. All Rights Reserved. *Reprinted by Permission of Hal Leonard Corporation.*

"It's Good To Be The Queen." Words and Music by Sylvia Robinson and William P. Wingfield Copyright © 1982 GAMBI MUSIC, INC., TWENTY NINE BLACK MUSIC and MAJOR SEVEN LTD. All Rights for GAMBI MUSIC, INC. and TWENTY NINE BLACK MUSIC Administered by SONGS OF UNIVERSAL, INC. All Rights for MAJOR SEVEN LTD. in the U.S. and Canada Administered by UNIVERSAL–SONGS OF POLYGRAM INTERNATIONAL, INC. All Rights Reserved. Used by Permission. *Reprinted by Permission of Hal Leonard Corporation.*

"Jesse." Words and Music by Melvin Glover and Sylvia Robinson. © 1984 GAMBI MUSIC, INC. All Rights Administered by SONGS OF UNIVERSAL, INC. All Rights Reserved. Used by Permission. *Reprinted by Permission of Hal Leonard Corporation.*

"Just Don't Give A Fuck." Written by Marshall B. Mathers; Mark Randy Bass; Jeffrey Irwin Bass. Published by Eight Mile Style LLC. Administered by Kobalt Music Services America Inc.

"Monster." Words and Music by Kanye West, Mike Dean, William Roberts, Shawn Carter, Onika Maraj, Justin Vernon, Malik Jones, Patrick Reynolds and Ross Rick. © 2010 EMI Blackwood Music Inc., Please Gimme My Publishing Inc., Papa George Music, Sony/ATV Songs LLC, 4 Blunts Lit At Once, Carter Boys Music, Chrysalis Music, Money Mack Music, Harajuku Barbie Music, Plain Pat What Up Publishing, Universal Music Corp. and Jabriel Iz Myne. All Rights on behalf of EMI Blackwood Music Inc., Please Gimme My Publishing Inc., Papa George Music, Sony/ATV Songs LLC and 4 Blunts Lit At Once Administered by Sony/ATV Music Publishing LLC, 424 Church Street, Suite 1200, Nashville, TN 37219. All Rights on behalf of Carter Boys Music Administered by WB Music Corp. All Rights on behalf of Chrysalis Music Administered by Chrysalis Music Group Inc., a BMG Chrysalis company. All Rights on behalf of Money Mack Music and Harajuku Barbie Music Administered by Songs Of Universal, Inc. All Rights on behalf of Plain Pat What Up Publishing Administered by Universal Music Corp. All Rights on behalf of Jabriel Iz Myne Controlled and Administered by Universal Music Corp. International Copyright Secured. All Rights Reserved. *Reprinted by Permission of Hal Leonard Corporation.*

"One Love." Words and Music by Jalil Hutchins and Lawrence Smith. © 1986 Universal Music–Z Tunes LLC, Funk Groove Music Publishing Co. and Imagem London Ltd. All Rights for Funk Groove Music Publishing Co. Controlled and Administered by Universal Music–Z Tunes LLC. All Rights for Imagem London Ltd. in the U.S. and Canada Administered by Universal Music–Z Tunes LLC International Copyright Secured. All Rights Reserved. *Reprinted by Permission of Hal Leonard Corporation.*

"Rappers Delight." Written by Bernard Edwards & Nile Rodgers © 1979 Sony/ATV Music Publishing LLC, Bernard's Other Music. All rights on behalf of Sony/ATV Music Publishing LLC administered by Sony/ATV Music Publishing LLC, 8 Music Square West, Nashville, TN 37203. All rights reserved. Used by Permission.

"Scapegoat." Written by Slug (S. Daley for Upsidedown Heart Music–ASCAP). Used courtesy of Rhymesayers Entertainment, LLC.

"Self Destruction." Words and Music by James Smith, Lawrence Parker, Derrick Jones, Joseph Williams, Dwight Myers, Carlton Ridenhour, Arnold Hamilton, Glenn Bolton, Douglas Davis, Mohandas Dewese, William Drayton and Marvin Wright. Copyright ©1991 by Universal Music–Z Songs and Universal Music–Z Tunes LLC. International Copyright Secured. All Rights Reserved. *Reprinted by Permission of Hal Leonard Corporation.*

"Shine." From the Alan Lomax Collection at the American Folklife Center, Library of Congress, Courtesy of the Association for Cultural Equity.

"Sippin' On Some Syrup." Written by Paul Beauregard, Jordan Houston, Bun B and Pimp C © 2000 TEFNOISE PUBLISHING LLC (BMI)/Administered by BUG MUSIC, UNIVERSAL MUSIC–Z TUNES LLC and PIMP MY PEN INTERNATIONAL. All Rights for PIMP MY PEN INTERNATIONAL. Administered by UNIVERSAL MUSIC–Z TUNES LLC. All Rights Reserved. Used by Permission. *Reprinted by Permission of Hal Leonard Corporation.*

"Takeover." Words and Music by Rodney Lemay, Lawrence Parker, Shawn Carter, Kanye West, Eric Burdon, Alan Lomax, Bryan Chandler, Jim Morrison, Raymond Manzarek, Robert Krieger and John Densmore. © 2001 LONDON MUSIC U.K., UNIVERSAL MUSIC–Z TUNES LLC, BDP MUSIC, EMI BLACKWOOD MUSIC INC., LIL LULU PUBLISHING, UNICHAPPELL MUSIC INC., SLAMINA MUSIC, LUDLOW MUSIC, INC., CARBERT MUSIC INC. and DOORS MUSIC CO. All Rights for LONDON MUSIC U.K. Controlled and Administered by UNIVERSAL-POLYGRAM INTERNATIONAL PUBLISHING, INC. All Rights for BDP MUSIC Controlled and Administered by UNIVERSAL MUSIC–Z TUNES LLC All Rights for LIL LULU PUBLISHING. Controlled and Administered by EMI BLACKWOOD MUSIC INC. All Rights for SLAMINA MUSIC Controlled and Administered by UNICHAPPELL MUSIC INC. All Rights Reserved. Used by Permission - contains elements of "Sound Da Police" Words and Music by Rodney Lemay, Lawrence Parker, Eric Burdon, Alan Lomax and Bryan Chandler and "Five To One" Words and Music by Jim Morrison, Raymond Manzarek, Robert Krieger and John Densmore. *Reprinted by Permission of Hal Leonard Corporation.*

"The Breaks." Words and Music by James B. Moore, Lawrence Smith, Kurt Walker, Robert Ford, and Russell Simons. Used courtesy of Music Management, Neutral Gray Music and Funk Groove Music.

"The Revolution Will Not Be Televised." Written by Gil Scott-Heron. Used by permission of Bienstock Publishing Company.

"Through The Wire" by Cynthia Weil. © 2003 Dyad Music Ltd. (BMI) admin. by Wixen Music Publishing, Inc. All Right Reserved. Used by Permission.

CHAPTER 1

WHAT IS HIP HOP?
WHAT IS RAP?

Learning Objectives

When you have successfully completed this chapter, you will be able to:

- Understand the different definitions of hip hop and how they developed.
- Identify the key players in hip hop.
- Describe the development of hip hop from its roots to mainstream success.
- Define hip hop's four key art forms: art, dance, music, language.
- Trace the African and Latino influences in hip hop culture.

The term "hip hop" has been incorporated into the everyday speech of mainstream America for several decades. It has been used in a variety of ways: to describe a musical genre in which the lyrics are delivered in a rapping style; to name sample-driven pop or R&B tunes that have no rapping at all; or to connect to an urban subculture that emerged in the 1970s.

At other times "hip hop" is used to designate dramas or musicals that are framed in urban African American or Latino ghetto experiences, like the 2008 Tony Award–winning musical *In the Heights*. Sometimes "hip hop" is used to describe a category of fiction about gang life and street realities, like 50 Cent's G Unit book series or James Earl Hardy's B-Boy Blues series. Similarly, the term "hip hop poetry" has been used to describe the spoken-word performances of Ursula Rucker or the poets on *Def Poetry Jam* (which aired on HBO between 2002 and 2008) designed to appeal to a younger, modern audience. The name "hip hop fashion" has been used to market the designs of Marc Ecko, Sean John, and Rocawear. Arguably, it is possible to drink hip hop with beverages like 50 Cent's Smartwater, Nelly's Pimp Juice, or Lil Jon's Crunk Juice. For all practical purposes, hip hop has become so pervasive that it has been linked to anything that has the slightest connection to urban, African American pop culture within the last 35 years.

Cover of the "Hip Hop Shop" video.

In a recent visit to a chain megabookstore, I came across an instructional dance DVD, *Hip Hop Shop* (2001), that promotes "Britney [Spears]" and "Justin [Timberlake]" as dance heroes of hip hop culture, while one of the featured instructors on the video, Rock Steady Crew b-boy icon Richie "Crazy Legs" Colón, is barely mentioned on the video's box. I was fascinated by the way products like this disconnect hip hop from its roots. It reminded me of an observation that anthropologist Claude Lévi-Strauss made: "The more a civilization becomes homogenized, the more internal lines of separation become apparent; and what is gained on one level is immediately lost on another" (1978: 20). In this case, the more industry moguls try to homogenize hip hop culture, the more "original school" innovators and particular frames of cultural reference become disconnected from it, further marginalizing hip hop from contemporary enthusiasts and consumers. These examples demonstrate a lack of knowledge or concern for the vibrant culture that created hip hop.

Definitions tend to blur over time and in different cultures; being dynamic in practice, they are not meant to remain static. In the classroom, students have a hard time defining "hip hop," or distinguishing it from rap. To help clarify this issue, we will begin by examining some statements made by practitioners of both art forms, exploring how hip hop culture, like the various musical styles of rap music, has changed. While reading these many different definitions, you should consider your own experiences with hip hop culture and how varied definitions of rap, rap music, rapping, and hip hop are. It is at this point that we can begin to frame what hip hop was, is, and can be.

A Few Definitions to Guide Our Study

Here are three definitions I have developed with my students that have helped guide our approach to the study of hip hop culture:

1. **Hip hop** is the product of inner-city African American, Caribbean, and Latino communities that were plagued by poverty, community decay, and the proliferation of drugs and gang violence in the 1960s and early 1970s.

2. **Hip hop** includes four related art forms—DJing, MCing, breaking (b-boying), and graffiti—that are the product of a unifying ideology.

3. **Rap** is the musical product born of the urban—particularly South Bronx—subculture's DJing and MCing performances, but especially the commercial

product that gave priority to the rapper. Rap music has, at times, been called hip hop by the industry and fans alike, who make little distinction between the culture and the recordable product.

The Key Players

Just as hip hop culture and rap music have developed and changed considerably over the past decades, the key players in the creation of the music and culture have had evolving roles. It is important to differentiate the roles of each performer in a typical crew as this musical art form first developed.

The DJ

Initially, the **DJ** was the party organizer and one-man show accompanied by a couple of friends. He (usually the DJ was a man; women had limited opportunities in the early days of rap, a topic we will return to later) created the musical soundtrack. Besides selecting and playing the music, the DJ originally also stirred up the crowd by shouting phrases designed to inspire people to gather around and enjoy the music.

There were many influences on the development of the DJ. Most often cited as one predecessor were the Jamaican DJs of the 1960s. These DJs built impressive mobile, sound trucks that they could drive to an event. Thanks to their loudspeakers and sophisticated equipment, they could draw considerable crowds for their dance parties. One of the influential early DJs in the Bronx—DJ Kool Herc (see Chapter 5)—was born in Jamaica, and his development of a large sound system for hosting outdoor parties was inspired by the culture he had experienced growing up there and his father's recollections.

Another key ancestor for rap were radio DJs, or "disc jockeys." Prior to World War II, radio stations mostly featured live musical performers. But, after the war, stations began to play recordings to save the cost of hiring musicians. In order to differentiate themselves, they hired "radio personalities" to spin the records and provide information and patter between the selections. In the early days of R&B and rock and roll (late 1940s–mid-1950s), DJs began to develop distinct personalities in order to attract listeners. These DJs copied the teenage slang of the "hip" crowd—that, in turn, copied the slang of jazz and R&B performers—to appeal to their youthful listeners.

Besides mainstream popular radio, there were local stations aimed at particular communities, including African Americans and Latinos. Here, DJs mirrored the community's taste in music and used local slang. DJs such as Jocko Henderson and Jockey Jack Gibson kept listeners' attention with innovative rhymes rapped over music. Drawing on a rich tradition of African American verbal arts (see Chapter 4), these DJs were in turn copied by white announcers like Alan Freed of Cleveland, Ohio, who also began to play R&B records for their suburban audiences and later coined the term "rock and roll."

The DJs played vinyl records using a phonograph, which had three key parts: a tone arm, needle, and turntable. The records had grooves that ran from the outer edge of the disc up to the central label; as the record turned on the turntable, the needle tracked these grooves, sending the signal up the tone arm to an amplifier where the sound was processed and sent to external speakers. Although some composers had experimented with using turntables as musical instruments—notably John Cage in the mid-'40s—few had realized that by manipulating the turntable (spinning it in reverse, stopping it with the hand, or dropping the needle on the breakbeat of a disc) new musical sounds could be created. This "discovery" formed the basis of the DJ culture in hip hop. Grandmaster Flash is generally credited with popularizing many early DJing techniques, including backspinning and scratching (see Chapter 5).

The MC

As the hip hop DJs' job became increasingly complex, it became more difficult for them to handle the duties of announcing and stirring up the crowd and creating the music for dancing. Around 1975, several DJs, including Kool Herc and Grandmaster Flash, began adding **MCs** to their crews to take over the job of speaking to the crowd, so the DJs could focus on music making. These MCs themselves became competitive and began to develop their verbal skills, which eventually evolved into complex raps. The separation of the DJ and MC functions allowed rap to grow where it otherwise might have been left unexplored. (See Chapters 3 and 4 for a discussion of the growth of the MC culture.)

Breaking (B-Boys/B-Girls)

Early on, DJs discovered that certain parts of a song were more attractive to the dancing crowds than others. The instrumental **breaks** that emphasized the rhythm section over the more melodic verses were most popular with the dancers. By stringing together or repeating these popular breaks, the DJs could inspire the crowd to dance. Eventually, DJs built their crews to include dancers who could perform in these breaks; they became known as **b-** (or "break") **boys** and **b-girls**. Breaking changed into a separate, commercial art form, called **breakdancing**, with highly developed routines.

Hip Hop Chronology

In this book, we will study the development of hip hop culture since it first emerged in the late 1970s. Following other histories of this style, we will divide this history into three basic periods:

- Proto–hip hop and old school (1950s–1970s)
- Commercial rap music (1979–mid-1990s)
- Hardcore and the mainstream (mid-1990s–2000s)

Of course, these periods are somewhat flexible and represent only the most broad outline of how hip hop developed.

During the first, proto–hip hop/old school period, hip hop developed from a variety of roots and enjoyed its first commercial success. We will trace the roots of hip hop in African and African American culture and show how it developed in a specific time and place—the 1970s-era South Bronx—to include several related art forms. These art forms broadly speaking are:

- Art (graffiti writing)
- Dance (b-boying/breaking/breakdancing)
- Music (DJing)
- Language (MCing/rapping)

We will trace how gang culture shaped the original social clubs and organizations that became the seedbeds for hip hop and rap music through the work of several key organizers and leaders, including Afrika Bambaataa (see Chapter 2), Kool DJ Herc, and Grandmaster Flash (see Chapter 5). We will take a close look at the related arts of graffiti and breakdancing (see Chapters 3 and 4) as they developed alongside early rap. We will then show how rap became commercialized through the success of early recording groups, notably the Sugarhill Gang, and how this commercialization of the music transformed the culture for participants and the audience (see Chapter 5).

Following this chronology, our attention turns to the second phase of the commercialization of rap music as it crosses over into the mainstream in the mid-1980s. We see the explosion of different styles and hybrid forms, and the domination of hardcore styles, especially as the messages shift from street-reality tales to gangsta rap (see Chapters 6 and 7). The last chapters of the book focus on the most recent periods of hip hop culture, including hardcore and mainstream styles. These chapters address several issues that arose from the dominance of gangsta rap, globalization, and hip hop in the new millennium (see Chapters 8 and 10). What was once an underground musical movement based on beats and rhymes has turned into a "hip hop" that is the most image-driven part of popular music and popular culture.

Hip Hop's Roots

Hip hop culture has its roots in the spread of African and Latino peoples from their original homes to the Americas. Ethnomusicologists, anthropologists, folklorists, and other social scientists define this movement as a diaspora. The term **diaspora** originally referred to the settling of scattered colonies of Jews after their captivity in biblical times. Diaspora is now defined more broadly as the breaking up and scattering of a people, as in the African *diaspora*, in which people settled far from their ancestral homelands—by force in the case of the Americas as a result of the slave trade. However, in addition to recognizing the global-intercultural aspects of a diaspora (e.g., Africans living in the Americas and Caribbean by way of the slave trade), the term is also applied to migrations within a country; for example, the *black diaspora* from the rural South to northern cities in the United States after World War II, and the social, linguistic, economic, cultural, and political causes and consequences associated with this migration.

The diaspora to the Americas began with the capture of millions of Africans. Once the Africans arrived in the Americas, they were transformed from African

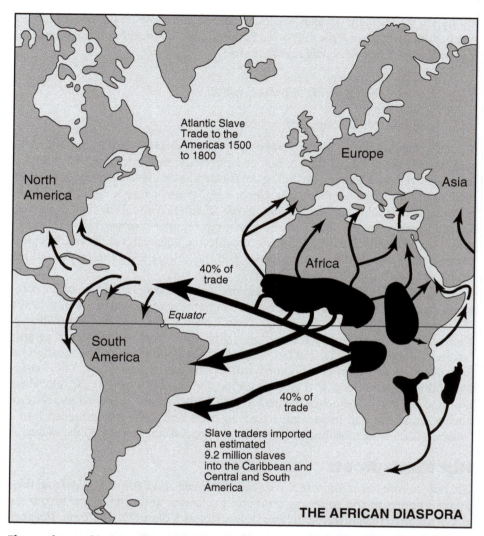

The tracks on this map show the African diaspora during the past 2,000 years, as African people and ideas spread to regions and countries around the world, which scholar Paul Gilroy refers to as the Black Atlantic.

captives into American slaves. Over three to four years, veteran slaves or white overseers trained the new arrivals, even those most resistant to this **domestication process**. The specific system varied from colony to colony. In the northern colonies, slavery existed on a smaller scale, and many of the slaves lived and worked in close proximity to their European slaveholders. However, in the farms and plantations of the South, only house servants, specialty-skilled slaves, and those living on small farms had regular contact with whites. The majority of slaves lived on large farms or plantations located some distance from the master's house. This environment allowed the slaves to maintain traditional cultural values and preserve a sense of self and identity that would provide the foundation for the development of an African American culture. Despite the severe repression and violent enforcement to assimilate European cultural traditions, slaves maintained and creatively transformed their African heritage in these new territories. Their cultural values and traditions sustained them in the struggle against slavery.

Practicing lore and passing it from one generation to the next, from one environment to another, lends itself to culturally valuable and valid variation. As Amiri Baraka (1966) observed, **tradition** is the "changing same." Tradition is dynamic, not static, and can adapt to new situations.

The experience of the enslaved also varied depending on where they settled and which other cultures they encountered. For example, in Brazil a distinctive African-centric dance-battle tradition emerged known as capoeira (see Chapter 4). This tradition was influenced by African practices that the enslaved brought with them, but also mixed with both native and Latino cultures that were already present in Brazil. Other combat traditions that share the same cultural roots were developed in the Caribbean and North America. Similarly, African rhythms mixed with Latino influences in the Caribbean and South American musical landscapes to form the basis of the dance styles of rumba, mambo, tango, and samba.

Hip hop shares this wealth of cultural influences, mixing in subtle and changing ways. So whether we are talking about the outdoor sound system of Jamaica or the Afro-Latin rhythms incorporated into DJ sets, the creative milieu of the South Bronx was flavored by African American, Latin, and Caribbean cultures. Peoples of the African diaspora borrow from each other, revising and recycling traditions. Afrika Bambaataa, a founding father of hip hop culture, articulates the cultural convergence of youth culture, ethnicity, and race in this nascent music scene: "Now one thing people must know, that when we say Black we mean all our Puerto Rican and Dominican brothers. Wherever the hip hop was and the Black was, the Latinos and the Puerto Rican was, too" (quoted in George 1993/2004: 50). Ghettocentricity remains key to understanding the formation of the youth party scene's embryonic journey to hip hop. This differs from the ghetto-thug narratives glorified and glamorized by the commercial rap music industry since the 1990s.

CHAPTER SUMMARY

The phenomenon we call hip hop in the following chapters is not one uniform thing. Between 1973 and 1981, it was a vibrant and ever-developing music subculture that garnered structure from a collective of leaders like Afrika Bambaataa, DJ Kool Herc, and Grandmaster Flash. Interactions between DJs and audiences eventually bore a convergence of styles, with the Bronx style becoming the most dominant DJing party style. It is to this phenomenon that we will speak in the following pages.

STUDY QUESTIONS

1. What are the possible ways to define hip hop?

2. How has hip hop been commercialized by outside forces?

3. Is there a distinction between hip hop and rap? Explain your answer.

4. Identify the primary ethnic groups who lived in the South Bronx and contributed to the emergence of hip hop culture.

5. What are the four defining elements of hip hop?

KEY TERMS

B-boy/b-girl	Diaspora	Hip hop
Break	DJ	MC
Breaking	Domestication process	Rap
Breakdancing		Tradition

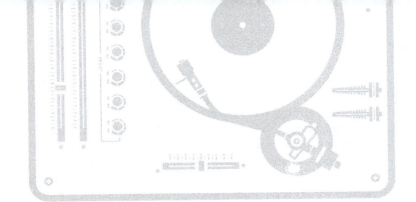

HIP HOP'S GROUND ZERO: THE SOUTH BRONX AND URBAN AMERICA

Learning Objectives

When you have successfully completed this chapter, you will be able to discuss:

- The social, economic, and political conditions that gave birth to hip hop culture.
- The role street-gang culture had in hip hop.
- Afrika Bambaataa's importance in transforming street gangs into social clubs.

> We use to break up the monotony of all the tension building up in the neighborhood. 'Cause there was a lot of times where the only event that everyone had was gangs. Before we were on radio, we would hold parties in the park, and hold 'em hostage, and make 'em have a good time.
>
> —Flavor Flav

Most histories of hip hop culture and rap music cite one neighborhood in New York City—the South Bronx—as the birthplace of these styles. Of course, proto–hip hop, DJing, and rapping cultures were found in other cities, and there were many influences that came together to make the South Bronx an ideal breeding ground for hip hop and rap.

While we will focus on the South Bronx in this chapter, it is important to remember that similar forces were reshaping African American, Caribbean, and Latino cultures throughout the Americas. The graffiti art that would become connected to the South Bronx party scene of the 1970s had its antecedents in Philadelphia as well as every borough in New York City, with contributions made by kids of varying economic class, race, ethnicity, and gender. The South Bronx dance innovation breaking (b-boying/b-girling) was informed by a battle-dance craze coming out of Brooklyn called uprocking, as well as by watching the Los Angeles dance group the Lockers do their thing on television's *Soul Train* in 1972. The art of hip hop DJing has Jamaican outdoor sound systems as just one important antecedent (see Chapter 1). In fact, African American club DJs, such as Grandmaster Flowers (Brooklyn), King Charles (Queens), and Pete DJ Jones (Bronx), were instrumental in establishing a slicker, rapping style on the mic and using dual turntables at adults-only night clubs throughout the city before and *during* the South Bronx youth music scene. However, the DJs in other boroughs were playing funk and soul records in the nightclubs and out in the parks; they did not focus their mixes to include obscure and rare beats or create rhythms or sound effects in their sets by cutting, scratching, or chirping the vinyl.

As we noted in Chapter 1, in its most basic definition, hip hop began as an inner-city subculture that created its own graphic art (graffiti; see Chapter 3), dance (b-boying/breaking; see Chapter 3), and musical styles (DJing and MCing; see Chapters 4 and 5) and was connected to particular cultural, social, and economic contexts. Hip hop is the product of inner-city African American, Caribbean, and Latino communities that were plagued by poverty, community decay, and the proliferation of drugs and gang violence in the 1960s and early 1970s.

The South Bronx: Where Hip Hop Was Born

To understand how that subculture emerged, we must travel back in time to the period following World War II in the South Bronx, New York. Today, the South Bronx is often associated with the urban problems of drugs, crime, and poverty that much of the nation faces. However, prior to WWII, Jews, Italians, Germans, and Irish inhabited the South Bronx, at a time when industrial jobs were plentiful. Indeed, the South Bronx was considered a safe, comfortable working-class neighborhood.

After the war, major changes in policy by the government of New York City resulted in unintended changes to the Bronx and its people. Two notable events transformed the neighborhood that were the outgrowth of the work of city planner Robert Moses, who did much to change the face of New York during the postwar period:

1. The city's slum-clearance projects displaced poor Manhattan families—mostly Puerto Rican—from the Upper West Side (known as Spanish Harlem) to the South Bronx. Although the city promised to relocate these people to subsidized housing, they ended up seeking shelter with friends and family, often living in substandard-sized apartments located in the southern neighborhoods of the Bronx, which already had small pockets of African Americans, West Indians, and Hispanics living there.

2. The Cross Bronx Expressway, which first opened in 1955 and was completed in 1963, cut through the heart of the Bronx. Residents who had lived there for generations began to move out in droves. Those who could not afford to leave—predominantly the working-class and poor African Americans, West Indians, and Latinos—remained in the southernmost neighborhoods. In 1960, there were

350,781 blacks and Hispanics residing in the Bronx, with almost 266,988 living in the South Bronx neighborhoods.

As a result of skyrocketing vacancy rates, some landlords quickly sold their property to slumlords—or hired professional arsonists to burn buildings down so they could collect on insurance money. Landlords could not make a profit off their buildings, because the city strictly controlled the amount they could charge for rent. Meanwhile, many tenants were unable to keep up with their payments. Tenants also set fires so that they would be eligible to move into public housing. In the 1970s, fires in buildings and apartments raged through the

The Cross Bronx Expressway, 1974. The building of the expressway cut neighborhoods apart. The Third Avenue elevated subway ran above the expressway.

Source: Photo by Jack E. Boucher, Library of Congress Prints and Photographs Division

South Bronx. During this time New York City was teetering on the edge of bankruptcy. The city had to cut back on its services (including closing all but one fire station in the South Bronx) and provided little or no support to poor neighborhoods.

Loss of housing and jobs inspired a growth in street gangs. Gang confrontations escalated in the late 1960s, with the year 1968 marking a rise in youth gangs. Some of these youth started terrorizing the neighborhoods and would dominate the South Bronx for the next six years. The introduction of drugs into the neighborhood helped fuel the growth of gangs, whose members often played a key role in the sale and distribution of illegal narcotics.

One of the pioneering South Bronx gangs was called the Savage Seven. They were a group of seven youths between the ages of 12 and 15 that wreaked havoc in the neighborhood surrounding the Bronxdale Community Center. Their activities in the neighborhood received mixed reviews: when they beat up winos and vagabonds that their neighbors did not welcome, they were praised; they were appreciated less when their targets were local business owners, renters, or regular "upright" citizens.

As their ranks swelled, the Savage Seven renamed themselves the Black Spades. They modeled their uniform after the Hell's Angels motorcycle gang: Lee jeans, Garrison belts, and engineer boots, with a large spade emblem sewn onto their jean jackets. The Black Spades' emblems were also spray-painted throughout the hallways of the Bronxdale Projects. Often, gang members' nicknames were scribbled on the walls as well to mark the territory as Black Spades turf and intimidate any trespassers (see the graffiti section below). They took on street names, nicknames that allowed them to adopt a different identity or persona to present to the outside world.

Rival gangs from other projects began to emerge. According to Disco Wiz, a Puerto Rican–Cuban DJ, the Bronx was largely a self-segregated region: "Blacks and Latinos were not united" (2009: 39). Preserves were often established according to ethnic affiliation more so than skin color alone, especially regarding the ways Caribbean youth negotiated "blackness" with "Latino-ness." Latinos—mostly Puerto Ricans, but including Dominicans and Cubans—were the largest population in the South Bronx, but there were also white gangs, such as the Italo-American Golden Guineas that ruled the area north of the Grand Concourse above 183rd Street. Steven Hager reported (1984) that by 1970, estimates of gang membership ran as high as 11,000. Gang-related assaults had risen from 998 in 1960 to 4,256 in 1969. So, why did these kids join gangs?

The Lure of the Gang Lifestyle

In general, a **gang** can be defined as a loosely organized group of individuals who collaborate for social reasons. Gangs provide protection to members and help give them status in a larger society that has often denied them a seat at the table. For gang scholar Eric Schneider, a key element in defining a gang is engagement in a pattern of conflict with other gangs or society as a whole.

Since the 1960s, scholarship on **gang culture** has focused primarily on urban, minority populations, typically African Americans and Latinos living in the poorest, inner-city neighborhoods, and ignored the activities of white gangs. Gangs have been viewed primarily as a social problem. Furthermore, there is a long-standing debate on a single definition of the street gang, among researchers and gang members themselves. Many of the youth in the South Bronx referred to their organizations as clubs and not gangs.

In order to understand the gang mentality better, let's consider what gang scholar Steve Nawojczyk calls the "Three R's": reputation, respect, and retaliation. All three will remain important to the foundational ethic that will give us the hip hop clubs.

One's **reputation** is of critical concern to individual gang members, as is the reputation of the gang as a whole. To obtain a reputation a gang must prove itself to be tough, powerful, and numerous. Getting "jumped in" is a common initiation practice for gang membership in which full gang members beat a prospective member until the leader calls for it to end. This ritual and what it exactly entails varies from gang to gang. The purpose is to evaluate a prospective member's toughness and willingness to fight. Toughness, in theory, translates into the prospective member's willingness to defend the group and maintain a strong and fierce reputation. Once accepted into the gang, the new initiate is embraced by members. These intimate actions—extremely violent at one end and highly affectionate at the other—are meant to bond the members together as a family. Earning a reputation is arguably less problematic than maintaining a reputation. Once a gang member has earned and maintained a "**rep**," plenty of young men and women will challenge him or her to defend it. This component of gang culture is important as it will translate into the battle-culture ethic of hip hop culture.

Respect is sought not only for the individual but also for one's gang, family, and territory. All gangs and individual members want and need respect. Some gang members carry their desire for it to the extreme. A gang might require its members to show disrespect, or to "**dis**," rival gang members. This concept is reflected in the battle culture of hip hop b-boys (breakdancers) and MCs in particular. Once a dis has been issued and witnessed, then the third "R" becomes evident.

Retaliation, or revenge, is not only warranted, it is expected. For example, if a dis is issued, the crew determines what needs to be done in order to keep the reputation of the insulted member and gang intact. This may occur immediately or follow a delay in order to plan and obtain the necessary equipment or weapons to complete the retaliatory strike.

Many acts of violence were the result of bad drug deals or infringement on a rival gang's turf or drug territory. While drug trafficking might have helped finance the economic survival of some gangs, gang chronicler James Haskins (1974) noted that many members turned to heroin and marijuana because of their accessibility and their potential to relieve the misery of poverty and the pressure of gang life. However, gang scholar Eric Schneider (1999) claims that gangbangers did not tolerate heroin addicts among their members for two reasons: (1) heroin users would not be effective fighters, and (2) using heroin would affect the gang's profits considerably.

The Gang Leader

Gangs generally have a leader or group of leaders who issue orders and benefit from the gang's activities; they also bring a sense of order to a chaotic world. Within the context of this era, a prez (president), a VP (vice president), a warlord (a sergeant-at-arms), a peacemaker (one who attempts to pacify a rivalry), and a masher (best street fighter) led most organizations. Youth gangs were by no means kids' play. Their orientation was turf protection and brotherhood but also drug trading and general thuggery. Nonetheless, the need to organize, recognize members' individual contributions, and compete would also inform the alternative social clubs that emerged after 1973.

From Street Gangs to Social Clubs

Some gang members sought to improve social relationships between gangs and to improve inner-city life. Several became involved in community self-help projects funded by government grants. These activities were influenced by the self-help, community empowerment, and black pride ideologies of the **Black Power movement**. In the late '60s and early '70s, organizations like the Black Panthers promoted these ideas through slogans like "Black is beautiful." Others formed **social clubs** designed to encourage constructive rather than violent forms of competition. From these clubs emerged various forms of creative expression such as graffiti writing, breaking, DJing, and MCing.

By the early '70s, gang membership started to wane. Some claim it was the girls who left first; others grew tired of the potential for death or imprisonment. Perhaps more importantly, the decline could be attributed to the 1971 truce initiated by members of the Puerto Rican gang the Ghetto Brothers, in collaboration with other gangs and the police. The Ghetto Brothers were among the earliest gangs to promote peace and self-sufficiency in the neighborhood through live performances by their salsa-rock band and the release of their album *Power Fuerza* in 1971. These were early attempts at establishing a healthier and more stable environment for the youth in the area; nevertheless, gang activity resumed and would peak in 1973.

Spawning from gang members' need for respect, a strong reputation, and re-taliation, the spirit of aggressive competition carried over into these new gang-alternative social clubs and continued to be an integral part of hip hop. For example, fights between rival gangs could be substituted with "battles" between rival b-boy crews (dancers of the breaking or b-boying tradition) to determine who had the better skills; an audience of peers evaluated performances and deter-mined a winner. The "apache line" used to jump gang members in and out would be utilized in a b-boy battle, but now the initiate would travel down the line to do "battle" with each member verbally (not physically). Those who earned a "rep" eventually became targeted by up-and-coming b-boys in an effort to usurp the current "b-boy king" or crew in the neighborhood—very similar to the gang cul-ture from which many of these kids came. Battles also took place between the growing numbers of DJs.

Gang leadership roles were also transformed (recall the gang titles of prez, VP, masher, peacemaker, and warlord). The desire to be a part of a group remained at the core of creating crews, and these crews assigned leadership roles to those with supe-rior skills or the ability to manage a group of energetic teenagers. While these clubs emerged and began to organize over time into crews for DJs, b-boys, graffiti writers, and lastly MCs, gangs, poverty, crime, and other bad elements of the ghetto life did not disappear, nor did every crew member totally give up those grimier aspects of street life. However, the attempt made by these social clubs to move in a positive direction had a profound influence on the growth of hip hop.

A key person in transforming gang into club culture was organizer/DJ Afrika Bambaataa (see Chapter 5). Inspired by the hero of the 1964 film *Zulu*, Afrika Bambaataa (a.k.a. Bambaataa Kahim Aasim) renamed himself after the rebel Zulu chief of the turn of the 19th century who fought against the British imperialists. Although he was a high-ranking member of the Black Spades, Bambaataa spent most of his time scouring record bins and collecting obscure R&B records as well as rock and roll, jazz, and German electronic music . . . anything he could find with a good beat.

Although Bambaataa did his share of gang-related activities, as a gang member he was also known for his communication and diplomacy skills. Former Black Spade Jay McGluery told journalist Steven Hager that Bambaataa knew at least five mem-bers from every gang in the South Bronx. In times of conflict, he would try to squelch all grievances among the gangs before they turned to violence. Because Bambaataa's mother was a nurse and often not in the apartment, his home became a center for his friends to party. His record collection was the heart and soul of his house parties.

When he was 12 years old, Bambaataa spent much of his free time at the Black Panther Information Center, and he later became involved with the Nation of Islam. Both movements introduced him to a soulful positivism that was reflected in the music of performers like James Brown (e.g., songs like "Say It Loud, I'm Black and I'm Proud" and "I'll Get It Myself," which promoted self-sufficiency and pride in African American heritage) and Sly and the Family Stone (the peace-and-harmony lyrics of songs like "Everyday People" and "Stand"). Bambaataa had also participated in the Truce of 1971 as a representative of the Black Spades.

These associations also influenced him to be a proactive member of the community and helped him frame an ideology of self-actualization through a performing group, the Bronx River Organization, which was made up of former Black Spades. This new organization had a motto: "This is an organization. We are not a gang. We are a family. Do not start trouble. Let trouble come to you, then fight like hell" (quoted in Chang 2005: 96). The Bronx River Organization was an alternative to the Black Spades and eventually became the model for the emergence of the hip hop community.

In 1974, the Bronx River Organization was renamed the Universal Zulu Nation, and it remains active to the present day. This social club first brought together:

Afrika Bambaataa and his crew, ca. 1980. Top, l. to r.: G.L.O.B.E., Bambaataa, DJ Jazzy J. Bottom, l. to r.: Pow Wow, Mr. Biggs.

Source: © Pictorial Press Ltd/Alamy

- Graffiti writers
- Mobile DJs
- B-boys and b-girls (breakers, known outside the community as breakdancers)
- MCs (later known as rappers)

These four elements formed the core of an emergent music-centered youth movement.

This new culture—known as "hip hop" today—produced both entertainment for inner-city youth and a new forum for competitive nonviolent gang warfare. At block and house parties, in schoolyards, and later in clubs, current and former gang members used their creative talents to transform their marginal existence into a meaningful social and cultural experience. By 1977 hip hop culture, especially DJing and MCing (the foundations of rap music), dominated the expressions of inner-city youth.

CHAPTER SUMMARY

The South Bronx is generally viewed as the birthplace of hip hop culture. In the post–World War II era, a combination of slum-clearance projects in Manhattan and the construction of the Cross Bronx Expressway led to a decline in the area. Displaced blacks and Latinos replaced earlier ethnic groups, and housing fell into the hands of slumlords who did little to maintain their properties. Lack of jobs and the introduction of drugs in the mid-'60s led to a growth in gang culture. Gangs were built on the "Three R's" of reputation, respect, and retaliation. Gangs helped give individuals a sense of belonging to a greater organization, reinforcing self-respect and providing protection in an often hostile environment. In the early '70s, individuals like Afrika Bambaataa helped transform gang cultures into social clubs that became the breeding ground for the new hip hop culture. Bambaataa's Bronx River Organization (later the Universal Zulu Nation) brought together the four basic elements of hip hop culture: graffiti writers, mobile DJs, b-boys and b-girls, and MCs. Gang life did not come to an end, but it is important to recognize the youth in these violent neighborhoods who sought and constructed alternatives to it. This fledgling subculture was supported by a mission to not let each other become another statistic.

STUDY QUESTIONS

1. Prior to World War II, which ethnic groups dominated the South Bronx neighborhoods?

2. Explain how the city's plans for improvements changed the racial and economic composition of the neighborhood.

3. How and why do we make a distinction between youth gangs and youth clubs? Discuss other possible ways to identify an organized group of young people.

4. What were the social and cultural functions of the early party scene as its members transitioned away from street-gang mentality?

5. How did Afrika Bambaataa take a leadership role in transforming the gang the Black Spades into an organization promoting nonviolent activities and self-expression?

KEY TERMS

Black Power movement

"Dis" (disrespect)

Gang/gang culture

Reputation/rep

Respect

Retaliation

Social clubs

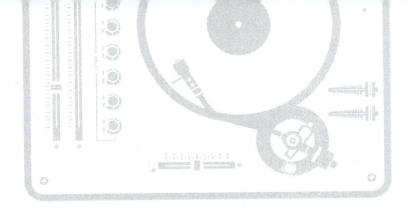

CHAPTER 3

GRAFFITI ART AND BREAKING

Learning Objectives

When you have successfully completed this chapter, you will be able to:

- Discuss the art of graffiti in the hip hop tradition.
- Describe how graffitists were accepted into the world of fine arts and how this affected their work.
- Trace the development of b-boying and breakdancing from their African and African American roots.
- Understand the importance of the dance-fight traditions in African culture and how they have spread through various locations.

Graffiti Art

Although DJing started the party culture, graffiti writers had the greatest initial impact on the mainstream public. An important element of hip hop culture, graffiti tagging was adopted from the street gangs to become a means of both asserting self-identity and spreading the hip hop message across the city.

The term **graffiti** typically refers to short, anonymous, unauthorized writing or drawing on a surface that is meant to be seen by the general public. Graffiti can be a slogan, limerick, or epithet scribbled on a bathroom stall—known as *latrinalia*. Graffiti can also be a scrawl of someone's name or nickname on the side of a building. This form of graffiti is known as **tagging** because the artist is making his or her presence known and proclaiming his or her identity through a unique mark. Graffiti is always public, visually confrontational, and illegal. Some graffiti can also be elaborate enough to be viewed as an art form. In the hip hop context, stylized lettering, such as bubble letters or interlocking letters, and dramatic color schemes belong to the sophisticated outlaw graffiti artist who referred to their style as **writing**. These young pioneers would not call their work graffiti art until they received attention from the media in the late 1970s and early 1980s.

Why was it that graffiti had such a great impact beyond the Bronx in the early years of hip hop culture? Graffiti writing was placed on public and private property, especially subway cars that traveled throughout the many boroughs of New York City, and so was seen by millions of public transit users; this art form eventually covered almost every car, inside and out. Visual art has the power to capture attention and asks viewers to place a value on its form, color, statement, purpose, and place. Graffiti art forced New Yorkers to acknowledge the disenfranchised and marginalized inner-city black, Latino, and white youth.

The Emerging Youth Graffiti Scene

Around 1950, street gangs began to use graffiti for self-promotion, group identity, and marking territorial boundaries by scribbling their nicknames on walls. It also served as a warning while spreading news on current gang activities. In the late 1960s, gangs used graffiti for purposes of intimidation. For example, in the South Bronx, if a rival gang member walked into an area with "Savage Skull" or "Seven Immortals" written a hundred times, followed by the name of every member, and warnings such as "Do not enter," the rival knew that he or she was trespassing and was not safe.

As early as 1967, graffiti became more than a gang-related activity or a thoughtless moment of vandalism. It became a way of life with codes of behavior, secret gathering places, slang, and aesthetic standards. Although Philadelphia, Pennsylvania, was the original site of this larger-scale graffiti writing, the development of simple tags into full-blown works of art went furthest in New York. In fact, of the four elements of hip hop, graffiti writing has had the most racially, ethnically, geographically, and economically diverse participants. While many of these artists associated with writing groups and the hip hop community, many other were totally independent or aligned themselves with the punk culture emerging simultaneously in New York City.

Tagging

A **tag** is a graffiti writer's personalized signature or logo. Originally, graffiti artists used spray paint to make their mark. However, in the late 1960s tagging got a big technological boost with the invention of the Magic Marker, which was much easier to conceal than spray paint. One of the first to take advantage of this was a Greek immigrant teenager named Demetrius who lived in the Washington Heights section of Manhattan. He is credited for popularizing the earliest graffiti tradition by writing his tag "Taki 183" everywhere. He used a shortened version of his Greek nickname, Taki, and his street address, 183rd Street, to create his tag; Taki's approach became the basic formula for others to follow. Because he was so prolific, Taki 183 got the most exposure; on July 21, 1971, the *New York Times* printed an article written about him and this new youth craze.

Although we credit Taki 183 for popularizing tagging, he is not the originator of the style. In an interview with Don Hogan Charles (1971), Taki 183 stated that he took the form from "Julio 204," a teenager who lived on 204th Street and had already been tagging for a couple of years. Artist and graffiti chronicler Jack Stewart cites Julio 204 as the first to add his street number under his name, which became the formula for the first generation of taggers. Julio 204 was a territorial writer, in that he invaded gang territory and wrote his name and street address as if to say, "I just bombed your turf." However, other writers expressed a desire to avoid gangs as a reason to do graffiti. Graffiti gave early writers a community to belong to besides the gangs.

Early targets were school walls and playgrounds. Buses and delivery trucks followed, but most writers avoided the interior walls of subway cars at first since Transit Authority officers could trap them inside if caught. Since tagging was illegal, the notion of being an outlaw became an important feature to the tradition, and artistic achievement increased as the obstacles became more difficult. Some of these young men and women remained taggers, limiting their skills to their personalized logos. Others became writers, artists who expanded on the basic idiom of tagging, creating the most elaborate of art pieces. At the bottom of the hierarchy were "toys," or inexperienced writers who lacked or never developed skills.

Graffiti Clubs

Although most writers tended to be fairly independent, it was not long before loose-knit groups began to evolve, such as Tragic Magic (TM), Latin Action (LA), and Out to Bomb (OTB; a play on New York City's Off Track Betting legalized gambling). They set up "writer's benches" and "writer's corners" around the city, especially in subway stations, where they compared notes, lettering styles, and methods for avoiding transit police. The earliest writer's bench in New York was located at 149th and Grand Concourse where the numbers 2 and 5 trains ran.

The Ex Vandals were the earliest writing organization. Their name was short for Experienced Vandals and played with the notion that they were vandals-turned-artists. Founded in Erasmus Hall High School in Brooklyn by seven graffitists, they modeled themselves after the neighborhood gangs, decorating their jean jackets with their logo painted on the back. They introduced a script-like tag that was known as the Brooklyn style. The Ex Vandals were largely a nonviolent street gang, and as their membership grew, they functioned more as a social club than a writing club. They disbanded in 1973, although many of the original members continued to write together as a group called the Sultans. Phase 2 was the president of the Bronx chapter of the Ex Vandals. He later formed a new crew called the Independent Writers, which included prominent writers such as Super Kool and Stay High, and he is credited for developing the "softie," or "bubble," letters.

The Importance of Style

In time, subway-car graffitists became more concerned with style, content, and placement than their predecessors had been. The objective was to develop one's own unique technique, capture the attention of passengers, and, of course, to "**bomb**" the city (i.e., to write on or cover as many subway lines as possible). By 1973, more elaborate tags began to surface; first it was an outline filled in with color, then an elaboration of the traditional shapes, followed by more complex color schemes. For example, a "throw-up" (cf. "tag") is a quickly drawn piece with one or two colors and bubble letters. Writers also incorporated polka dots, clouds, and fire motifs into the lettering. Cartoon characters, like Beetle Bailey, Charlie Brown, and Mickey Mouse, started to appear, too. More importantly, the pieces on subway cars grew in size: first pieces appeared that could fit from the window downward, then artists worked to cover subway cars top to bottom (T to B), followed by end to end (E to E), which covered the length of the car, and finally a whole car. Each trend built on the last innovation.

Graffitists in the New York tradition had always referred to themselves as writers, but the younger crews began to adopt the term "graffiti artist" in an attempt to recognize that their pieces could be called art. Writers went beyond scribbling simple tags all over town. They competed to "get up" their impressively elaborate, colorful pieces known as "burners," which comes from slang for beating the competition with your style, as in "that burns!"—i.e., "that is a great piece." Highly visible spaces, such as bridges and billboards, remained desirable, but the sides of train cars allowed pieces to go "all-city" in a way that transformed the art form because, as trains travel from one end of town to the other, a writer's audience expands. Writing on trains provided writers a mode to communicate with one another. Trains became their primary canvas and their own mobile gallery.

In 1974, Tracy 168 began appending "WS"—an abbreviation for "wild style"— to his name in reference to new tumbling script developing among the writers. **Wild style** is a complicated construction of interlocking letters, with lots of connectors or arrows, and is the hardest style to master. Tracy 168, Blade 1, and Phase 2, among others, continued to develop this new lettering style into the 1980s until their names grew completely undecipherable to nonwriters.

Style Wars

The style wars were a period when anyone who wanted to get the appropriate respect from his or her peers as the best writer had to paint with great style and be prolific. To be a "king" or "queen" required tremendous creativity and radiance, and meticulous craftsmanship. Graffitists couldn't simply rest on the reputation they had earned through their name alone. Instead, originality, style, color, clean outlines (work with no drips), and overall aesthetic talent were all factors for evaluation. However, during this period, kings and queens of a tradition were easily deposed.

Each year a new generation of writers appeared, and these younger writers tended to be more ambitious, energetic, and willing to take risks than the graffiti masters before them. The same value system of respect, reputation, and retaliation that drove the gang mentality drove the writing tradition. How does a writer show up the last piece? How does a writer best the reigning king or queen? These challenges inspired both the novices and the established masters to push the art form further, a culture trait that reappears in the other hip hop traditions. In these battles, there were rules of engagement and codes: a writer could paint over simple tags with a multicolored piece, but not the other way around—at least, not without repercussion.

The Second Generation

Graffiti activity peaked in 1976 and marked the second wave of this particular art tradition. An elite writing club, the Fabulous Five (TF 5), emerged, naming themselves after the number 5 IRT (Interborough Rapid Transit) Lexington Avenue line they bombed regularly. Membership was drawn from both black

Fab 5 Freddy in 1986.
Source: *Photo © Ebet Roberts*

and Latino gangs, showing how graffiti overcame racial and social barriers. They quickly established themselves as the premier writing crew in the city, mostly by their December 1977 masterpiece: a 10-car whole train with a mural painted on every car.

In 1979, a member of the Fabulous Five named Lee met a graffiti artist from Brooklyn, Fred Brathwaite, better known as Fab 5 Freddy or Freddy Love. (In 1988, Fab 5 Freddy became hip hop's greatest pitchman and the host of MTV's first hip hop music program, *Yo! MTV Raps*.) In June 1980, Fred and Lee participated in a very important art show, the Times Square Show, which took place in an abandoned massage parlor and brought together young, independent artists displaying graffiti, punk art, erotica, and political manifestos. Keith Haring, a recent art school dropout, also exhibited at that show. He claims that he used to "follow" Lee's graffiti when he first moved to New York from his native Pennsylvania. Soon after that show Haring began producing the "graffiti art" that made him famous.

Fab 5 Freddy appeared in an influential *Village Voice* article in December 1980. Journalist Richard Goldstein, with Fab 5 Freddy's assistance, connected the graffiti art that New Yorkers were viewing to the underground musical party scene in the South Bronx. Furthermore, Goldstein presented these kids as something other than antisocial pariahs living among the civilized:

> The big lie is that graffiti is confined to "antisocial" elements. Increasingly, it is the best and the brightest who write on subway walls, tenement halls. They travel in bands with names like the Crazy Inside Artists (CIA), Children Invading the Yards (CITY), Rolling Thunder Writers (RTW), Out to Bomb (OTB). Unlike the newspaper that has called for their demise, these bands are racially integrated, which gives writers access to the same cross-cultural energy that animates rock 'n' roll. In fact, the graffiti sensibility has a musical equivalent in "rap records"— another rigid, indecipherable form that can sustain great complexity.
> (1980: 58)

Goldstein's awareness of the emerging hip hop music scene—MCs rapping over DJs' beats—was probably limited at that time, as it was for many of his readers. However, explaining that hip hop music sprang from the same cultural and social conditions as graffiti was correct.

Graffiti in the Marketplace

Around 1981–1983, art lovers worldwide began to look at New York City graffiti differently, and a demand for "authentic" graffiti art on canvas began to emerge in the elite galleries in lower Manhattan, such as the Fun Gallery in the East Village. Poor graffiti writers were more than willing to fill this demand. Street graffiti crossed over easily in the early 1980s to the fine arts world for several reasons. By 1980, film, performance art, and sculpture had dominated the art scene for almost a decade. As the art of painting was lying on its presumed deathbed, the market began to boom again as a result of wealthy art collectors looking for undiscovered artists. Impoverished young writers rushed to the major galleries to sell their work painted on canvases instead of subway cars. While the beauty of shape and color could be fashioned within the borders of a canvas, the massive impact of outlaw art painted on a subway car could not be reproduced.

Despite the fact that both schooled and unschooled teenagers had transformed graffiti into the hottest art commodity in the United States and abroad by 1982, most of these outlaw artists found it difficult to make the transition from guerrilla writer to studio painter. The power of graffiti art depends largely on size, color, and constant movement, and while the aerosol pieces on small canvases were beautiful, much of their impact vanished, as did the element of "outlaw" artist. By 1983 many collectors of graffiti art treated the work as a fad. To add insult to injury, the large number of entrepreneurs selling graffiti paintings began to market them as if they were quaint, simple trinkets or "outsider art." While some aerosol artists survived, the most successful were the more traditional, non–street artists, such as Keith Haring and Jean-Michel Basquiat. Their reinterpretation of "graffiti" was the only artwork of the period that would maintain its aesthetic and monetary value. In fact, these two artists are the only representatives of the graffiti art movement discussed in H. H. Arnason's *History of Modern Art* (2003), in which the author appropriately appoints Haring the "dean of the art-school graffiti artists" and not a "writer" in the New York street tradition.

Graffiti and the Transit Authority

Another factor in the decline of graffiti art was the New York City Transit Authority's campaign to eradicate graffiti from its subway trains. As early as 1972, concerted attempts were made to remove graffiti through chemical washing that turned the colorful murals into a murky gray mess. However, this inspired the writers to use better-quality paints and finish off their pieces with clear enamel. By 1976, the entire fleet of nearly 7,000 subway cars had been covered. That same year, an anti-graffiti squad was formed. As early as 1984, the success of the city's annual $42 million anti-graffiti campaign was becoming apparent. In 1980, more than 95 percent of the subway cars had been covered inside and out; by 1984, 86 percent of the 5,956 cars had been rendered graffiti-free. Arrests for graffiti vandalism dropped from 2,400 in 1984 to 300 in 1987.

There were other factors that transformed graffiti culture, including the rise of crack cocaine and firearms in the inner city and the economic systems that accompanied them. In the 1980s, writers had to contend with newer categories of violence by gang-bangers and Metropolitan Transportation Authority (MTA) officers alike as they crept around subways and train yards. For example, graffiti tagger Michael Stewart was arrested by police when he was caught spray-painting on a station wall at about three o'clock in the morning on September 15, 1983. While the details of the incident have never been totally clarified, Stewart apparently resisted arrest and was subdued by the officers, who perhaps used excessive force; Stewart subsequently died. Eleven officers faced two different indictments and trials, but none were convicted, despite the community's outrage at the event. Meanwhile, violence among competing graffiti artists was a growing problem. In 1988, graffiti writer Mr. Reals told journalist Fox Butterfield that graffitists of his generation would fight more fiercely over turf or the quality of their work than previous writers. "The bottom line is, I'll kill you, that's it," he explained. "It can happen any night." The art of writing shifted from the sophisticated mural pieces that covered entire cars to quick throw-ups and Magic Marker tags.

The End of the Graffiti Era

Graffiti art was the first element of the developing hip hop culture that the public had to acknowledge because of its in-your-face presentation style. Any surface could be a writer's "canvas." Although its popularity waned by the late 1980s, graffiti did not disappear, and the style most associated with this early hip hop period still dominates global graffiti aesthetic sensibilities. In examples found throughout the globe—in Europe (Barcelona and Paris), the Middle East (Beirut), and Asia (Bangkok)—artists construct incredible works of colorful, thematic, meaningful art on property that is not their own, following the graffiti-style aesthetics associated with the hip hop tradition. The aerosol art that emerged from the East Coast of the United States is being reproduced all over the world, much like its musical counterpart.

B-Boying and Breaking

A key element in hip hop culture was a new dance form that was originally called b-boying or breaking (breakin' in the vernacular). In this section, we will focus on this dance movement style, which evolved into the media sensation "breakdancing." First, we'll trace its African and African American roots, and then we'll discuss how the style evolved from the early '70s into a brief period of wide public acceptance and popularity.

No one will deny the original b-boys' claim that breaking started in the South Bronx. However, it is important to understand the cultural traditions that made the dance style especially relevant to African American and Caribbean youth. KRS-One, in the documentary *The Freshest Kids* (2002), beautifully expressed how breaking drew from "old, old" African traditions:

> *Nobody really knows. It's some old, old, old human thing. The feeling to want to get on the ground and spin and dance, and, really, become one with the earth, with the ground. Imagine that was before concrete. You was breaking and spinning on the earth.*

KRS-One speaks to the ways cultural traditions are embedded in our memories and transmitted from one generation to the next, forever preserving and re-creating our ancestors' beliefs. The transmission of folk traditions is typically by word of mouth or by demonstration; that is, cultural knowledge or tradition is learned, preserved, and passed on through practice. For example, enslaved Africans brought skills to the Americas, such as animal husbandry or the cultivation of rice and tobacco, and passed that knowledge on to progeny, peers, and slaveholders alike (see Chapter 1).

Capoeira

The Brazilian martial art form **capoeira** has been compared to breaking in part because both forms fluctuate between dance and combat, and between theater and sport and both are in constant interaction with the music produced simultaneously. Capoeira is a fight-like dance or dance-like fight created by enslaved Africans in Brazil. It is what the anthropologist Clifford Geertz refers to as a "blurred genre"; although practitioners refer to it as a "game," it mixes elements of martial arts, dance, folklore, sport, ritual, and training for unarmed fighting. There are many different styles of capoeira. The traditional "Capoeira Angola" shares many b-boying aesthetics and attitudes, especially in the no-contact fighting ideal. In some versions of capoeira, the fighters are forbidden to make physical contact; instead, their skill is measured by their ability to intimidate without touching, and to evade their opponent's attacks.

Ologund capoeira dancers in performance.

Source: *Photo © 2003 Jack Vartoogian/Front Row Pictures*

Kongo scholar K. Kia Bunseki Fu-Kiau thinks that capoeira is really a transformation of the Bantu Kikongo term *Kipura* (also, *Kipula*), which describes a rooster's movements while fighting. It is more likely, however, that the absence of hand techniques is based on an ancient Kongo tradition in which the hands should be used for good work, that is, creative activities, while the feet should be used for bad work, that is, punishment and destruction. The militaristic dexterity of these people led to the development of a combat technique in which warriors stood on the hands to draw a manual connectedness to their ancestors. This call on the ancestors by "touching hands" was a way to conjure their power into battle—echoing KRS-One's assertion about breakers' connection with those who came before them. Practitioners were taught not only kicks and sweeps but also agile evasiveness or trickery, called *sanga*, that was considered central to preparation for warfare. During the era of enslavement, many of these highly trained warriors were taken to the Americas, transporting with them cultural knowledge of this military art and its related practices.

By the early 1800s, in Brazil, this fighting-dance form came to be known as capoeira. It was practiced largely by both Afro- and Euro-Brazilians, especially those living in the lower economic strata. Not surprisingly, the authorities were not happy with the proliferation of this practice; in a statement made circa 1878, the chief of police in Rio de Janeiro said, "Capoeira constitutes one of the strongest moral infirmities of this great and civilized city" (quoted in Almeida 1986: 26). Official repression of capoeira intensified in the late 1800s through the 1920s, and clandestine capoeira groups (called *maltas*) formed secret meeting places, initiation rituals, and rules of membership as a result. However, by the 1940s, the martial art form had found new acceptance and was co-opted by politicians and others seeking to appeal to populist sentiments. Many idealized the dance form as the perfect blend of African and European traditions and therefore a symbol of Brazilian national culture. Capoeira became a "mulatto" ideological symbol of a perfectly mixed society and was a uniquely Brazilian art form (Almeida 1986: 20).

While capoeira, specifically, did not develop in other areas of Latin America and the Caribbean, it would be logical to assume that similar fight-dance traditions emerged in other areas exploiting enslaved Africans. Because capoeira was brought into the mainstream, it has appeared to be a unique tradition, but the Kikongo traditions could have persisted in the Caribbean and North America and taken different forms. For instance, similar fight-dance customs materialized in the Caribbean, such as *mani* in Cuba and *danmyé* in Martinique. Another fight-dance practice called knockin' and kickin' appeared in South Carolina and Georgia. For knockin' and kickin', two combatants entered a circle accompanied by music, just as in capoeira (and later breaking). Knockin' and kickin' is still practiced today but remains marginal and secretive.

Many of these fight-dance traditions have been blended into other ceremonial practices. In one example, this art form gradually became part of the Christian praise-house societies on Sea Island plantations. In this tradition, the initiate cannot participate in the ring shout until passing through a required phase of "seeking," which parallels African initiation rituals. The initiate is guided into "the wilderness" and enters "spiritual traveling." When these journeys are complete, the initiate is reborn into the praise-house community through baptism by immersion. Then the individual is free to join in the ring shout, which may be used as an outlet for secret display of knockin' and kickin'.

Comparing the Martial Art and the Dance

The *jôgo de capoeira*, or "play of capoeira," takes place as a ritual activity in a circular area, called a *roda* (pronounced *ho-da*), which translates as wheel, circle, or social group (compare with the breakers' "cipha," described in the section on "B-Boying as Performance Spectacle"). The *roda* is the performance site in which capoeiristas gather and play capoeira. The players and onlookers form the *roda*. At the top of the circle is the *bateria*, which is an ensemble of musicians and singers. Music is central to the practice of capoeira; singing folk and improvised songs, accompanied by clapping, enhances the energetic environment and enjoyment of the *rodas*.

Two combatants engage in a cycle of attacks, defenses, and counterattacks in a flow that allows them to display their technique, trickery, and finesse. The performance is characterized by a series of dynamic movements: cartwheels, handstands, spinning kicks, and spontaneous acrobatics. Only one's hands or feet are allowed to touch the floor; touching the floor with any other part of the body disqualifies a player. Unlike full-contact martial art forms, the object of the game is for the capoeiristas to use flair, cunning, and technique to render their opponent open to a kick, sweep, or punch as opposed to actually kicking, tripping, or punching an opponent. An implied blow is more admired than actual contact. Manipulating the opponent into an indefensible position demonstrates greater skill. The encounter ends when one is placed in an indefensible position or both feel that their battle has come to completion. The two then rejoin the circle to allow another pair to enter it.

Similar to the *roda*, b-boy battles also become enclosed in a circle by the audience and the other competitors. Compare the capoeiristas' performance to Sally Baines's description of breaking in the Bronx:

> The format of the dance was at first quite fixed. The dancers and onlookers formed an impromptu circle. Each person's turn in the ring was very brief—ten to thirty seconds—but packed with action and meaning. It began with an entry, a hesitating walk that allowed him time to get in step with the music for several beats and take his place "onstage." Next the dancer "got down" to the floor to do the footwork, a rapid, slashing, circular scan of the floor by sneakered feet, in which the hands support the body's weight while the head and torso revolve at a slower speed, a kind of syncopated, sunken pirouette, also known as the helicopter. Acrobatic transitions such as head spins, hand spins, shoulder spins, flips, and the swipe—a flip of the weight from hands to feet that also involves a twist in the body's direction—served as bridges between the footwork and the freeze. The final element was the exit, a spring back to verticality or a special movement that returned the dancer to the outside of the circle.
> (1981: 15)

African American Roots of Breakdancing

The story of African American dance is as complex and rich as that of African American music. Many influences, from Africa and Europe, have been combined to form a number of popular dance forms that themselves can be seen as ancestors of b-boying and breakdancing. While we cannot detail all of these styles here, we will focus on African American tap dance, particularly the highly athletic styles developed in the '20s and '30s.

Tap Dancing

Tap dancing itself has roots in various traditions, from clog dancing brought to America by Irish, Scottish, and English settlers to African forms of dance movement. Like the earlier fight-dance traditions already discussed, in tap the upper body—including the hands and arms—are less active than the lower body (from the waist down). This rigidity of the upper body may be rooted in the same traditions that helped form capoeira in Brazil and is also found in traditional Irish dance. The virtuosity of movement is focused on the lower legs and feet, which form a powerful percussion instrument.

As in breaking, there is a tradition in tap of "combat" where individual dancers trade steps in an attempt to "one up" each other. While played out in a semiserious manner, the fight tradition is clearly seen in the way the dancers challenge each other by upping the ante with each subsequent display of rhythmic prowess. The idea is to outdance your opponent by creating increasingly complex foot movements and rhythms. There is both dialogue—in the sense that each dancer responds to the challenge laid out by the previous dancer's routine—and battle, because the winner must ultimately vanquish all comers through his superior footwork. These battles are sometimes called "cutting sessions," underscoring the ruthlessness of the combatants that underlies each encounter.

Although there were many famous tap dancers active from the 1910s through the 1950s, the Nicholas Brothers were perhaps the most athletic, melding traditions of the fight dances like capoeira with the high showmanship of a nightclub act. Fayard and Harold Nicholas danced together from the time they were teenagers in the 1930s, and developed a unique ability to precisely mirror each other's movements. Like other dancers of the era, they created an elegant style of dance, using limited arm and hand movements to emphasize the rhythmic tap patterns that they created with their feet.

Most notably, the Nicholas Brothers' routines took tap beyond the basic foot work to include stunt work that emphasized precise timing and movements that seemed to defy gravity. For example, they performed precisely timed splits, dropping slowly and evenly to the floor and lifting themselves up in a perfectly synchronized return to standing positions in a single, smoothly executed movement. They could leap effortlessly between nightclub tables and take gravity-defying leaps landing in their famous splits, both illustrated in a famous routine from the film *Stormy Weather* (1943). That routine ends with an incredible series of leaps down a flight of stairs, with the brothers successively jumping over each other, landing in a split, and then returning to full height to leap again.

Jitterbug and Dance Contests

Simultaneously with the golden age of African American tap dancing, a new craze arose in the ballrooms of major cities for a highly athletic couple dance known as the jitterbug. The term was used rather loosely to describe a number of dances that involved precision movement and athletic skills, most notably the Lindy Hop.

Dancers performed in couples, executing movements like the man guiding his female partner between his legs in a gliding movement; athletic leaps; overhead flips; and other synchronized movements. But they also demonstrated solo virtuosity, such as falling to the ground to perform spins and other movements. The descriptions of Lindy Hoppers in the popular press—as performing "jerky" or "spasmodic" movements—were remarkably similar to how early b-boys were described by outsiders. Popular ballrooms, like New York's Savoy, sponsored contests for dancers to "battle" for the title of best Lindy Hopper. Again, the athleticism and competitive structure of these performances were reminiscent of earlier African dances. Although the Lindy Hop was originally performed by amateur dancers, show troops were also formed, notably Herbert White's (a.k.a. Whitey) Lindy Hoppers, featuring dancer Frankie Manning, who can be seen in an amazing dance sequence in the film *Hellzapoppin'* (1941) and the short *Hot Chocolate* (1941) with the Duke Ellington band.

Some early b-boys, such as the fraternal duo the Nigger Twins (later known as the Nigga Twins), claim the Nicholas Brothers as direct influences on their style. Other breakers may not have specifically been aware of these earlier dancers and dance forms. However, acts like the Nicholas Brothers, performers like Sammy Davis Jr., and dances like the Lindy Hop helped create the environment in which athleticism and dance could be combined to form the kind of gravity-defying moves that would become a central part of the hip hop dance tradition.

The Rock Steady Crew performing in the Bronx.
Source: *Photo © 1983, 2010 Linda Vartoogian/Front Row Pictures*

James Brown

The most influential of all African American entertainers in the pre-breaking years was singer/dancer/bandleader James Brown (1933–2006). Putting aside his musical contributions—which were themselves immensely influential on the growth of funk—the singer created an incredible series of dance moves that were widely copied by early b-boys. Brown's most famous move—a series of rapid foot movements executed while his body from the ankles up remained seemingly unaffected—showed his incredible physical control and prowess. This movement, associated with Brown's hit "Good Footin'," became the basis for top rockin', which we'll discuss later in the chapter.

B-Boy, Breaking, and Breakdancing

Now that we've examined the African and African American roots of breaking, we can look specifically at the history and development of b-boying to see how these same forces came to create a vibrant cultural tradition.

Kool Herc's Contribution

In the early days of the party scene, Herc noticed that the dancers at his parties waited for the most rhythmic, percussive moments of a song to perform their best dance moves. In kind, he responded to the kids' love of the breakbeat by bringing two turntables to his parties and duplicate copies of the same record to extend the break by playing the same breakbeat back to back. He called his technique the **merry-go-round** and the Incredible Bongo Band's "Apache" (1972) was the first record he used in this way. Herc began stringing together different songs with matching break sections to create a continuous dance rhythm. This unspoken communication between the DJ and the dancers developed the music, *b-beat*, and the dance movement, *breaking* or *b-boying*, of the party scene.

This unspoken dialogue between DJ and dancers mirrors a traditional African artistic form called **call and response**. For example, a leader will perform or call out to the audience and the audience will respond in kind; such an exchange can develop a dialogue. The call-and-response structure encourages performer-audience interaction. Herc intuitively took the traditional knowledge of outdoor entertainment in Jamaica and applied it to a new social context in the South Bronx. The dancers' attention to the breakbeat started the dialogue between music-making (call) and dance movements (response). The DJ was able to create a longer conversation with the addition of the second turntable and duplicate copies of the same record. The repetition of this dialogue at each party inspired a more finalized product and performance: something Herc and the kids would call b-beat music and b-boying.

The Term "B-Boy"

The term "b-boy" has been taken to be an abbreviation for, at times, "Bronx boy," "bad boy," and "boogie boy" and has been associated with anyone participating in this underground music-dance culture. However, in the 2002 documentary *The Freshest Kids: A History of the B-Boy*, Herc explains that he coined the term "b-boy" for "break boy" because of the way the kids danced, fierce and untamed. "Break" or "break out" at that time was a slang term meaning to go berserk. Early b-boy dance moves have been described as jerky, sporadic, wild-spirited, and lightly choreographed. They were mostly a chaotic combination of movements. Breakin' thus describes the frenzied moves of the b-boys. "Rockin' " and "breakin' " became the names for the dance these kids performed. There were also b-girls in this scene, such as Daisy "Baby Love" Castro of the Rock Steady Crew, but they were in the minority.

Some of Herc's set favored by b-boys include Jimmy Castor Bunch's "It's Just Begun" and the Incredible Bongo Band's "Apache," Johnny Pate's theme to *Shaft in Africa*, Dennis Coffey's "Scorpio," and the Babe Ruth Band's "The Mexican." But it was James Brown's live version of "Give It Up or Turnit A Loose" from the *Sex Machine* album that was considered the b-boy anthem.

⓪ Listening Guide

Listening to James Brown

"GIVE IT UP OR TURNIT
A LOOSE"

COMPOSED BY Charles Bobbitt

PERFORMED BY James Brown and the JBs

Appeared as a single, 1969 King
Records 45-6213; peaked at no. 15 on
Hot 100 and no. 2 on R&B Charts.

James Brown's "Give It Up or Turnit A Loose" became a classic b-boy anthem during the early days of hip hop. Its consummately funky groove and tight instrumental arrangement provide complex polyrhythmic layers of activity that make this one of the most danceable tracks of its era. The song is built on a main **groove** that is characterized by a number of interlocking melodic riffs and Brown improvising on the song's tagline, which alternates with a bridge that introduces a different rhythmic feel highlighted by syncopated guitar stabs throughout and the introduction of new lyrics.

The main groove of the song contains a strong polyrhythmic feel: the repeated bass line and guitar riffs interlock in counterpoint and are tied together by the active drum groove that has noticeably strong accents on the snare drum and open hi-hat throughout the vamp. Punctuated horn figures appear throughout the song's main groove and usually serve in a call-and-response role with Brown's vocals. As the band continues to vamp throughout this section, Brown also vamps vocally, improvising rhythmically around the song's repeated tagline while leaving room for the horn section to respond throughout. This stylized vamping is prototypical of the minimalistic funk of Brown's bands, typically with one instrument improvising sparsely over the vamped groove. In this case, the improvising instrument is Brown himself, rhythmically embellishing the song's lyrics with his voice, alternating percussive and raspy timbres accented with grunts and screams, in a manner that has often been compared to another percussion instrument.

The bridge of the song (which first appears at 1:08) introduces a new, contrasting vamp with Brown singing a new, more extended, set of lyrics. While the bridge still depends on a polyrhythmic feel to give the groove motion, the main groove's contrapuntal guitar line is here replaced by a repeated **telegraph** guitar stab that resembles the electronic beeping of a telegraph machine. The drums tighten up, with less motion on the cymbals than was present throughout the main groove, and the horn section plays a sustained chord at the end of their percussive repeated figure. The song cycles through the main groove and the bridge again, but the horns are not repeated in the second iteration of the bridge figure.

"Give It Up or Turnit A Loose" fades out as the main vamp of the song continues, returning to the original musical material. A listener might imagine that the song continues as an extended vamp. These extended workouts were characteristic of Brown's live sets, such as his performance of "Doing It to Death," which was known to extend for 15 minutes in a live setting. The tight funk groove that enables the song's vamp to continue and remain interesting is a key reason this song was so highly appreciated by b-boys and b-girls everywhere. It is a prime example of the rhythmic action that led Brown to become arguably the most sampled artist in hip hop.

Rap music from the late 1980s to the present has reinvented many of the sounds produced by Brown and the JBs. While Clyde Stubblefield's drum break "Funky Drummer" (1969) might be the most sampled item in hip hop, "Give It Up or Turnit A Loose" would appeal to a variety of hip hop styles, such as the political sonic explosions in Public Enemy's "Bring the Noise" (1987), where a sample of the phrase "Turn It Up" is heard at around 1:36 and again at around 2:25 in the instrumental background; the X-rated rap of Live Crew's "With Your Bad Self" (1988), which punch-phrases Brown's grunt ("Ugh!"), shout ("Baby!"), and the phrase "your bad self" atop a sample of the bass line from around 0:03 to 0:20, 0:37 to 0:57, 1:26 to 1:42, and 2:01 to the end of the song; and Miles Davis's jazz–hip hop fusion "Blow" (1992), which samples the bass-line beginning at around 0:14 and runs through the song.

0:00	"Yeah . . ."	The song begins with one of James Brown's characteristic screams.
0:02		The bass guitar plays the first two notes of the vamp and the rhythm section enters. The guitar and bass are playing contrasting lines in counterpoint to one another, while the drummer plays a funky groove with heavily accented snare drum and hi-hat patterns.
0:09	"Baby . . ."	The band vamps on the song's main groove. Brown repeats the "Give It Up, Turnit A Loose" tagline with some lyrical and vocal embellishment.
0:13		The horn section is first heard playing its main vamp accompaniment line, in response to Brown's vocal call. This horn section line returns throughout the main vamp.
0:39		The horns begin to crescendo, initiating a gradual build.
1:03		There is increased activity among the horns and within the rhythm section, building to the song's bridge.

Continued

Listening Guide

Listening to James Brown **Continued**

1:08	"Ayyyyyy. . . . All night long . . ."	The bridge begins here, featuring a repeated bass line and "telegraph" guitar stabs.
1:14		A new horn figure enters, building throughout the bridge.
1:39	"Baby, give it up . . ."	The band returns to the song's main vamp. The band is still locked into the groove tightly but is playing a bit louder now.
2:16	"Hold ya tight . . ."	The band returns to the bridge. The horn figure does not appear this time.
2:37	"Baby . . ."	The band returns to the main vocal and instrumental vamp before the song fades out.

Listening Guide

Listening to the Jimmy Castor Bunch

"IT'S JUST BEGUN"

MUSIC AND LYRICS CREDITED TO Jimmy Castor, Johnny Pruitt, Gerry Thomas

ARRANGED BY Jimmy Castor and Gerry Thomas

PERFORMED BY the Jimmy Castor Bunch

Recorded 1972; released on *It's Just Begun*, 1972, RCA Victor LSP-4640.

With its relentless rhythmic activity, variety of textures, and ever-changing musical structure, it is no wonder that the Jimmy Castor Bunch's "It's Just Begun" has provided a rich source of samples through hip hop's musical history, on par with some of the tracks of James Brown and George Clinton. In the days of b-beat, the Jimmy Castor Bunch's "It's Just Begun" and the Incredible Bongo Band's "Apache" were among the top songs to b-boy.

"It's Just Begun" provides a DJ or producer with a wealth of interesting material for sampling, as it includes a number of distinct rhythmic patterns and textures. This record is full of musical breaks—textural shifts that interrupt the main groove of the song (which is first introduced in its entirety at 0:08)—which provide a rhythmic punctuation of the primary musical material. These breaks—the most percussive or rhythmically complex sections—are particularly useful moments for sampling in other songs, as they contain short, funky musical ideas that can be easily combined within a new context. These textural shifts are often indicated by changes in the instrumentation, as occurs at 0:33 when bass, vocals, and drums drop out, leaving only horns and **wah-wah** guitars. Portions of "It's Just Begun" have been sampled by a variety of artists, ranging from Grandmaster Flash to Mos Def, and the song itself engages in some musical "borrowing," as Castor quotes Kool and the Gang's "Give It Up" in the opening measures of his saxophone solo.

"It's Just Begun" is characterized by unrelenting polyrhythmic activity, with the main groove and the breaks taking on layers of complex rhythmic textures (see the drum kit and timbale break at 1:59). The vocal lines and musicians' solos are ultimately subject to the multilayered sense of groove—there are few notes in this song that last longer than one beat. The textural contrasts that occur throughout also are largely governed by the song's driving rhythm. The bridge of the song (beginning at 1:07), injecting new rhythmic energy in juxtaposition with the polyrhythmic pattern that governed the preceding verses, is brief and quickly returns to the main vamp. In addition to the multilayered rhythms that occur throughout the song, the multilayered instrumental sounds are notable; for example, the guitars are processed with **distortion** and wah-wah effects, which add richness.

The recording techniques used to create this song also are multilayered. Jimmy Castor himself is credited with saxophone, timbales, and vocals; since these instruments are heard playing together at various points in the record, Castor would have had to overdub these parts in the studio. This is especially noticeable when two saxophones play simultaneously during horn breaks. The recording has been processed with a further addition to the song's texture, as the echo that occurs at the end of the recording was likely a studio-added tape-based effect.

0:00		The song begins with a saxophone introduction, characterized by short, staccato lines that inflect a strong 16th-note funk groove. The horn section gradually slows down before the rest of the band joins.*
0:11		The bass line and drum groove are introduced with a slowly ascending horn section glissando. This common glissando effect resembles the sound of a train whistle.
0:18	"Watch me now . . ."	Bass and drum groove stay the same. Wah-wah guitar enters, along with a second, distorted electric guitar that plays a repeated funk riff.
0:27		Punctuated horn section line provides a break between verses.
0:35	"Here we come . . ."	Musically, this is the same as the first half of the verse.
0:44		The rest of the band drops out for a break with the horn section and wah-wah guitar.
0:52	"Day or night . . ."	The band is playing the same groove as in previous iterations of the verse.

Continued

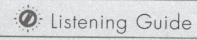
Listening Guide

Listening to the Jimmy Castor Bunch Continued

1:02		Another break in the verse groove. The horn section issues a musical "call"; guitar and bass "respond."
1:07	"Peace will come . . ."	The bridge, composed of musical material that contrasts with the verse groove, arrives. The walking bass and syncopated guitar provide both a textural and rhythmic contrast to the verse groove.
1:17	"Day or night . . ."	The verse groove returns, ending with the tag line of the song's title.
1:27	"It's just begun . . ."	The final line of this chorus is extended for three bars, allowing the band to vamp before the saxophone solo begins.
1:33		Tenor sax solo. Castor plays in a choppy, riff-oriented style that is reminiscent of Maceo Parker, tenor saxophonist for James Brown's band. Castor imitates Parker's short, rhythmic lines throughout this solo. He only plays one note in the middle of the solo that lasts longer than one beat, a technique that Parker used to create dramatic interest in many of his solos, before returning to short, repeated riffs. Additionally, Castor begins his solo by borrowing his initial melodic riff from Kool and the Gang's 1969 song "Give It Up."
2:10		The guitarist plays a wah-wah glissando and a drum break begins. The syncopated timbale pattern is prominent throughout the break.
2:17		The guitarist plays a solo and the full drum kit returns. This solo, like the prior saxophone solo, is characterized by short, staccato musical phrases and repeated notes. This playing style contributes to the established polyrhythmic groove and keeps the groove funky.
2:33	"It's just begun . . ."	The final line of the chorus (and the song's title) is repeated as a refrain while the guitar solo and drum groove continue.
2:40		The bass groove returns and the guitarist finishes his solo.
2:50		The band continues vamping, with the guitar now serving as accompaniment. The reiteration of the song's final line continues.
3:02		The guitarist begins to play controlled electronic feedback. The band crescendoes as this feedback ebbs and flows through the texture of the mix.
3:32	"It's just begun . . ."	The final iteration of the lyric sounds, accompanied by a whistle, and is echoed by a tape delay effect, gradually fading away.

*The iTunes version is from the greatest-hits collection, *16 Slabs of Fun,* and omits this horn break.

Early Style

Early b-boy style was influenced by the dance-like stage moves James Brown performed for his song "Good Footin'." The b-boys imitated and adapted Brown's moves to create a dance, known as **top rockin'**, that was done standing upright. The structure and form of top rockin' absorbed other influences, including Brooklyn uprocking, tap, the Lindy Hop, salsa, and Afro-Cuban and various other African and Native American dances. Later in its development, it incorporated moves by the Lockers on *Soul Train* and Hong Kong martial art films of the 1970s. The pioneering b-boys included the Nigger Twins, Sasa, James Bond, Clark Kent, Timmy Tim, Spy, and Trac 2.

By 1974, Herc's parties moved from the community center to the neighborhood parks, incorporating the b-boys as part of the DJ's crew. Summertime block parties were nothing new to the South Bronx neighborhoods, but by making his parties open to the public, Herc simultaneously introduced his DJ style and b-boying to a larger audience. More importantly, he had a ready-made audience with the Latino kids. Latin rhythms with heavy horns and deep bass were familiar to them from the salsa records that were popular at that time. Latinos, mostly Puerto Ricans, now became part of this budding music-dance scene.

The Foundational Years: 1974–1977

As the dance form became standardized and participants grew in numbers, b-boy crews started to emerge. The first were Afrika Bambaataa's Zulu Kings, made up of former Black Spades; Starchild La Rock, Salsoul, Crazy Disco Kings, the Bronx Boys, and Seven Deadly Sins followed. The competitive sensibilities of gang life were translated into the battle-like nature of these dances. Soon, top rockers took their moves to the ground. Sally Baines (1981) described a typical choreographed piece for a *Village Voice* article. The dance started with top rocking followed by the dancer dropping to the ground, going into leg shuffles, and then performing a **freeze** (i.e., a pose within the dance) before coming back to his feet. Though choreographed to a certain degree, there was always room for improvisation, especially if one's competitor was challenging. A b-boy's opponent might have to do twice as much floor work or a better freeze to win the battle. The fancy leg movements done on the ground, supported by the arms, were eventually defined as **footwork** or **floor rockin'**. In time, an impressive vocabulary of footwork, ground moves, and freezes developed.

According to Jorge "Popmaster" Fabel (2006), top rockin' combined with floor rockin' were key elements in the dance's execution. Some dancers claim that they could determine competitors' style and finesse by their top rockin' even before they dropped and floor rocked. According to scholars Joseph Schloss and Raquel Z. Rivera, top rockin' or uprocking, more specifically, was a move first introduced in the late 1960s by young Puerto Ricans in Brooklyn. That transition between top and floor rockin' became known as the "drop," and that too was incorporated and stylized. There were front swipes, back swipes, dips, and corkscrews. The performance of the drop was as important as other components of the dance. Flow is crucial: the smoother, the better. The way dancers moved in and out of a freeze was equally significant, in that the b-boy had to demonstrate control, power, precision, and, at times, humor. Some of the foundational moves that became established in this period were the chair freeze, CC [side-to-side] rock, Russian, neck move, backspin, and butt spin.

Latinos Contribute to the Dance Form: 1976–1977

While the African American kids' participation in b-boying began to wane, Puerto Rican crews such as the Rock Steady Crew, the Floor Masters, the New York City Breakers, and the Rockwell Association kept the tradition alive—engaging in the dance when b-boying was believed to be "played out" or "kids' stuff." Richie "Crazy Legs" Colón of the Rock Steady Crew first saw b-boying at age 11 watching his cousin Lenny Len dance with his friends. Crazy Legs would invent the continuous backspin, the "windmill," and is credited for giving birth to new forms of athletic aesthetics that developed into the '80s. While African American kids pioneered the form, the Latino kids made the form popular and introduced new innovations that would thrust b-boying into the mainstream.

Battling

The consensus among the kids themselves was that battling on the dance floor offered an alternative to battling with fists, knives, and guns. For example, journalist Sally Baines (1981) reported that a b-boy by the name of Tee told her, "In the summer of '78, when you got mad at someone, instead of saying, 'Hey man, you want to fight?' you'd say, 'Hey man, you want to rock?'" In dance battles, showing off and competing for respect were encouraged. Of course, scuffles between warring b-boys still took place, but that was probably no different than a scuffle that breaks out on the court of your local game of pickup basketball. Some of the fights that did break out at parties were a result of warring fans supporting their favorite b-boy crew.

While many of the battles took place at parties and clubs, both impromptu and organized battles also took place on street corners and in subway halls in broad daylight. The more visible breaking became, the more pedestrians and other outsiders had to confront it. At first, breaking was not always understood as a sportive spectacle. Much of the attention it received was negative, with outsiders believing that these dance battles were actual gang warfare. Soon, the battles garnered a lot of media attention, and journalists tried to explain this "bizarre" dance form and the complex subculture from which it came.

Hitting the Clubs

The popularity of breaking spread as it became apparent that white, downtown audiences would flock to any club associated with this fascinating musical subculture. Negril, a small basement nightclub, was among the first to cultivate a following, and Danceteria was another popular venue. These downtown clubs invited and *paid* Herc, Bambaataa, the Funky Four Plus One More, the Treacherous Three, Cold

Crush Brothers, the Rock Steady Crew, and others to perform. Breaking's popularity grew quickly and it moved to the much larger Roxy nightclub.

B-Boying as Performance Spectacle

Although the more historically accurate docudrama *Wild Style* came out in 1983, the commercially successful film *Flashdance* (1983) introduced breaking to mainstream America. The film featured a performance by the Rock Steady Crew, but its presentation misrepresented the actual setting of their street work. Structurally, these dance battles took place within an enclosed circle, called a **cipha** (also, cipher), made by spectators. However, the need to stage b-boying for an audience or a camera breaks the spirit created by the cipha. Choreographer Rennie Harris explains, "the movement is an improvisational, spiritual thing. When you're onstage you're in a box with people looking at you, so you have this different type of relationship with your movement. When you're at a club, you're in a circle—in the round—and energy surrounds you. It's difficult to re-create that feeling onstage" (quoted in Gottschild 1999: 61).

As the form became popular and, later, marketable, the lure of making money through b-boying allegedly turned more gang members away from troublemaking and towards dancing. There was much cultural and commercial interest in the new urban dance form following the success of the Rock Steady Crew in *Flashdance*. Other well-known crews started appearing on TV talk shows and in commercials as well as in more Hollywood movies. So much positive media attention led to b-boys participating in the 1984 Olympic closing ceremonial spectacle and in a performance for President Ronald Reagan. Through its commercialization, the dance was separated from its roots in hip hop and lost much of its cultural power.

West Coast Style

In the early '80s, the media merged Bronx b-boying with other popular urban African American dance styles, using the name "breakdancing" to encompass them all. Many of these hip hop dance forms, such as **popping** and **locking**, originated and developed on the West Coast in the early 1970s. In fact, the West Coast funk culture remains overlooked and underrated in the development of hip hop even though it was as powerful a force among the youth there as the party culture in the South Bronx.

Throughout the 1970s, the West Coast was engaged in creating its own cultural movement. This scene was nourished by soul, R&B, and funk music at outdoor functions and discotheques. This resulted in new and innovative dance movements that became part of the new breakdancing form.

Popping and locking debuted as early as 1973, when the L.A. Lockers performed on nationally televised programs such as *Soul Train* (1973) and *Saturday Night Live* (1975). Los Angeles native Don Campbell—a.k.a. Don Campbellock—is credited with inventing the dance form known as locking, which incorporated an effect of locking the joints of the arms and body. In Fresno, California, Sam "Boogaloo Sam"

Solomon, Nate "Slide" Johnson, and Joe "Slim" Thomas formed the Electronic (later Electric) Boogaloo Lockers in 1977. Some of the most common Electronic Boogaloo moves included isolating the body into sharp angles, funky hip rotations, and an attempt to use every part of the body. Much of their inspiration came from Chubby Checker's "Twist" and a James Brown dance called the Popcorn. Originally, "popping" was a term used to describe a stop-start muscle contraction executed with the triceps, forearms, neck, chest, and legs.

Many different regions of the West Coast were known for their own distinct styles, each with a rich history. Other cities on the West Coast, including Oakland, Fillmore, East Palo Alto, Richmond, Sacramento, and San Francisco, made regional stylistic contributions, such as strutting (a walk-like dance move), ticking (staccato dance movements), and hitting (gangsta-style or fight-like dancing).

"Breakdancing"

Theatrical film and music video productions in the mid-'80s celebrated the "breakdancing" phenomenon but compromised and diluted the hip hop dance forms in the process. Interest in breakdancing peaked in the mid-'80s as a result of popular films like *Breakin'* (1984) and *Breakin' 2: Electric Boogaloo* (1984), which were among the hip hop exploitation films of the time that merged West Coast funk dance styles into the New York dance traditions. This fusion was not necessarily a bad thing, but at the time breakdancing separated b-boyin' and breakin' from the hip hop culture that nurtured them. By the mid-1980s, both the mainstream and many rap artists felt breakdancing was "played out" as yet another dance craze. However, the improvisational, competitive b-boy performance that later became a choreographed, staged dance would not die. It persisted in the underground scene and reemerged in the 1990s.

CHAPTER SUMMARY

In this chapter, we've shown how both graffiti and b-boying and breakdancing developed from traditional African and African American art forms through the diaspora of the original African peoples in the slave trade. Each was originally an integral part of hip hop culture, but as they were commercialized they were divorced from their original source of inspiration. While each enjoyed brief notoriety in the mainstream media, each faded as the public attention was grabbed by the next "latest thing." Each has survived to some extent within the hip hop community, but neither is as visible as it once was. On the other hand, as we shall see in the following chapters, the art of setting words to music—which became known as rap—did survive its ultimate separation from the hip hop world to become the major popular musical style in the late 20th–early 21st centuries.

STUDY QUESTIONS

1. How do you reconcile moral integrity with the social response of graffiti writing (whether it is tagging and making the city notice the invisible and/or the socially conscious messages of some of the art pieces and/or the morality of painting such incredible works on public and private property)? There is no right or wrong answer. Make an argument and defend your position.

2. What is the difference between a b-boy and a breakdancer? Where does this dance tradition fit in hip hop dance style today?

3. Who and what were the models for the development of the breaking?

4. How did breaking cross over into the mainstream?

5. In this chapter, how are hip hop elements connected to a cultural continuum of Africa and the African diaspora?

KEY TERMS

Bomb

Call and response

Capoeira

Cipha (Cipher)

Distortion

Footwork or floor rockin'

Freeze

Graffiti

Locking

Merry-go-round

Popping

Tag/tagging

Telegraph

Top rockin'

Wah-wah

Wild style

Writing

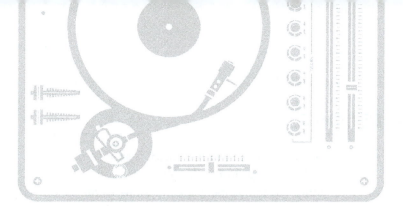

CHAPTER 4

RAP'S AFRICAN AND AFRICAN AMERICAN CULTURAL ROOTS

Learning Objectives

When you have successfully completed this chapter, you will be able to:

- Discuss rap's cultural roots in African American spoken and musical traditions.
- Understand the narrative traditions in West African societies as they relate to African American storytelling.
- Describe ways speech can be transformed into a heightened performance art.
- Discuss the ways pop cultural antecedents inform MCing.

Although graffiti art and breaking were important elements in the initial growth of hip hop culture, eventually rap—the spoken-word tradition begun by the DJs and expanded through the microphones of the MCs— would become hip hop's most visible and commercial product. Rap has been a presence on the pop charts since the mid-1980s, and its popularity shows no signs of declining. Rap music has had a particular relevance to African American consumers because rapping is part of a larger lyrical tradition rooted in other African American folk traditions, as well as verbal art and musical aesthetics that can be traced to West Africa. These traditions have been passed on from one generation to another. They are performed in communal spaces and account for a shared cultural heritage that exists beyond specific geographical boundaries.

Rapping is not the same as everyday speech. The term can be used to refer to normal conversation, as in, for example, "let's rap about politics." However, hip hop rhymes were conceived as a poetic form accompanied by music and not as music with words. Therefore, we can make a distinction between **speech as practice** (everyday life communication: getting business done) and **speech as performance** (heightened experience: artful communication). Hip hop poetics demonstrate a distinction between simply talking over music and a heightened experience of speaking; that is, a speech performance that places emphasis on style, cadence, wit, and musicality.

Rap's Pop Culture Roots

Rap draws on many cultural and pop culture traditions, including:

- Jamaican toasting
- African American preachers, particularly in Holiness churches
- Scat singing and other vocalization styles developed in jazz
- R&B singers using dramatic spoken interludes
- "Personality" DJs on the radio in the '50s, '60s, and '70s
- Recordings by the Black Arts Movement poets of the '60s and '70s
- Risqué or "blue" recordings

Jamaican toasting emerged from outdoor parties of the 1960s in which DJs talked over recorded music, inserting their own catchy words and phrases, playing off the lyrics and rhythm of the original track. Native Jamaicans call it "chanting 'pon the mike." Parties were held outdoors, and mobile DJs used large homemade sound systems in the battle of "volume" to compete for dancers. While spinning records, DJs announced songs, praised dancers on their appearance, and promoted upcoming dance parties.

To appeal to DJs and dancers, Jamaican record labels began placing on the flip side of a popular song an instrumental-only version, with the rhythm track (bass and drums) boosted to emphasize the dance beat. These tracks became known as "**dubs**" (or doubles), because they were variants of the original recording. "Toaster" U-Roy recorded his melodic talk, or "verbal riddims," over an instrumental track to create one of the first major reggae hits, "Wake the Town" (1970). Some sound engineers began making more elaborate dubs, phasing in and out the vocal and instrumental parts of the original recording, adding echo, reverb, or other effects, and adding new spoken vocal parts. By the mid-'70s, producers like Lee "Scratch" Perry were typically producing double-sided singles: "Surfer's Time," performed by vocalists the Heptones with backing by the Upsetters, had a flip-side instrumental-only version credited to the Upsetters alone titled "Surfer's Dub."

Jamaican DJs were heavily influenced by the personality disc jockeys from the United States, such as Jockey Jack Gibson, Dr. Hep Cat, and Douglas "Jocko" Henderson, who were active on radio in the 1950s–1960s. These disc jockeys' fascination with the sounds of words, vocal inflections, and rhythmic play at times took precedence over textual meaning. Jocko Henderson's radio shows were all the rage in Philadelphia and in New York City. He was not the first to perform rhymes on the radio, but he was one of the important popularizers of this genre. Here's a transcription from one of Jocko's radio shows recorded in the 1960s:

> *Once again it's rocketship time.*
> *And those that aren't boardin'*
> *Must be out of their mind*
> *The rocketeers are lined up side-by-side*

Ready to take the most exciting ride
From the EARTH to the moon
You gotta GO
With the rocketship commander—Jocko.
We'll be on the moon,
If the fuel will last
And let [us] leave the earth
with a big baaad blast
[Rocket blasting sound/Flying saucer ascending sound]
and way up here
in the stratosphere
we gotta holla mighty loud and clear.
Eee-tiddlee-yock
HO! This is Jock
And I'm back on the scene
With the record machine
Saying go Papa-doo
We'll be swinging for you [begin Temptations "The Way You Do the Things
*   You Do" (1964)]*

Jocko's use of space travel as a metaphor for African ascendancy is a particularly early example of the kind of utopic images of Afro-futurism that would have an enduring influence on the R&B and hip hop that followed: George Clinton's Parliament Funkadelic Mothership in the 1970s; Afrika Bambaataa's Universal Zulu Nation cosmic philosophy, as well as his Pan-African music-electronica mixes and comic book album cover for *Renegades of Funk* or the intergalactic *Planet Rock* in the 1980s; and Outkast's vision of Afro-futurism in the 1990s.

African American preachers developed a style of "heightened" speech in which they combined elements of chant, rhythmic speaking, rhymed phrases, and audience participation that have all influenced the development of rap. A good example is Rev. F. W. McGhee's 1930 recorded sermon "Nothing to Do in Hell." It demonstrates the antiphonic speech device, call and response, that describes the back-and-forth performance relationship between the preacher and his audience. Similar heightened speech effects can be heard in the political speech of great African American orators, including the Rev. Martin Luther King Jr. and Rev. Jesse Jackson.

Louis Armstrong is generally credited with being among the first jazz musicians to record **scat singing**. On songs like "Heebie Jeebies" (1926), Armstrong imitates the melodic and rhythmic delivery of a musical instrument, ignoring the song's words and using instead vocalizations to imitate both the sound and syncopations of jazz music. "Minnie the Moocher" (1931) demonstrates the scat or "freestyle" singing popularized by swing-era jazz icon Cab Calloway. Calloway's colorful stage personality—including his eye-catching zoot suits—became a model for countless other African American entertainers, and his fancy dress is echoed in the emphasis on exaggerated wealth or "bling" among contemporary rappers. Scat is just one bodily percussive style that anticipates the era of beatboxing, another vocal percussive style that was conceived as a human version of the Vox drum machine and the modern soundscape.

Rhythm & blues performers of the '50s and '60s began incorporating dramatic dialogues into their recordings. For example, Isaac Hayes's "By the Time I Get to Phoenix" (1969) features Hayes using an introductory narrative to set up the lyrics sung to the song's melody. In a less commercial but more radical setting, the sociopolitically charged messages of the '60s/'70s–era Black Arts Movement poets, like Gil Scott-Heron's "The

Poet Gil Scott-Heron, photographed in 1981.
Source: *Photo © Ebet Roberts*

Revolution Will Not Be Televised" (1970) or Sonia Sanchez's "So This Is Our Revolution" (1971), presented another early model for rappers to emulate.

The Black Arts Movement arose out of the frustration of young black poets and writers with the appropriation of black culture by the Beat poets of the '50s and '60s, along with the passivity and lack of political involvement of urban blacks. LeRoi Jones (a.k.a. Amiri Baraka) formed the Black Arts Theater in 1965 to feature contemporary black speech and to address cultural and political issues affecting African Americans. Performances using black vernacular English celebrated the working and underclass but also called for political, revolutionary action. The theater combined elements of speech, music, and political oratory into a new form of expression.

One of the performers who came out of this movement was Gil Scott-Heron of the Last Poets, who wrote and performed "The Revolution Will Not Be Televised," accompanied only by drums. This poem uses sardonic wit to chastise traditional civil rights activists like Roy Wilkins for their passive, nonviolent approach to addressing discrimination, but also challenges younger blacks, whom Scott-Heron criticizes for their lack of political engagement:

> *. . . The revolution will not be brought to you by Xerox*
> *In 4 parts without commercial interruptions. . . .*
> *There will be no slow motion or still life of Roy*
> *Wilkins Strolling through Watts in a Red, Black and*
> *Green liberation jumpsuit that he had been saving*
> *For just the proper occasion.*

*Green Acres, The Beverly Hillbillies, and Hooterville
Junction will no longer be so damned relevant, and
women will not care if Dick finally gets down with
Jane on* Search for Tomorrow *because Black people
will be in the street looking for a brighter day. . . .*

Scott-Heron embeds news reporting rhetorically and calls on disengaged young black people to participate in a more radical movement. As the artistic siblings of black nationalism, these poets' socially conscious, jazzy, funky sensibilities would be incorporated in the late '80s/early '90s as rap artists begin to politicize their lyrics and move away from party themes.

Finally, the sexually liberated themes and sometimes-raunchy lyrics by performers including Millie Jackson in songs like "All I Want Is a Fighting Chance" (1974) were also influential on later rap artists. In fact, Jackson's risqué raps were acknowledged as models by artists like Lil' Kim and Foxxy Brown in the 1990s. Although women participated in rapping (Lisa Lee, Pambaataa, Sha Rock of Funky Four Plus One More, the Sequence, and Mercedes Ladies), b-girling (Daisy "Baby Love" Castro of Rock Steady Crew), DJ'ing (DJ Jazzy Joyce), and writing (Eva 62, Lady Pink, Lady Heart, and Lil Love 2), they remained a minority for a variety of reasons. Female graffiti writers, for example, faced many obstacles not encountered by men. The late hours and desolate locations in which most writing is done can be particularly dangerous for teenaged girls. Some of the female hip hoppers were discredited for imitation, or were accused of having boyfriends write their graffiti pieces or compose their rhymes. As with many male-dominated fields, the social atmosphere can be extremely harsh. Similarly, female DJs were often subjected to all kinds of harassment and physical threat, such as having their equipment stolen and battered, often leaving them without the tools to pursue their craft. While women's participation in hip hop has often been treated as an imitation of the male rappers' themes, styles, and posturing, closer observation reveals feminizing modifications to the genre: clothing choices, samples and DJing mixing style, and rhymes that challenge the social norms of female roles (see Chapter 7). Whether acknowledging a political agenda or not, women in hip hop have used rap music as a platform for female empowerment and raising awareness of a wide spectrum of women's issues ignored by the stereotypes perpetuated by many male rappers.

Beyond these pop antecedents, there is a rich tradition of oral poetry that came to America via the African diaspora (for more on the African diaspora, see Chapter 2). It is important to understand these African roots as a key influence on the development of hip hop culture.

African Roots of Rap as Oral Expression: The Jeli Tradition

African storyteller-musicians are one of the antecedents for rap's MCs. The **jeli** (the indigenous Mande term) or **griot** (the more common colonialist French term) is an itinerant poet-musician who is the custodian of his society's historical and cultural knowledge. Performances come in different forms—oral historical or fictional narratives; praises of patrons; advising; historical chronicles—that are sung or recited. These storytellers wield great power because they have the ability to shape the cultural past for the cultural present. Typically, a griot's performance takes place outdoors in a shared public space, so the community is invited to share in its history. He chronicles the patron's lineage and—while the history belongs to a specific individual—the entire community participates. The communal event connects members to a shared sense of heritage. Jelis/griots often accompany themselves on a kora, which is a harp instrument. (Female jelis or griots are a minority, and when they do participate, they are more likely to sing than recite.)

Elements of the jeli's or griot's performances and role in African society correspond to the party-culture ethic and the role of the DJ or MC in the South Bronx. Similarities include the following:

- The party takes place in the outdoors, in an open, shared, or public space.
- The event is inclusive: the entire community is invited to participate, as the main character's personal history is part of the community's history.
- Storytelling events are accompanied by music.
- The jeli is set apart by his extensive memory of cultural knowledge: while community members might know the basics, jelis are master performers and skilled storytellers.

When Jamaican-born DJ Kool Herc (see Chapter 5) took his parties outside he mirrored an age-old African tradition. In part there were practical reasons—it made sense to move out of the community centers during the hot and humid New York City summers—but he also was following his homeland's tradition of partying outdoors. By putting the party in a public space, he welcomed the whole neighborhood—Caribbean, African American, and Latino kids—to participate and have a good time.

While it is true that important points of continuity with the past persist, we cannot simply view MCs as direct descendants of jelis or griots. Alteration and adaptation of African lore was inevitable in the New World given the co-mingling with Europeans and indigenous people. Therefore, much of the MC's and DJ's style and formulaic conventions speak to pan–African American characteristics of verbal art traditions and musical tastes.

Storytelling Genres

Following the pattern set by the jeli/griot tradition, folk stories can be nonfictional (family lineage, hero's achievements, or historical events) or fictional, usually comprising stock characters, like the **trickster** (a clever person or animal who is able to manipulate others to get what he wants), that move the narrative along. We'll consider African American cultural narrative conventions holistically, especially with regard to changes in those cultural traditions as precursors to hip hop lyricism.

Toasting

A **toast** is a popular African American verbal art tradition that can be an enactment, a recasting, or an exaggeration of an actual event. A toast can be performed in rhymed couplets or prose and tends to celebrate the acts of an outlaw. An "outlaw" might refer to a bad man committing acts of violence, but it could also be a "**baadman**" who is getting things accomplished within an unjust social system; that is, overcoming obstacles in an America that observes institutionalized racism and supports discrimination and segregation. His outlaw status enables him to overcome Jim Crow laws. Here's a popular toast called "Shine" that emerged soon after the sinking of the grand passenger ship *Titanic*. It was told to the folklorist Alan Lomax by Charles Haffer in Coahoma County, Mississippi, and reprinted in his book *The Land Where the Blues Began* (1993):

It was on the fifth of May[1]
When the great Titanic went down.
Po Shine was on the bottom of the deck.
The captain and his mate was havin a little chat.
Po Shine ran up to the top of the deck,
Say, "Captain, captain, the water is now
Coming in the boiler room door."
He say, "Go back, Po Shine, and pump the water back;
We got one hundred and fifty-two pumps to keep the water back."
Po Shine dashed his black ass overboard and began to swim.
The captain say, "Come back, Po Shine, and save po me.
I'll make you just as rich as any son-of-a-bitch can be."
Po Shine looked back over his shoulder and said,
"What good is money to me, in the middle of the sea?"
Went right ahead.
Just then a millionaire girl walked from the bottom of the deck.
She say, "Come back, Po Shine, and save po me.
I might turn your wife, it's true."
He looked back over his shoulder and said,
"Honey, you're purty-lookin jelly roll, it's true,"
He said, "There are a thousand
In New York as good as you."
He swim right ahead.
Just then a whale, he jumped up and grinned.
Po Shine looked back

---

[1]The Titanic sank on April 15, 1912, not on May 5.

Over his shoulder again at him—
Jumped up and walked the water
Like Christ did in Galilee.
When the Titanic went down,
Po Shine was down in Harlem,
Almost damn drunk.
The Devil was laying across his bed.
He got up and walked to the door
And looked out and he said,
"They been a long time comin,
But they welcome to Hell."

"Shine" fits our definition of a toast in that the narrative praises an anti-authority, anti-establishment heroic figure (someone who is not a typical hero). Shine worked in the belly of the ship as a stoker, feeding coal into the furnace that powered the great boat's engines. As an African American working on board a boat reserved for America's elite class, he was able to survive using his wits and sheer will against all obstacles.

The story of Shine has survived in many forms, including a poem titled "Dark Prophecy" by the Black Arts Movement poet Etheridge Knight—who himself served time in prison. Brooklyn poet Lemon Andersen performed Knight's poem on the first *Russell Simmons Presents Def Poetry Jam* in 2002, explaining to his audience, "I'm a prison-type Mother F——er. . . . This is for my peoples in jail who taught me to read and write poetry." Andersen draws a parallel between himself and Shine, citing his own "outlaw" past by thanking "my peoples in jail" for inspiring him to write poetry.

Toasting is one of many African American oral folk traditions that are foundational to the emergence of the rapping that became more formalized in the 1970s South Bronx tradition. Similar to African American storytellers, MCs pay homage to the deeds of real or imagined heroes or baadmen/baadwomen. Many hip hop MCs celebrate the defiant acts of individuals. In the early party days, these toast-like stories usually took form without developing a full narrative. The idea was to celebrate the baad skills of a crew's DJ; for example, Melle Mel venerating the masterful skills of Grandmaster Flash, or Grandmaster Caz praising Charlie Chase's skills on the turntables. However, in the commercial era, that trend changed as the MCs' lyricism expanded.

Listen to Grandmaster Melle Mel's song "Jesse" (1984). On this record, Melle Mel praises the defiant acts of Jesse Jackson, an African American man and advocate for civil and human rights, as he takes on the establishment by running for president in 1984. Jesse Jackson's run for office had a profound effect on both the minority population in the United States and the mainstream culture. Similar to the toasting tradition, in this rap, Melle Mel recounts Jackson's history, reminding us that Jackson started with nothing and through determination and wit rose to be a great leader—now running for the highest office in the land. This short excerpt gives a sense of the whole song:

> *[Melle Mel]*
> *Hypocrites and Uncle Toms are talkin' trash/(Let's talk about Jesse)*
> *Liberty and justice are a thing of the past/(Let's talk about Jesse)*
> *They want a stronger nation at any cost/(Let's talk about Jesse)*
> *Even if it means that everything will soon be lost/(Let's talk about Jesse)*
>
> *[Chorus: performed by Sylvia Robinson and Ronald Isley]*
> *He started on the bottom*
> *Now he's on the top*
> *He proved that he can make it*
> *So don't never stop*
> *Brothers stand together and let the whole world see*
> *Our brother Jesse Jackson go down in history*
> *So vote . . .*

Jesse Jackson is portrayed as a baadman in what could be perceived as a defiant act in mid-1980s America; that is, he had the audacity to challenge the status quo of the white politicians running the country. Later in the song, Melle Mel refers to President Ronald Reagan, the most powerful man in the country, as someone who will eventually show Jesse Jackson the respect he merits. In the rap, Jackson becomes a kind of folk hero who overcame the obstacles that leaders like Reagan stacked up against African Americans. The song also served as a public service announcement to encourage African Americans to register to vote and make a change.

While the song "Jesse" is *not* a toast, listeners can hear how early oral traditions like toasting influenced the rhyme style and content of rap music. The subtleties of "defiant acts" are metaphorically in line with what a baadman character must do in order to overcome an unjust political system that maintains minorities in the lower economic stratum. The baadman sensibilities became more dominant, even exaggerated, in the gangsta era of the 1990s. "Urban folktales" of gangsta life often were personalized and narrated in the first-person voice, as in Scarface's "Jesse James" (1994). These later rap songs also underscored the blurring of this genre with another, related one: boasting.

Boasting (Praising Oneself)

The **boast** is another African American narrative form that celebrates oneself, usually by bragging about one's prowess and riches (real or exaggerated). The boast amplifies reality, sometimes testing the boundaries of believability. The impact is one of surprise; the boaster's exaggerations exude freshness, humor, and shock. A boast's form can be as simple as a one-line commentary; for example, "Mess with me and I'll stick my foot so far up your ass when you brush your teeth you'll shine my shoes." Other forms are lengthier narratives. The folk narrative boast "A Harlem Jive Spiel," collected during World War II, shows many typical attributes of the boasting tradition, including the narrator's claims of sexual prowess, "baadness," and incredible feats of strength and cunning, as can be seen in this excerpt:

> Looka here, Babes, I'm too busy to spiel too long to any one hen.
> But I wanna put it down for you once and for all
> I'm too hipped for any small beg acts,
> And I ain't never in the mood to be so crude
> As to drop my gold on a chick that's bold. . . .
> I'm a hustler, a rustler,
> The solid hipster they all boost,
> and the King of the Robber's Roost.
> I've put down issues and solid action
> for the whole world's complete satisfaction,
> from the Golden West to the Righteous East!
> I'm a cool fool, to say the least. . . .
> I'm really BAD, Babes. I'm rough and I'm tough.
> I've climbed the Rocky Mountains, fought the grizzly bear;
> I've trailed the wild panther to his hidden lair.
> I've crossed the great Sahara Desert, Babes, I've swam the Rio Grande;
> I fought with Pancho Villa and his bloodthirsty band.

Compare this with rap MCs' bragging about their personal attributes, material possessions, and verbal and technical skills as a form of competitive play. For example, in the Sugarhill Gang's "Rapper's Delight" (1979; see Chapter 5), the rappers celebrate their style and skills, bragging about their wealth.

> You see, I got more clothes than Muhammad Ali and I dress so viciously
> I got bodyguards, I got two big cars
> That definitely ain't the wack
> I got a Lincoln Continental and a sun-roofed Cadillac

They even claim to be more potent than Superman:

> He may be able to fly all through the night
> But can he rock a party 'til the early light?
> He can't satisfy you with his little worm
> But I can bust you out with my super sperm!

While male rappers dominated this genre, female artists also demonstrated their rapping skills. Another old-school example comes from Sugar Hill Records president Sylvia Robinson in "It's Good to be Queen" (1979)—a boast about her skills both as a rapper and as the person who put rap music on the map:

> It started back, in seventy-nine
> My whole darn future, was on the line
> I created, a brand, new sensation

Through my mind and the whole darn nation
With the Big Bank Hank, the Wonder Mike
And this kid called Master G (That's me)
Well would you believe their "Rapper's Delight"
Went down in history, hahaha!

Listen carefully to the raps of many hip hop artists from the old-school era and compare them to current hip hop stars. As you'll see, the art of boasting remains central to the tradition. Nevertheless, it is not just about bragging; rather, it is the *way* the story is told. Toasting and boasting are forms of storytelling that are rooted heavily in the rhythmic and lyrical complexities provided by the performer, and lend themselves as models for the more contemporary art form: rapping.

Playing the Dozens/Signifyin'

Thus far, we have discussed two of the three verbal art forms—toasting and boasting—that have set the stage for hip hop's lyrical and musical form. In Chapter 2, we discussed the importance of a ritual combat that may very well be the root of African diasporic fight-dance traditions such as capoeira and b-boying. In my own research and discussions with Ghanaian youth, I learned about a kind of ritual verbal dueling practiced by Ghanaian boys that requires combatants to go back and forth, reciting traditional proverbs from their repertoire. Verbal art value systems such as this one and the beauty found in ritualized battles—all performed according to a cultural rhythmic plan—gave birth to African American ritual insult traditions: **playing the dozens** and **signifyin'**.

Traditionally, African Americans have viewed ritual insults as entertainment and a form of competitive play, and its boastful "baadness" has its roots in the toasting tradition. Playing the dozens can be defined as insults often directed toward the significant women in the lives of the males involved in verbal dueling. The objective of the duel is to anger one's competitor to the point that he (or she) "loses their cool" and concentration and thus loses the battle. Across the country, there are many names for playing the dozens, such as capping, cracking, dissing, joning, ranking, ribbing, serving, signifying, sounding, snapping, and yo mama. While the names vary, the rules of the game remain remarkably standardized.

Two common formats for playing the dozens are the following:

1. Duel: To win a battle, a competitor needs to have a large repertoire of insults and be prepared to launch an attack when necessary and adjust when appropriate. Even while being attacked, the competitor must prepare a counterinsult.

2. Round: A group session, in which anyone can take a turn displaying verbal skill (compare to the hip hop verbal art tradition, cipha). This allows a novice to build a repertoire.

Humorous imagery and wit, especially directed at the opponent's mother, is key. Ritualized insults have to be delivered properly in order to work effectively. Standardized expressions ("Your Momma's so fat"; "Your Momma's so easy"; or "Your Momma's so old") typically frame the event as a game of ritual dueling (i.e., not serious). It is in completing the insult that the speaker shows creativity and humor; for example, the ritual opening "Your Momma's so fat . . ." might be completed with ". . . that when her beeper goes off, people think she's backing up." Flow is important in that the delivery of a series of insults requires a rhythm.

Members of the audience serve a number of fundamental roles in playing the dozens. First, they are needed to witness the event. Second, they are responsible for recording the verbal history of the battle as well as spreading it throughout the community. Third, they fuel the conflict by responding to the insults (with oohs and aahs, laughter or reproof), and it is their reaction that determines the ultimate winner.

In the commercial rap era, the MCs attempt to gain an edge on competition by exchanging insults about the appearance, character, personality, material possessions, physical attributes, and other personal qualities or activities of competitors or their family members. In the old-school song "Ya Mama" (1982) by Wuf Ticket, we have a mock battle between crew members and a literal interpretation of playing the dozens, but this time accompanied by a studio recording. Another commercial recording example, The Furious Five Meets the Sugarhill Gang's "Showdown" (1981), the two groups demonstrate the style of a pre-commercial MC battle. This song is a good example of the sensibilities behind the South Bronx MC battle tradition because the rappers are bragging about their skills more than verbally attacking one another.

Signifyin' is another ritual insulting art form that has many variants and also has its roots in the toasting tradition. Signifyin' can be the exchange of indirect insults during verbal dueling or a way of subtly implying indirect messages intended as insults. For example, you might tell a friend, "What a lovely coat. They sure don't make coats like *that* anymore." While this sounds like a compliment, the implied meaning is that your coat is out of style.

More broadly, signifying is a way people (usually in a weak position) play with language to trick other people (usually in a position of power) who don't understand the language play. Ethnomusicologist Cheryl Keyes explains that signifying occurs "when one makes an indirect statement about a situation or another person; the meaning is often allusive and, in some cases, indeterminate" (2002: 24). In this manner, the dozens and signifying can be seen as part of the "raw material" of longer storytelling traditions (toasts and boasts).

African American Girl Culture

Black cultural aesthetics acknowledge a symbiotic relationship among oral, aural, and kinetic elements. Up to this point, much of our attention on hip hop performance and expression has focused on male-centered, folkloric genres such as signifying, toasting, boasting, and playing the dozens or even (loosely) breaking. However, the ideals of African American cultural performance in girl culture—specifically, ring games, handclapping games, and double dutch jump rope, games that use oral, aural, and motor skills all at once—have also been influential in the development of hip hop.

According to ethnomusicologist Kyra Gaunt, African American girls' musical games promote the skillful development of music and authority that reflects blackness, gender, individual expressive ability, and the very musical styles and approaches that later contribute to adult African American musical activities. Our primary interest here is how the games African American girls play provide insight into African American women's "ambivalent" participation in hip hop music.

For example, the lyrics from the handclap game "Mailman, Mailman" as analyzed by Kyra Gaunt reveal the powerful idioms of verbal skill and female sexuality:

> *Mailman, mailman, do your duty, [delivering the "male"; play on the "male" and "mail"]*
>
> *Here come the lady with da African booty. [pride in sexual attractiveness, and African-ness]*
>
> *She can do da wah-wah, she can do da splits, [perhaps the Watusi? she can entice the male with her sensual moves]*
>
> *She can do anything to make you split, so split! [she can drive a man crazy, but does not need a man]*

Gaunt notes that clapsies and jump-rope rhymes are testimonies to the power of the body, because they match such lyrics with coordinated physical action. There is always a kinetic connection between verbal play and physical play in these rhymed games (unlike playing the dozens).

Salt-n-Pepa's video for "Push It" (1987) demonstrates the influence of the games of African American girls on hip hop performance. Salt-n-Pepa spin, hop, twist and drop and kick while reciting their rhymes, and their moves are reminiscent of a double dutch performance. Such female oral-aural-kinetic play is influential in terms of visualizing the transition from the more masculine "b-boying/breaking" as the dominant dance tradition to the feminine combination of double-dutching with Jamaican women's dancehall dancing that defines much of "hip hop dance" from the 1990s to the present.

MC Battles

In the early, pre-commercial days, MCs gained their fame through live battles with other MCs. MC battles took place live at a party with a DJ and an audience. Many MCs kept notebooks of their rhymes, but proving oneself meant skillfully making up a rhyme on the spot (**freestyle**) to win the respect of the crowd. Lyrical strategies included praising the DJ, boasting about one's rhyming skills, and engaging the audience to respond with shout-outs. The winners were the crew that got the most crowd response and participation in the battle. The battle was built on the structure of playing the dozens, but without directly insulting anyone.

Structurally, MC battles differed in the first-wave and the second-wave eras. In the first-wave, old-school era, the MC battles put into practice the original mission advocated by Herc and Bambaataa: nonviolent competition. For example, on July 4, 1981, at the Harlem World Disco, the Cold Crush Brothers battled the Fantastic Five. The Cold Crush Brothers went on first, wearing matching pinstriped gangster suits and brims, along with prop machine guns. The Fantastic Five (a.k.a. the Fantastic Romantic Five) came out in their trademark white tuxedos. The crews took turns on the mic.

The Fantastic Five's initial performance did not stray too far from the catchphrases that would get the crowd participating in their routine, asking them for example to repeat a catchphrase ("Say, 'Number one!'") or to take a specific action

("Throw your hands in the air!"). The crew's boasting was validated by the audience through its repetition of these key phrases or actions. As typical in a battle, there was no harsh, direct attack on the other crew. That's not to say that an indirect jab might not be thrown, as when Caz of the Cold Crush commented on the Fantastic Romantic Five's trademark tuxedos: "You got to give a performance, because now you should know/That you're giving a party not a fashion show." However, this is a minor insult at best.

Battles like this were the proving ground for rival MCs and up-and-coming crews. Verbal dueling was nothing new; it is another long-lasting African American oral tradition. It differed in this context, especially when compared to playing the dozens, in that the MC's job in a battle was not to attack opponents personally, although an occasional jab here and there did occur. This orientation to battle reflects the ideology of the subculture that was originally guided by Bambaataa and Herc; that is, to have a good time, even in a "battle." As a result, verbal battles were primarily judged on the skill of an MC to excite the crowd. Each MC interacted with the audience while his opponent stood back and waited to perform; the two MCs did not interact with each other while the audience participated by shouting out in response to the MC's performance. In this particular battle, the Cold Crush Brothers might have had cleverer rhymes, but the Fantastic Five prevailed because they got the crowd excited and the audience participated in their rapping routine. On the other hand, fans are loyal, and the Fantastic Five might have been able to gather more supporters for that show than their competitors.

In the second-wave era, the Christmas 1981 MC battle recorded at the same Harlem World club between Busy Bee and Kool Moe Dee would forever change the rules of play in MC battles. Busy Bee, a.k.a. Chief Rocker Busy Bee Starski, incorporated the call-and-response technique to deliver his famous rhymes and crowd-

pleasing favorite chants ("What's your favorite restaurant? Is it . . ." or "What's your zodiac sign?"), a shout-out to DJ AJ ("Nobody can do it like this DJ can. Come on!"), and a bouncy, rhythmic flow that was signature Busy Bee ("Bow-diddy bow ba dang, ba dang . . .). The audience was immersed into the music-making process and responded to Busy Bee's call-outs.

Kool Moe Dee and Heavy D, 1981.
Source: *Photo © Ebet Roberts*

Kool Moe Dee of the Treacherous Three was the host of the event but also the last battler to come on stage. Of course, he bragged about how great an MC he is, as the tradition calls for, and he paid respect to Busy Bee's crowd-rocking skills. But next he changed his tone, quickly

firing a barrage of lyrical bullets aimed at Busy Bee's style. Kool Moe Dee came out
with hard lines of disrespect:

> *. . . Every time I hear it I throw a fit*
> *Party after party the same ole shit*
> *Record after record, rhyme after rhyme*
> *Always wanna know your zodiac sign*
> *He changed the shit to your favorite jeans*
> *Come on Busy Bee tell me what that means?*
> *Hold on brother man don't you say nothin'*
> *I'm not finished yet, I gotta tell you somethin' . . .*

Kool Moe Dee delivered these rhymes like a machine gun, rhythmically faster and
more forcefully than Busy Bee's bouncy cadence; his aggressive delivery style foreshadowed the next generation of rap artists. This was a profound moment in MC battle
culture because it was the first time an MC attacked another MC personally. In traditional old-school battles, the combatants' relationship to one another was parallel in
that the dialogue was between the MC and his audience (as depicted in the diagram,
left). Kool Moe Dee initiated a new relationship between the two MCs, in which the
trading back and forth of boasts and insults occurred between them, with the audience
becoming spectators to the battle (see diagram, right). Attacking one's opponent brings
rapping closer to the ritual dueling traditions like playing the dozens.

To be clear, Busy Bee and Kool Moe Dee were friendly before and after this battle.
In fact, the two battled again on New Year's Eve, but due to technical difficulties, no
recording exists of the match. Even though this was a move away from the nonantago-
nistic logic of the earliest party culture, there was no animosity; the frame of this event
still cued the combatants that this was play.

The mixtape of this Christmas battle was passed around and played on the radio. It
introduced hip hop fans to the new, more aggressive approach to battling. It was probably the catalyst for Roxanne Shanté and her producer Marley Marl to record "Roxanne's
Revenge," an answer record to UTFO's "Roxanne, Roxanne," on which she dissed the
members of the group. It shows the transition of MC'ing out of the old-school style
(party rap) and into a new generation of rap music making, the new-school style.

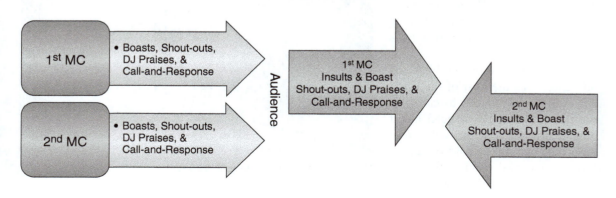

Like playing the dozens, MC battles were more than a game. MCs battled for respect. Battling is an exhibition of emotional strength and verbal agility, a confrontation of wits instead of fists: a war of words. Hyperbole and flair in these insults demand a lot from the listeners' imagination, especially when the insults are anchored in reality—as in the very personal verbal assault made by Kool Moe Dee against Busy Bee.

CHAPTER SUMMARY

Our discussion of African American folklore provides us with a glimpse of the ways youth from the South Bronx developed their word play as artistic communication rooted in African and African American traditions. More important is the way musicality guides the rhythmic logic behind African American speech. Creativity and change are encouraged in language artistry and oral tradition; because there is also a kinetic application, alongside oral-aural engagement, the same invasive musicality guides other elements of hip hop. This diagram graphically charts the development of three of the hip hop elements, as verbal art and kinetic art were incorporated by musical sound.

The sounds of hip hop are derived from a heterogeneous sound ideal that reflects the cultural values and social practices of an African cultural heritage. The concept of an aesthetic represents the ideas people express about values for beauty in musical sound as well as visual and kinetic display. Music of Africa and the diaspora is characterized by the layering of varying tonal qualities or timbres, and polytextured and polyrhythmic sounds, which some critics have interpreted to be "noise" or uncivilized sounds. Furthermore, musical performances within an African context are conceived as social events where people come together and actively participate in the music-making process as both performers and dancers.

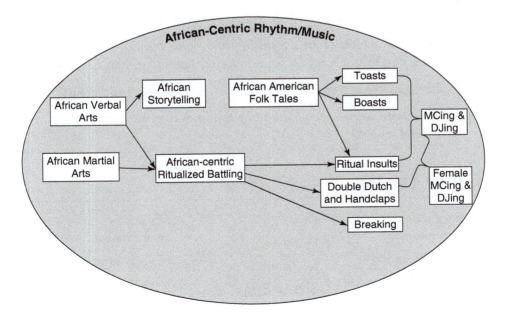

These unique and varied musical sounds and textures that characterize African and African diasporic music performances reflect the aesthetic values of this culture group. In the production of these sounds, musicians aspire for what composer Olly Wilson (1983) labels the "heterogeneous sound ideal": varying sound qualities and textures; singing or playing of instruments in a percussive manner; participating by way of call-and-response performance structures; and incorporating physical body motion as an intrinsic part of the music-making process. The polytextured and poly-rhythmic sounds are analogous to the many different effects that DJs create mixing two or more sound sources and manipulating the turntable to create new rhythm patterns. Responsorial collaboration between DJ and dancers encourages emergent or improvisational performances. MCs use different inflections, accents, and manipulation of vocal qualities (raspy, throaty, nasal, percussive, melodic) to deliver their rhymes. The cumulative result is a production that satisfies the heterogeneous sound ideal.

STUDY QUESTIONS

1. How do the black oral traditions discussed in this chapter represent traditions in hip hop culture?

2. What are the components of the African American toasting tradition discussed in this chapter that differ from the Jamaican toasting tradition discussed in Chapter 3?

3. How might the bardic tradition of the jeli/griot be compared to aspects of the early South Bronx party community?

4. What is the function of storytelling and ritual insults in African American folk culture? What is their function in hip hop culture?

5. Can you identify the oral traditions in contemporary rap songs?

6. How were women positioned in hip hop during the early days of the old school?

KEY TERMS

baadman/ baadwoman

Boast/boasting

Dozens/playing the dozens

Dub

Freestyle

Jeli/griot

Scat singing

Signifyin'

Speech as performance

Speech as practice

Toast/toasting

Trickster

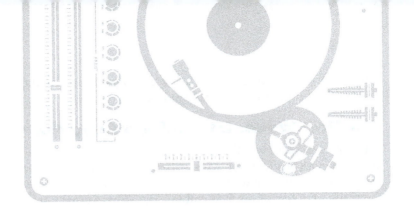

CHAPTER 5

OLD-SCHOOL DJs AND MCs

Learning Objectives

When you have successfully completed this lesson, you will be able to:

- Discuss the emergence of the hip hop culture and the important roles of the DJ and MC.
- Identify the contributions of DJ Herc, Afrika Bambaataa, and Grandmaster Flash to old-school rap.
- Distinguish pre-1979 old-school hip hop (a.k.a. first wave) from the commercialization of old-school (a.k.a. second wave/commercial era).

There have been several distinct eras of development in the history of hip hop culture. Two broad periods—**old** and **new school**—have been identified, although it is often hard to distinguish where one era began and the other ended. Within these broad periods, we can make further distinctions based on developments in hip hop style. In this chapter, we will focus on the old school of hip hop culture, distinguishing two periods of development:

1. **First wave** (approx. 1973 to 1981), or the foundational years

2. **Second wave** (approx. 1979 to 1983), or the early commercial years

During the first wave, hip hop was a local and informal artistic scene. Cassette tapes were home produced and circulated by individuals; graffiti and breaking were a part of community artistic expression. Events were advertised by word of mouth and flyers. Performers of hip hop music "dressed up" for shows emulating the R&B and space-oriented attire of the funk and disco traditions; others displayed exaggerated wealth, wearing heavy gold jewelry and leather attire. The second wave was ushered in by the commercial success of "Rapper's Delight" in 1979. MCs were elevated in status above DJs, with rap music overshadowing the other elements of hip hop. At first, live studio musicians replaced records as accompaniment to the rappers, but this changed over time as new technologies were introduced.

The First Wave: DJs and the Early Party Scene

Although graffiti art was the first component of hip hop culture to gain widespread attention, with breaking/b-boying arising next to become immensely popular in the New York City disco and club scenes (see Chapter 3), it was the DJ who was in fact the major architect of hip hop culture. The DJ was usually the leader of the social club or organization out of which hip hop emerged (see Chapter 2). In particular, three DJs played seminal roles in the creation and development of hip hop culture: DJ Kool Herc, DJ Afrika Bambaataa, and Grandmaster Flash. These DJs pioneered the key techniques that would be passed on to following generations.

DJ Kool Herc

Following the 1962 termination of Britain's Commonwealth Immigrants Act, which made it more difficult for colonials to enter the United Kingdom, a wave of West Indian expatriates headed for the United States in search of a better life. Among those expatriates leaving the West Indies between 1965 and 1970 were 12-year-old Clive Campbell and his family, who left Kingston, Jamaica, for New York City in 1967. As a youth in the South Bronx, he hung out with the formidable graffiti crew the Ex Vandals and assigned himself the tag "CLYDE IS KOOL" because his new American friends called him Clyde and never Clive. He was also nicknamed Hercules by his classmates in school because of his massive stature; however, he did not like the nickname until it was abbreviated to Herc. Clive's first public performance occurred when his sister Cindy asked him to DJ her back-to-school party in August 1973 held at the community center on 1520 Sedgwick Avenue. More parties followed, first in the recreation centers and then out into the parks, which brought him much local fame.

Clive became known for his DJ system, which was inspired by a Bahamian Fordham University student DJ who called himself Amazing Birth, his awareness with outdoor sound systems in Jamaica, and his father's support; his DJ gear included twin turntables, a McIntosh amplifier, and huge Shure speaker columns. He was also known for playing soul, funk, and R&B music that was not being played on the radio. Over time, he took on the stage name DJ Kool Herc (also, Kool DJ Herc). Although Herc began to charge for his parties, the price of admission was affordable for almost every kid in the neighborhood. In fact, the first parties matched the going rate for a pack of Wrigley's chewing gum. DJ Kool Herc provided the kids with a venue where gangster activities were separated from the party-people mentality. For example, Herc's flyer for his party at a club called Sparkle (April 7, 1978) clearly stated: "NO DRUGS, WEAPONS, ALCOHOLIC BEV, SNEAKERS, IN AND OUT."

Herc's parties provided the blueprints for three of the most identifiable features of the party DJ:

- The Jamaican oral tradition of toasting (see Chapter 4)
- The Jamaican-inspired outdoor sound system
- The creation of b-beat music (the musical inspiration for b-boying, or breaking; see Chapter 3)

Herc's Blueprints

Herc knew that the DJ's primary job was to rock the crowd, appeal to the crowd, and control the crowd. Controlling the crowd would become especially important as the parties grew larger. Herc began talking over the music similar to the Jamaican toasting tradition at first to make simple announcements: someone's mom at the door, or the date of his next party. He would also praise the dancers and audience and boast about his DJing skills. African American friends, like Coke La Rock, joined him on stage, adding rhymed couplets and shout-outs since the first party.

African American styles of rhymed speech are derived from African traditions (see the discussion of the jelis/griots of Gambia in Chapter 4). There are many other similar oral traditions found throughout sub-Saharan Africa. Through the African diaspora (see Chapter 2), these traditions came to the Caribbean and the United States and took root in various forms (see Chapter 3 for more on these oral traditions).

DJ Kool Herc's toasts inspired more elaborate raps performed by his crew the Herculoids (a.k.a. the Herculords). Herc differentiated his toasting style from MCing. The MCing tradition of shout-outs and boasts as well as rapping full narratives built on Herc's and his crew's toasting style. Following Herc's toasting style, one Herculoid in particular started lightly rhyming over records. His name was Coke La Rock and his style took toasting to a new level.

> *Transcription of Herc's toast:* "*You never heard it like this before, and you're back for more and more and more of this here rock-ness. 'Cause you see, we rock with the rockers, we jam with the jammers, we party with the partiers. Young lady, don't hurt nobody. It ain't no fun till we all get some. Don't hurt nobody young lady!*"

> *Transcription of Herc's toast given to him by his friends Coke La Rock (first rhyme) and Dickie (second rhyme):* "*There's no story can't be told, there's no horse can't be rode, and no bull can't be stopped and ain't a disco we can't rock. Herc! Herc! Who's the man with a master plan from the land of Gracie Grace? Herc! Herc!*"

Although Herc's friends, like Coke La Rock, Dickie, and Timmy Tim, were not yet "MCing" in the more sophisticated rapping style of the late '70s, the development of their style as indicated in the two examples formed the blueprint for MCing in terms of its use of rhymes and rhythmically similar phrase structures. In the first example, Herc seems to be stringing together a random series of boasts. In the second example put together by Dickie, we see him building an argument for the supremacy as leader and metaphor. The "land of Gracie Grace" is a reference to Gracie Mansion, which was most famously a residence for New York's mayors, suggesting that Kool Herc was the mayor of the Bronx. In building on Herc's original DJing, Coke La Rock talked on the mic, toasted, and called out expressions that would become standardized, such as, "And ya don't stop" and "To tha beat y'all." Soon, other DJs and their crews modeled themselves after Herc and the Herculoids, competing for the attention of the audience. As a result, the early MCs continued to make general announcements and praise the dancers but also began celebrating their DJ's skills, and later their own crew's style, which would eventually lead to what is more identifiably hip hop MC'ing today.

Competition and the Ensuing DJ Battle Culture

Herc is the father of the South Bronx DJ party scene, and its first "king," but many upstarts would challenge him and two would prove to best him. DJs competed for the favor of the crowd by finding the most unique and danceable beats on the records that they were playing. Herc learned an important lesson from his father to protect his reputation: he peeled off the labels of his records, so other DJs couldn't steal his sources. His followers also applied this strategy. Two former Black Spades, Kool DJ D at Bronx River and Disco King Mario at Bronxdale, followed Herc's style and took on Afrika Bambaataa as their apprentice. Bam started throwing his own parties soon afterwards and built an audience at the Bronxdale Community Center (for more on Bambaataa's early life, see Chapter 2). Bambaata was the son of Jamaican immigrants and was familiar with the toasting tradition. He continued to take the Jamaican style and adjust it to American records.

In 1977, DJ Afrika Bambaataa came up against Herc at the Webster Avenue Police Athletic League in the Bronx. They became fierce competitors for the South Bronx audiences, with Herc controlling the West Bronx while Bam held the South. This was the beginning of Herc's retreat from his leadership role in the still-developing rapping scene. Some of his associates from that era believe his retreat resulted in part from a stabbing Herc received in 1977 trying to break up a fight outside the Executive Playhouse, where he was performing. Soon afterwards, Herc's performance venue burned down. It has been suggested by various members of that early community that Herc never fully recovered from those events. In his own words, "Papa couldn't find no good ranch so his herd scattered" (quoted in Hager 1982).

Another upstart, calling himself Grandmaster Flash, claimed that—despite all of his innovations—Herc's mixing skills and turntable tricks were limited. In the short period that he reigned as king, Herc's limited skills became a handicap in competing with younger, more dexterous DJs like Grandmaster Flash.

Afrika Bambaataa

In Chapter 2, we discussed how Afrika Bambaataa established the Bronx River Organization, which became the first club to unite gangs of writers, b-boys, DJs, and later MCs. The Organization also gained the support of the community, opening more and more chapters throughout the Bronx. It eventually changed its name to the Zulu Nation (currently the Universal Zulu Nation), a promise Bambaataa made to himself in honor of the Zulus who fought for their land and freedom. This new organization was committed to not being a violent street gang; its motto was "Peace, Love, Unity and Having Fun" (Chang 2005: 96–105).

Like many of the DJs in the South Bronx party tradition, Bambaataa's parties were taped on audiocassettes (a.k.a. **mixtapes**), to be sold on the streets, that showcased his DJ skills and captured his live performances. Other DJs sold their tapes as well; David Toop reports that Flash supposedly sold his tapes for "a buck a minute" (2000: 78). However, creating a commodity was not the focus for Bambaataa; his parties remained largely responsible for integrating rival African American and Latino gang members and showing them an alternative to the disintegrating and self-destructive life of the street gangs.

Grandmaster Flash

Joseph Saddler went to Herc's jams not to party but to study his work: the DJ technique, the crowd, the equipment, and the music. He knew he could not compete with Herc's massive and superior sound system, so he sought to outdo Herc with superior DJing skills. He apprenticed under Pete "DJ" Jones, whom he felt was more skilled at mixing than Herc. Like many in his neighborhood, he was poor but savvy.

Grandmaster Flash and Melle Mel, 1983.
Source: *Photo © Ebet Roberts*

He studied electronics at Samuel Gompers Vocational High School. With his soldering iron, screwdriver, and curiosity he adjusted the cheap turntables he already had and put them together with other equipment, turning them into machines comparable to Herc's incredible sound system. He wanted to turn beat-juggling and crowd-rocking into a science. For his DJ work, he took the name Grandmaster Flash.

"Quick Mix Theory" and Other DJ Techniques

Flash's first innovation was "quick mix theory," a technique in which he stopped the record with his hand and reversed its direction to replay that portion of the record. DJs would call this technique **backspinning**. At this time, touching the vinyl to control the record's revolutions and counterrevolutions had never been done. This technique proved to be very useful, advancing what Herc had created with the merry-go-round (see Chapter 3) and creating the foundation for scratch art. However, it had a serious downside: the more you backspin, the more you destroy that part of the record, and some records are too rare to be played like that. Plus, the turntable itself is designed to spin in one direction, and its motor could be damaged or destroyed by the DJ constantly reversing its direction.

Flash advanced the art of mixing and evolved the **punch phrase** concept, where he took a musical phrase or vocal fragment from one record and punched it in over another record as it played. To do this, Grandmaster Flash developed what he called "**clock theory**" (and sometimes clockwork theory). In order to find the break of a recorded song quickly, by eye, on the vinyl record, Flash marked on the label with Magic Marker exactly where the tip of the sound was (the markings resembled the minute marks on a clock). He also popularized **scratching**, the manual spinning of a record back and forth with the needle in the groove to create a rhythmic pattern. Theodore Livingston (a.k.a. Grand Wizard Theodore, of the Fantastic Romantic Five) is credited as the pioneer for this invention and is the younger brother of Flash's partner "Mean Gene" Livingston.

To further promote his new techniques, Flash built a crew, which eventually became Grandmaster Flash and the Furious Five. They became *the* super group of the old school. Flash's crowning moment came on September 2, 1977, playing for an audience of 3,000 people at Harlem's Audubon Ballroom. After audiences heard Flash, Kool Herc could not draw the same kinds of crowds again. Note that of the three founding fathers of hip hop, only Grandmaster Flash and Afrika Bambaataa would go on to record their music during old school's commercial period.

The Founding Fathers' Contributions

Herc, Flash, and Bambaataa are the founding fathers who inspired young teenagers from all over the Bronx to become hip hop DJs. Each made a special contribution to the growing movement:

1. **DJ Kool Herc, the Master of Sound:** As for DJing style, Herc is best known for his massive sound system and for playing old R&B and soul tunes, reintroducing this music to a younger audience, while also premiering new music, including the Jamaican group the Incredible Bongo Band. Most importantly, he was the one who highlighted the best part of the records: the break. His parties inspired the dance moves that would become b-boying, his breakbeat juggline developed into the DJing style that he called **b-beat**, and his encouragement to take on up-and-coming DJs inspired the competitive edge that kept the pulse of the emerging hip hop culture beating.

2. **Afrika Bambaataa, the Master of Records and the Great Unifier:** In the early days, Afrika Bambaataa was best known for his amazing and extensive record collection and for playing rhythms that made the people dance. He was a skilled collector of beats. However, he will forever be credited for giving the culture a focus and for offering the youth of the South Bronx an alternative to gang culture.

3. **Grandmaster Flash, the Master of Technique:** Flash was a technician about his work. For him, it was more than playing records that got people dancing. He was creating new mixes that went against the rules of the disco DJs. He did not use the equipment to *play* music; rather, he used the equipment to *create* an instrument.

Hundreds of DJs followed these three young men, trying to successfully conquer the crowds in the parks and clubs of the Bronx, but only a few stood out: DJ Jazzy Jay and DJ AJ (DJing for the Zulus); DJ Charlie Chase (a Puerto Rican DJ with the Cold

Crush Brothers); DJ Jazzy Joyce (one of the few dominant female DJs); DJ Red Alert (who would go on to radio DJ success); Grand Wizard Theodore (inventor of record scratching); DJ Afrika Islam (a.k.a. the son of Bambaataa); and Grandmixer D.ST. (a Zulu, but most famous for collaborating with Herbie Hancock on their 1982 release "Rockit"). Along with Herc, Bam, Flash, and their MCs, these youth were the progenitors of hip hop culture.

The Role of the DJ
"Digging the Crates": [Re]searching for the Perfect Beat

The hip hop DJ's overall mission was rocking the house, and to do this he or she needed an arsenal of records with danceable beats. The DJ's ability to keep a dance floor packed relied on his selection of beats. The DJ had to include radio favorites as well as his or her own collection of obscure beats, and keeping these sources secret was very difficult. Even though everyone removed the labels from their records, eventually other DJs would discover or decipher the names of those secret beats. So, to keep your uniqueness, you had to go digging—searching for new beats.

Other than the development of the MCs, **digging the crates** was one of the most crucial aspects of the DJ party subculture. These young DJs had to develop a vast understanding of music. They listened to all forms of music; no album was too serious or silly, regardless of the album cover or genre. As DJs became more knowledgeable about various musical forms, their record collections grew.

The DJ studied the record to learn exactly where the rhythmic break was on it. Developing DJ skills required hours of practice and training one's ear to know how to make the beats work together. The new beats had to be played in a way that would not reveal the original artist. If it was just a drumbeat, it was harder for other DJs to guess who made the record. So cutting off the beat before the other instruments or singers came in was critical, which meant that the DJ had to be fast and precise. The fastest way to go from one part of a song to another is **needle dropping** (the ability to place the needle in the same spot on the record at will)—a skill not every DJ could master.

Techniques and Gear

DJing techniques, such as needle dropping, cueing records, backspinning, and scratching, are skills that have evolved out of hard work and creativity. Developing one's own style is key to making a mark on the party scene. Good DJs always wanted to find something new to mesmerize the crowd, including incorporating other instruments into their sets; for example, Flash's **beatbox**, a programmable drum machine that played digital samples.

As technology advanced, the DJ gear grew larger and more complicated. At different times, a DJ might use a mic, two turntables, a mixer, a drum machine, a sampler, an amp, and two bass-heavy speakers. Of course, he also had assembled a catalogue of constructs from samples of songs that were the most popular with dancers, segueing them into one long musical collage.

Sources for Beats: Funk

DXT, the old-school DJ formerly known as Grandmixer D.ST., explained that DJs listened to all genres of music—rock, Latin, country, opera, and so forth—but funk and R&B were always the core source for beats: "Funk/R&B music is the closest source of music that resembles the original drum sounds from Africa." Funk is an urban dance style, based on a polyrhythmic groove that became popular in the 1970s. It emerged from soul and, at times, served as a counter to the pop phenomenon, disco. In fact, Flash was drawn to Herc's "antidisco" record-playing style. While disco was not anathema to the party scene, many b-boys considered it separate from the musical scene in which they participated. A category of 1970s dance music named for the discotheques where it first was popular, disco is essentially a homogenized and blanched funk that was embraced by the entertainment industry.

James Brown was a major contributor to the transformation of R&B into soul music (funk's predecessor) by adding a southern rawness and rhythmic intensity to the tradition. His percussive vocal timbres and repetitive phrases interjected with grunts, screams, and hollers, as well as his polyrhythmic instrumental structures, define the gospel foundations of the soul aesthetic. Furthermore, James Brown's landmark horn arrangements and vocals resulted in a new musical sophistication that underlies the '70s funk genre. Funk became one of the most sampled styles of music by rap DJs during the late '80s and early '90s, introducing a new generation to the music of their parents.

The DJ Needs an MC

DJs emerged at a rapid rate to supply music to the growing demand of b-boys and young eager party people. As the parties grew larger and DJ'ing performances became more elaborate, the DJs began to give more control to their crews. For example, around 1975, Herc added MCs to help him get the crowd involved but also to control them when they got too restless. Coke La Rock, Clark Kent, and Timmy Tim formed the first MC team, the Herculoids (Herculords). Their style of "MCing" was largely party shout-outs like "Kool Herc is in the house and he'll turn it out without a doubt." They also incorporated a call-and-response technique, shouting to the party people, "Clap your hands." While Kool Herc called their rapping style "toasting" as opposed to "MCing," Melle Mel and Kid Creole of Grandmaster Flash and the Furious Five pioneered a more sophisticated style that is comparable to hip hop today.

In late 1975 to early 1976, DJ Grandmaster Flash realized that he needed vocal accompaniment to help spark his clock theory. He brought in former Black Spade Robert Keith "Cowboy" Wiggins to praise the DJ and command the crowd to "throw your hands in the air and wave 'em like you just don't care!" He also added two dancers, Debbie and Terri, to go through the crowd and say "Ho!" Then he added the Glover brothers, Melvin "Melle Mel" and Nathaniel "Kid Creole." According to Flash, they were the first "rhyme technicians." He claims they were the first to toss a sentence back and forth. For example:

Melle Mel: "I"
Kid Creole: "was"
Melle Mel: "walking"
Kid Creole: "down"
Melle Mel: "the"
Kid Creole: "street"

They alternated words to form rhymed couplets.

The DJ was in control, deciding when the name of the DJ and crew would be announced, and he was responsible for any break in the flow of music. The MC had to control the crowd so that the DJ could be creative. The main job of the MCs was to praise the DJ and the crew. However, with time and the competitive spirit, the MCs began to embellish those shout-outs and entertain the crowd with greater verbal artistry. Then they too, battled each other for lyrical supremacy.

Keep in mind that live performances were not perceived as a series of songs because the idea behind good DJing was to smoothly transition from one song to another, blending in the appropriate amount of breakbeats, cuts, punch phrases, and scratches. The MC's job was to keep with the flow of the music and to excite the crowd. Since the performance was thought of as a three- to four-hour continuous set, MC performances did not narrate a complete story. Instead, the DJ gave MCs some musical space to celebrate the DJ's skill and the prowess of the MC crew, encourage group participation through repeated catchphrases, and, maybe, recite a string of rhymed couplets to show off individual verbal artistry. Lastly, this was a party-music scene, and old school became synonymous with party rap. Musically, DJ Charlie Chase appealed to the crowd by working the disco beat "And the Beat Goes On" by the Whispers, while Grandmaster Caz got the kids excited with rhymes about Charlie Chase's skills.

The MC Emerges

By 1977, the MC had become a fixture in every hip hop crew. There were many wannabes in the first crop of MCs. Some were roadies, carrying crates and equipment in hopes of becoming part of the crew to get the attention of the girls. Others were MCs in training trying to learn the tradition. As the number of MCs continued to increase, competition rose.

Just as the DJs had battled and raised the standards of excellence, turning their hobby into an art form, so began the craft of MCing. There were solo MCs (Busy Bee, for example, an MC who had a reputation for taking the mic at any party; see Chapter 4), groups (two or more MCs with a DJ, such as Grandmaster Flash and the Furious Five; DJs Breakout and Baron and the Funky Four Plus One More; Grand Wizard Theodore and the Fantastic Five; Charlie Chase and the Cold Crush Brothers), and female MCs (Sha Rock, Lisa Lee, Pebblee Poo), but only one all-girl group, the Mercedes Ladies, who had as many as 21 crew members, 6 of whom MC'd. According to Grandmaster Caz, performing at parties was perceived as the "big time," and they had to win the favorable opinion of very tough crowds. The prize was respect on the streets.

DJs Overshadowed by Their MCs

The success of the DJs, their crews, and the parties that they sponsored drew people from around the city. More outsiders became interested in the culture, recognizing the magnetizing effect this music scene had on the young crowds. Some recognized an untapped source for income among this audience. Outsiders, like the members of Blondie, used the term "hip hop" as a noun, as in "let's go to a hip hop"—meaning a happening or an event that showcased the DJ, MCs, and breakin'. They all played a part in the transformation (and some would argue the demise) of the original South Bronx party culture and pushed the DJ's shining light into the shadows.

According to DXT, the DJs themselves made the first critical mistake: giving away the sources for their beats. Club owners came to parties to meet DJs to hire them to play at their clubs. Sometimes DJs needed new copies of some of their rare beats, especially after repeated use, and these patrons/club owners would purchase new copies and thus learn the identity of the DJ's secret sources. Outside entrepreneurs began packaging premade selections of key breaks and beats for anyone to purchase. *Village Voice* journalists Leland and Stein credit Lenny Roberts for compiling 20 volumes of beats and breakbeats in the series *Ultimate Breaks and Beats*. This resource became available to anyone who wanted to be a DJ and marked the beginning of the hip hop DJ's transition to obscurity.

Second, as early as 1979, record companies began signing MC crews to make records. The DJ and his MC were two components of one music-making unit, and along with the b-boys' dancing, they all complemented one another. However, this collaborative artistic aesthetic was not important to record executives and not necessary for the production of a rap song. The MCs were all they needed to sell records, and as a result record companies pushed the MCs into the spotlight, pulling them away from their DJs and excluding the DJs from the musical production. This was the beginning of the rap music industry and the second wave of old-school hip hop (see Chapter 6).

The Hip Hop Name

The movement was not named "hip hop" until Afrika Bambaataa started using the term in the early 1980s. Originally "hip hop" referred to the MCs scat-style of rhyming. Lovebug (also, Luvbug) Starski was considered by many to be one of the best party rockers of the late 1970s, and he was one of the first DJ/MCs to integrate the expression "hip hop" into his rhymes; that is, "hip hop" was an integral part of his party shout-out "A hip hop, a hippy a hippy a hip hip hop. . . ." Coke La Rock and Robert Keith "Cowboy" Wiggins have also been credited as early MCs to incorporate "hip hop" to their shout-outs. Whoever was first, this catchphrase, like others before and after, was co-opted by other MCs for their routines. The compound construction may have a contextual purpose. Hop refers to an informal dance. Hip or hep was jazz-age slang of the 1930s meaning to be up-to-date, modern, aware. M.K. Assante has argued that hip has Wolof origins, a language spoken in parts of Western Africa. Xippi (hipi) can mean to open your eyes, wake up, check out what's happening. Therefore, the logic behind calling this youth subculture "hip hop" reveals enlightenment or awareness through dance and music, which ultimately echoes Bambaataa's mission statement: "Peace, Love, Unity and Having Fun."

The Second Wave: "Rapper's Delight" Changes Everything

"Rapper's Delight" by the Sugarhill Gang—the record that would place rap music in the popular music history books—didn't come directly from the South Bronx tradition. Joey Robinson (son of Sugar Hill Records founder Sylvia Robinson) happened to hear Henry "Big Bank Hank" Jackson rapping to a tape of Grandmaster Caz of the Cold Crush Brothers while working at a pizzeria in New Jersey. At the time, Hank was the manager of the Cold Crush Brothers. According to Grandmaster Caz, "I used to make practice tapes at my house, saying my rhymes and DJing my beats. Hank took the tapes to work with him. . . . They heard Hank rhyming along to the tape . . ." (Fricke and Ahearn: 182). Robinson told Hank that he was forming a group called the Sugarhill Gang and asked if Hank would like to join. Hank accepted, although he was not an MC.

Hank went to Grandmaster Caz and asked him for some rhymes. Caz laid his rhyme books on the bed and said, "Take whatever you want," with the understanding that Hank would compensate the Cold Crush Brothers later. A good portion of Caz's lyrics were used in "Rapper's Delight." At the time Caz thought it would be good for the group—that they would get good publicity. Hank did not alter the lyrics very much, most notably rapping: "But I'm the Grandmaster with the three MCs"—problematic in that the Sugarhill Gang had three MCs, not four like the Cold Crush Brothers. He should have changed it to "But I'm the Grandmaster with the two MCs" to match the number of the Sugarhill Gang. Hank also maintained the line "I'm the C-a-s-an the o-v-a and the rest is F-l-y," which celebrates Caz's stage name when he fronted the Mighty Force as Casanova Fly. It would appear that many of the rhymes were also borrowed from lines Caz had developed as early as 1977 or 1978, despite Hank claiming toward the end of the song that he did not "bite" a single word. Nonetheless, "Rapper's Delight" became a huge hit in October 1979 and was the first rap single to land on the top 40 charts. Caz never received any credit or compensation for the rhymes that he contributed.

Grandmaster Caz of the Cold Crush Brothers, 1989.
Source: Photo © Ebet Roberts

Listening Guide

Listening to the Sugarhill Gang

"RAPPER'S DELIGHT"
(LONG VERSION)

MUSIC AND LYRICS CREDITED TO Sylvia Robinson, Henry Jackson, Michael Wright, Guy O'Brien, Bernard Edwards, and Nile Rodgers

PERFORMED BY Henry "Big Bank Hank" Jackson, Michael "Wonder Mike" Wright, and Guy "Master Gee" O'Brien

Released as 12" single in 1979 on Sugar Hill Records SH-542. *N.B.*: "Rapper's Delight" was released in various versions, in both "long" and "short" (edited for radio play) releases. This listening guide is based on the long version that is on iTunes as a track on the album *The Sugar Hill Records Story*. A slightly longer version with a prolonged fadeout can be found on YouTube that ends with additional alternations of the "Here Comes That Sound Again" drum part with the "Good Times" bass riff.

It is easy to dismiss "Rapper's Delight," the earliest rap crossover tune, because it carries a stigma of inauthenticity. However, this song served as a gateway into the hidden hip hop subculture previously found only in the ghettos of New York City, and it announced the arrival of a new musical trend during the last days of disco. Those unfamiliar with the crews and DJs that started it all knew all 15 minutes of this song, and any kid worth his or her muster could recite it verbatim. The raps were performed more palatably for a wider audience so that everyone could appreciate this new dance tune, not just the b-beat kids familiar with the tradition and expecting to participate with the MCs.

Producer Sylvia Robinson and the Sugarhill Gang contrived a studio recording reminiscent of a b-beat party of the South Bronx by using three unknown rappers and live musicians and MCs in a recording studio. Perhaps in an effort to avoid paying the composers for permission, she did not bring a DJ using records into the studio. As an alternative, she hired an arranger, Jiggs Chase, along with the label's house band—Keith LeBlanc on drums, Skip McDonald on guitar, Doug Wimbish on bass, and other session musicians—who together became the human turntables looping the beat from Chic's "Good Times" and material from Love De-Luxe's "Here Comes That Sound Again" in one extended studio take.

Lyrically, the song follows traditional ballad meter, which lends itself to easy memorization of a relatively long song. Furthermore, the rhythm is related to iambic meter—and at times follows true iambic meter—which helped mold the melodic style that become synonymous with the

Sugarhill sound: for example, "The *BEAT* don't *STOP* 'til the *BREAK* o' *DAWN*." With few shout-outs and only minor call-and-response verbal play, the smoothed-out raps appealed to audiences familiar with longer narrative verses of pop and R&B radio hits. The form helps the storytelling event in this rap. Each rapper takes his turn telling his tale following the **boasting** storytelling technique (bragging about his verbal skills, sexual prowess, and implausible wealth), but also covertly celebrates an unnamed "DJ" or beat-maker in **toast**-like fashion, bragging about his ability to move his partygoers' toes, feet, body, and seat. Additionally, Wonder Mike even offers us a little scatting—anticipating the emergence of the human beatbox technique: "Skiddlee beebop a we rock a scoobie doo" (~04:15).

The first eight measures of the introduction to "Rapper's Delight" are a studio re-creation of an excerpt of "Here Comes That Sound Again." The studio band follows this introduction with the "Good Times" groove that continues throughout the rest of the song. While the musicians try to create a soundscape in the manner of a DJ at a party, there are subtle details that make the live musicians on this recording noticeable. For example, at some moments, particularly during the second half of the song, there is increased rhythmic activity in the bass and drum parts, which a DJ would have been unable to achieve using existing recordings. An attentive listener can also hear variation among the instruments on "Rapper's Delight." While some of these discrepancies may be noticeable, they ultimately do not detract from this song's effective use of the studio musicians to imitate the DJ's methods of mixing different recordings to create a coherent track.

The instrumental arrangement of the verses is formulaic, consisting of eight measures of bass and drums playing the "Good Times" groove followed by eight measures with guitar and keyboard added. A live DJ would have achieved similar contrast by switching between two copies of the same record on two turntables, a technique that allowed DJs to extend a song's break indefinitely. Live musicians simulate this effect on "Rapper's Delight" by using material from a break, or breakdown section (just bass and drums in this case), and from a full-band iteration of the same material (with guitars and keyboards added) to extend the groove; this maintains interest by creating contrasting textures every eight measures. The drum break that replicates the "Here Comes That Sound Again" introduction reappears halfway through the song (at 4:37); the band again imitates how a DJ would create interest in the midst of an extended groove by inserting musical material from another record with the same tempo and a similar rhythmic feel.

This basic groove is at times punctuated by what sounds like a string **glissando**, a coordinated sliding effect (with its first appearance at 0:26) that returns periodically throughout the recording to accentuate particularly dramatic moments in the

Continued

Listening Guide

Listening to the Sugarhill Gang **Continued**

music or lyrics. In an interview with Richard Budman, Chic guitarist Nile Rodgers suggests that this sliding sound at the end of the string line was overdubbed onto "Rapper's Delight" from his original recording of "Good Times." It is likely that this effect was created by overdubbing a perfectly timed excerpt of the glissando on top of the studio band's simulated "Good Times" groove. This creates further musical interest, like a fake backspinning sound effect, with punctuations at key moments, and it also recalls the song from which the soundscape of "Rapper's Delight" is primarily drawn.

The re-creation of the atmosphere of a DJ party in "Rapper's Delight" is further heightened by several other prominent elements of the song's soundscape. The return of the lines beginning "Hotel, motel . . ." throughout the song, chanted by a number of male and female voices, is reminiscent of the kind of call-and-response interaction between MCs and their audiences at DJ parties, especially the punctuated "Say what?" from a female party responder. These voices, likely overdubbed in the studio, serve to further enhance the illusion that the "party" that "Rapper's Delight" evokes is actually occurring in the studio—a formula applied to other Sugar Hill recordings, but performed most realistically on Kurtis Blow's "The Breaks" in 1980. "Rapper's Delight," clocking in at just under 15 minutes, is roughly five times longer than the typical single of its day, which serves as another tribute to the party scene that the song represents on record. It should be noted that a chopped-up, single version about five minutes long was also released. The song, in both the long and short versions, fades out rather than coming to a conclusive end, further implying the continuation of the party after the recording is over.

0:00		Eight-bar introduction: Studio re-creation of breakbeat from Love De-Luxe's "Here Comes That Sound Again."
0:17		Bass line from Chic's "Good Times" with drum set and handclaps.
0:27		String section slide—likely overdubbed from a recording of "Good Times."
0:35	"I said a hip, hop . . ."	Beginning of Wonder Mike's first verse, still with minimal bass and drum texture for eight measures.
0:52	"See I am Wonder Mike . . ."	Guitar and keyboards enter for eight measures, thicker musical texture creates interest.
1:10	"Now so far you've heard my voice . . ."	Return to bass and drum texture for eight measures—the alternation between this texture and that of bass, drums, guitar, and keyboards continues every eight measures throughout the song.
1:18	"Check it out, I'm the . . ."	Big Bank Hank enters with a new verse.

2:02	"Hotel, motel . . ."	Female voice "Say what," followed by crowd vocal—probably over-dubbed in studio—chanting, "Hotel, motel, Holiday Inn." These additional vocals heighten the party atmosphere by simulating interaction between MCs and a crowd of partiers.
2:23	"Well it's on and on . . ."	Master Gee enters, with his first verse.
4:06	"Hip, Hop . . ."	The "hip hop" refrain, first introduced at the beginning of the song, returns here. This also marks the beginning of Wonder Mike's second verse.
4:37		Drum break from "Here Comes That Sound Again" returns. This break lasts eight bars before returning to the main "Good Times" groove.
4:54	"Hip, Hop . . ."	The "hip hop" refrain again returns here, to transition from the drum break back to the verse.
5:12	"And do a thing, but a-rock . . ."	Electric piano and vibraphone sounds added to the eight-bar "Good Times" groove that previously contained bass, drums, guitar, and piano. This pattern continues to alternate every eight measures with the original bass and drum pattern.
5:28	"Well, I'm Imp the Dimp . . ."	Hank returns for his second set of verses.
7:04	"Hotel, motel . . ."	First return of overdubbed crowd vocals.
7:30	"It was twelve o' clock one Friday night . . ."	Master Gee returns for his second set of verses.
9:04	"A can of beer that's sweeter than honey . . ."	Wonder Mike returns for his third set of verses.
10:21	"You call your friend two weeks later . . ."	Guitar is absent from the regular eight-bar bass, drums, electric piano, guitar, piano, vibraphone pattern. Regular eight-bar alternating patterns return after this section.
10:30	"Hip Hop . . ."	This "hip hop" refrain returns again.
10:47	"I go to the balls and I ring the bell . . ."	Hank returns for his third set of verses.
11:52	"Hotel, motel . . ."	Second return of overdubbed crowd vocals.
12:18	"Well, like Johnny Carson on the late show . . ."	Master Gee returns for his final set of verses.
13:35	"At the age of eight . . ."	A number of other, overdubbed voices appear before the song begins to fade out. The illusion of an in-studio party is heightened by the addition of these voices.
14:07		The drummer plays a fill, and the voices continue dubbed over the "Good Times" groove, as the track fades out.

Despite what many believe, "Rapper's Delight" was not the first "rap song" to get played on the radio. That distinction goes to the Fatback Band, a Brooklyn funk band that celebrated the rapping skills of a radio personality jockey. Their single "King Tim III (Personality Jock)" was released in the summer of 1979. King Tim's style was a cross between the old DJ rapping style of radio personalities from the 1950s and 1960s (DJ Jocko Henderson, Jockey Jack Gibson) and the South Bronx style of the late 1970s (see Chapter 2).

Grandmaster Flash was approached as early as 1977 to record his music, but he declined. He claims, "I didn't think that somebody else would want to hear a record re-recorded onto another record with talking on it. I didn't think it would reach the masses like that. I didn't see it. . . . So here it is . . . later and I hear 'To the hip-hop, to the bang to the boogie,' and it's not Bam, Herc, Breakout, AJ. Who is this?" (George 1993). Flash's query also reminds us that the primary leader of the culture was the DJ. Not until the commercialization of the scene would it shift completely to a rap-centered musical art form.

The commercial success of "Rapper's Delight" opened the door for rap music to get national attention and cross over into the mainstream pop market. Furthermore, radio stations often played all fourteen and a half minutes of the song, which was unheard of by radio-play standards because the average length of a song was about three minutes; even the five-minute, shortened version was longer than the average song on the radio. However, it was considered short by party-culture standards, because a performance was not conceived in terms of songs but much more holistically. To Flash's credit, a "song" by the subculture's standards reflects an entire performance: about two to three hours. Arguably, "Rapper's Delight" offers a nod to the ever-extending nature of a live performance in that the song fades out at the end and the rappers simply stop rapping.

"Rapper's Delight" used a live studio band to perform the backup track, based on the summer 1979 disco hit, Chic's "Good Times." This distorted the performance style developed by the DJs and MCs of the South Bronx, who always used the actual records. While disco tunes like "Good Times" were used in DJ mixes

Publicity photo of the Sugarhill Gang, ca. 1979. Left to right: Big Bank Hank, Master Gee, and Wonder Mike.

Source: *Courtesy BenCar Archives*

to the party culture, disco was subordinate to funk and soul. Thanks to "Rapper's Delight," the era of the MC as a showman and entertainer and the DJ as production leader was just about over and the art form was about to be reduced to its barest elements, rapping.

However, regardless of the ways it might have strayed from the local, underground tradition, "Rapper's Delight" had important features that would guide rap lyrics in the commercial era, some still relevant to that original community: boasting, exaggerations of worldly possessions, and promoting a good time.

The New Guard: Early Commercial Old-School Rap

Early commercial rap songs followed the lead of "Rapper's Delight." The working formula at the time was to hire a studio band to perform a familiar disco tune and get the MCs in the studio to rap to it. The earliest competitor for Sugar Hill Records was the short-lived Enjoy Records (1979–1981) run by Bobby Robinson—no relation to Sylvia and Joey Robinson of Sugar Hill Records. Bobby Robinson signed Grandmaster Flash and the Furious Five—the crew that was on every record company's wish list—as well as other MC crews that had paid their dues in the underground party scene in the Bronx. Because the Sugarhill Gang was a trio put together by Sylvia and Joey Robinson with no previous street credibility, the Funky Four Plus One More's "Rapping and Rocking the House" in 1979 was the first studio recording by a crew from the Bronx tradition. Like Sugar Hill, Enjoy producers paired the young MCs with a studio band, in this case playing the instrumental segments of Cheryl Lynn's disco hit "Got to Be Real" (1978), debatably a not-so-subtle jab at the "less real" Sugarhill Gang rappers.

Another convention that surfaced in the commercial era is the addition of party scene activity to connect this music to the subculture from which it originally emerged. Take, for example, Grandmaster Flash and the Furious Five's "Freedom" (1980, Sugar Hill Records). In "Freedom," Flash and his crew brought friends to the studio to re-create the party atmosphere: audience cheers accompanied by kazoos. Even when the tunes were moving in a direction of socially conscious rap, such as Kurtis Blow's "The Breaks" (1980), rappers maintained that party ethic. *Vibe* magazine journalist Tom Terrell describes "The Breaks" as the "greatest party you never went to" (1999: 47). The old-school commercial rap years can be summarized as the "party rap" years: Get the people dancing and boasting about your skills. Among many examples are Kurtis Blow's "Christmas Rappin'" (1979); Lady B's "To the Beat (Y'all)" (1980); Funky Four Plus One More's "That's the Joint" (1981); and Grandmaster Flash and the Furious Five's "Birthday Party" (1981). Although some conventions from the underground scene became a part of rap music, the DJ was still missing from the production.

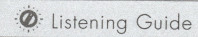
Listening Guide

Listening to Grandmaster Flash and the Furious Five

"THE ADVENTURES OF GRAND-MASTER FLASH ON THE WHEELS OF STEEL"

MUSIC AND LYRICS CREDITED TO Grandmaster Flash and the Furious Five

PERFORMED BY Grandmaster Flash and the Furious Five Recorded 1981

// The Adventures of Grandmaster Flash on the Wheels of Steel" was largely a re-versioning of Flash's routines at the clubs and parties where he performed before the commercial era. It only includes the other members of the group by way of songs they had recorded earlier ("Freedom" and "Birthday Party," both 1980) until the last two minutes of the record. While it did not have the crossover success that "White Lines" or "The Message" had on the pop charts, it made it to the 55th spot on the *Billboard* R&B singles charts and broke ground on what a DJ could do in the studio. This song is an incredible example of Flash's creativity and dexterity. It is composed of at least ten known records played on three turntables (though only six of the selections were acknowledged and copyrighted). This achievement is even more impressive when you consider that this record was created before the introduction of the sampler.

In "Wheels of Steel," Grandmaster Flash weaves his selections seamlessly, matching tempos and keys of the songs and maintaining a consistent pulse throughout; it's possible to tap one's foot on the beat and count measures of four beats from the beginning of this track uninterrupted until the end. Despite the fact that "Wheels of Steel" is a collage of snippets from several different records, Flash is able to keep the groove consistent, largely through his mastery of the technical elements of his craft.

Throughout the song, Flash is beat juggling in the tradition pioneered by DJ Herc. What makes Flash's approach different is that he incorporates backspinning (what he originally called quick mix theory) and his "clock theory" technique to accurately select the breakbeat or phrase to be punched in. Flash synchronizes disparate samples by effectively moving the needle in concert with the crossfader to switch between records at key moments, providing the sonic contrasts that characterize "Wheels of Steel" while maintaining a continuous rhythmic pulse throughout the song. A second key part of the continuous rhythmic pulse is the way Flash backspins records to repeat the same section of the groove. For example, using the record "Good Times,"

Flash backspins the record to repeat the bass line, seamlessly connecting the beginning of his chosen excerpts with the ending of the same excerpts, without interrupting the song's rhythmic pulse.

Flash also uses punch phrasing and baby scratching (the crisp sounds produced by moving the record back and forth in continuous movements while the crossfader is in the open position) to create percussive accents. These accents provide further layers of rhythmic activity, as though his punch-phrased or scratched records were another instrument that he could "play" along with the groove. Using these techniques, Flash creates a rhythmic counterpoint—a coherent combination of distinct musical material—by baby-scratching a second or third record in a rhythmic pattern that fills in gaps in the grooves that are playing. For example, at 4:43, to provide more rhythmic energy to "Good Times," Flash baby-scratches "8th Wonder" to create a type of percussive syncopation, sounding on the **off-beats**—the unaccented beats in this four-beat-per-measure song:

1-and-2-and-3-and-4-and

The off-beats are represented by "and" in the measure above.

Through Flash's masterful use of these techniques and his sense of what the most danceable portions of these records were, he was able to create a party-style DJ mix in the recording studio. It was unusual at that time to have a rap single bring the real sounds of a live DJ in performance, scratching and displaying the art of **turntablism**. With this song, Flash introduced the DJ as an artist for the emerging mainstream hip hop consumer culture.

The following is a list of the records used in "The Adventures of Grandmaster Flash on the Wheels of Steel" (in order of appearance):

1. "Good Times"—Chic
2. "Rapture"—Blondie
3. "Another One Bites the Dust"—Queen
4. "8th Wonder"—The Sugarhill Gang
5. "Birthday Party"—Grandmaster Flash and the Furious Five
6. "Monster Jam"—Spoonie G
7. "Apache"—Incredible Bongo Band
8. "Freedom"—Grandmaster Flash and the Furious Five
9. "Life Story"—The Hellers
10. "The Decoys of Ming the Merciless"—side 1 of *The Official Adventures of Flash Gordon*

Continued

☼ Listening Guide

Listening to Grandmaster Flash and the Furious Five **Continued**

0:00	Flash punch-phrases Spoonie G's "Monster Jam," then lets it play.
0:10	He blends this into Blondie's "Rapture," punch-phrases "Flash is fast," then lets it play.
0:20	He returns to "Monster Jam" and then transitions into Chic's "Good Times" bass line.
0:25	He begins baby-scratching a 16th-note pattern with "Good Times" bass line rhythm, as though his second turntable is another instrument in the groove's texture.
0:35	Flash crossfades into Incredible Bongo Band's "Apache"; continues baby-scratching rhythmically—this time scratching 16th-notes for the duration of the final bar of the four-bar "Apache" break pattern.
0:51	He punch-phrases Queen's "Another One Bites the Dust," then lets it play. He begins baby-scratching the "Good Times" record, providing a rhythmic motif in counterpoint to the main groove of "Another One Bites the Dust."
1:17	Flash returns to "Good Times," punch-phrases in his own group's song "Freedom" over the "Good Times" bass line.
1:51	He punch-phrases "Good Times" again, then lets it play.
2:09	He again uses a copy of "Freedom," on a second turntable, to develop a rhythmic figure in counterpoint to "Good Times."
2:13	He switches back to "Birthday Party" (brass section) and lets it play.
2:29	He pauses "Birthday Party" to punch-phrase in snippets of "Good Times" between the lines of the Furious Five's calls: e.g., Furious Five: "Everybody say one"/Crowd: "One!"/Furious Five: "Flash one time"[punch phrase "Good"]/Furious Five: "Everybody say two"/Crowd: "Two!"/Furious Five: "Flash two times"[punch phrase "Good. Good."], etc.
2:39	His punch phrasing morphs into more extended scratching of "Good Times" after the Furious Five says, "Flash three times."
2:43	He lets "Good Times" play, switching the crossfader between middle position (allowing "Freedom" to be heard with "Good Times") and the "Good Times" side.
3:14	Flash punch-phrases the roll call and zodiac sign from "Freedom" into the mix.
3:22	Flash creates a two-measure interlude by baby-scratching and punch-phrasing "Good Times," before letting the "Good Times" bass line play.
3:33	He moves the crossfader to the center position, plays "Life Story" by the Hellers with "Good Times."

4:02	Flash creates another two-measure baby-scratch interlude, then transitions into Sugarhill Gang's "8th Wonder." He lets it play.
4:25	Flash again scratches the "Good Times" record, in counterpoint to the handclap pattern on "8th Wonder."
4:34	He lets "Good Times" play.
4:43	Flash baby-scratches "8th Wonder" in counterpoint to "Good Times," filling in empty off-beats with syncopated scratches.
5:09	He lets "Good Times" play.
5:18	Flash mixes in children's record *The Official Adventures of Flash Gordon*.
5:24	Shout-outs by the Furious Five and party crowd. Flash returns on a second turntable, this time with an excerpt from the call-and-response section of the song.
5:57	Flash punch-phrases "Good Times," then he lets it play.
6:04	He adds a third turntable with another copy of "Good Times." Shout-outs by the Furious Five and party crowd and "Good Times" are playing uninterrupted, and more scratches are added on top of these records. Flash begins scratching and punch-phrasing this second copy of "Good Times" as a counterpoint to the copy that is playing uninterrupted.
6:44	He lets "Good Times" and the party section of "8th Wonder" play. Vocals fade out with a shout-out to Vicious Lee (the group's scratch artist). Additional baby scratches on the second copy of "Good Times" can be heard as the song fades out.

Crossing Over: The New Wave Connection

New Wave pop-crossover sensation Blondie recorded "Rapture" in 1980 and introduced the hip hop scene to a new set of consumers. The tune was the only "rap song" to reach number one on the *Billboard* chart during the 1980s. Blondie was never committed to the rap genre, and "Rapture" would be the group's one and only "rap song." The song lyrics celebrate two icons most notably, Fab Five Freddie and Grandmaster Flash, and the video includes Fab Five Freddie and Lee Quinones writing graffiti, as well as a young Jean-Michel Basquiat as a DJ. On February 14, 1981, Blondie were the musical guests for *Saturday Night Live*. They invited the Funky Four Plus One More to perform "That's the Joint" (1980) during their second set. It was the first time a South Bronx MC crew appeared on national television. The song's title recalls the b-beat era's party culture; the expression "that's the joint" refers directly to Herc's excellent parties.

New Technologies and New Experimentation

In 1982, Afrika Bambaataa signed with Tommy Boy Records and released the seminal hip hop tune "Planet Rock" with Soulsonic Force. Beginning in the late '70s/early '80s, Bambaataa and other DJs worked with computer programmers and experimented with synthesizers, drum machines, computers, analog and digital recording machines, and other equipment to create new and complex sound effects influenced by Kraftwerk's "Trans-Europe Express" (1977). Afrika Bambaataa introduced and popularized this technological production approach to hip hop in "Planet Rock."

Working with Soulsonic Force, Bambaataa made an effort to take the music and culture of the African American, Caribbean, and Latino Bronx into the punk and New Wave crowd, as if to announce to the world that this music can appeal to all audiences. In this song, Bambaataa blended musical fragments from sources that he felt both groups would appreciate, bringing the future into the past and celebrating the current: German electronic music pioneers Kraftwerk's "Trans-Europe Express" (1977) and "Numbers" (1981); the theme song from Ennio Morricone's *For a Few Dollars More* soundtrack (1967); and "Super Sporm" (1978) from the funky Captain Sky. He also encouraged his rappers to discard the staccato delivery of previous MCs in favor of extended notes and a chant-like style. He called his brand of hip hop music "electro-funk." "Planet Rock" is credited as the first song in the hip hop family of recorded music to use the Roland TR-808 drum machine. Grandmaster Flash and the Furious Five followed suit, releasing "It's Nasty" in 1982—which sampled rhythms from Tom Tom Club's "Genius of Love" (1980)—and "White Lines" a year later, sampling Liquid Liquid's "Cavern" (1983). In the same year the Cold Crush Brothers released "Punk Rock Rap," a tune that follows the New Wave dance trend (synthesizer and drum machine beats) and sung choruses that echo '60s pop like Gene Chandler's "Duke of Earl" (1962).

CHAPTER SUMMARY

During this brief 1979–1983 period (the second wave of hip hop's development), we can see how this early commercial era witnessed the four elements of hip hop converging and diverging as they became exposed to and appropriated into mainstream America. Hip hop music came to the fore, with the emphasis on the MC or rapper replacing the supremacy of the DJ. Second-wave rap music retained many features from the first wave, including themes, rhymes, and performance style and context. However, now it was recorded and popularized by small, independent, and mostly black-owned labels. Finally, synthesizers, drum machines, and computers became the primary instruments in the production of rap records, eventually replacing live musicians and arrangers in the studio.

The commercial forces that influenced the growth of hip hop culture favored those elements that could be most easily commodified. It was easier to bring hip hop dance to the screen or MCs to the recording studio than to represent and "sell" hip hop the grass-roots movement. Unlike graffiti and b-boying, rap music could be reproduced in a viable commodity, on rap records. In addition, rap's similarities to other African American verbal art traditions made it relevant to areas of the United States where those practices still persisted. Rapping as a convention for music making, especially among young African Americans, would grow and diversify especially in terms of regional musical variations and lyrical themes.

STUDY QUESTIONS

1. Identify the contribution of DJs Kool Herc, Afrika Bambaataa, and Grandmaster Flash to the development of hip hop music.

2. How did the rhyme and mixing battles of the DJs in the South Bronx contribute to the rise of MCs?

3. When and why did rap music shift from being exclusively an underground or street form to a commercial commodity for mass consumption?

4. Identify the musical features that characterize early old-school hip hop (early 1980s). What lyrical themes prevail in the old-school style?

5. What are the contributions of African American radio-personality DJs and Jamaican club DJs to the development of old-school hip hop?

6. In what ways did the following recordings change the studio production sound of rap music?

   Grandmaster Flash "Adventures of Grandmaster Flash on Wheels of Steel"

   Afrika Bambaataa & Soul Sonic Force "Planet Rock"

   Cold Crush Brothers "Punk Rock Rap"

KEY TERMS

Backspinning

Beatbox

Digging the crates

First wave [old-school hip hop]

Mixtapes

Needle dropping

Old-school

Punch phrase

Scratching

Second wave [old-school hip hop]

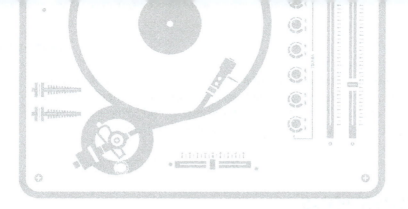

CHAPTER 6

THE GOLDEN ERA

Learning Objectives

When you have successfully completed this chapter, you will be able to discuss:

- The commercialization and crossover of rap music into the mainstream.
- The development of new styles, themes, and important artists in the 1980s through the early 1990s.
- The relationship of African American musical influences in this period of hip hop.

From Old School to New School: Concept of Rappin'

Hip hop was conceived as a poetic form *accompanied* by music, not as music with words; rhythm is its driving force. As we noted in Chapter 4, the delivery style of MCs draws from the traditions of African American preachers (improvised freestyle and rhymed couplets, syncopated rhythms, and call-and-response structures); the scat or free singing style of jazz performers; radio-personality DJs who rapped and rhymed in rhythm over recorded music; nationalist poets who told stories over drummed rhythms; and rhythm and blues performers who introduced their songs with extended narratives labeled "rapping." The lyricism of rap artists in the mid-1980s grew more sophisticated, both in terms of subject matter and the range of vocal styles, including more rhythmic phrasing and imitation of rhythm instruments (called **beatboxing**).

Second Generation of Rappers

Performers, fans, and rap scholars have labeled the second generation of rap variously as **new school**, the **golden era**, and **third wave**. This era is bookended by the commercial breakthrough of Run-D.M.C. in 1986 (some date it to 1984 with the crossover success of Run-D.M.C.'s video "Rock Box") and the explosion of gangsta rap with

1992's *The Chronic* by Dr. Dre. These years witnessed recordings from some of the biggest rappers in the genre's history, including LL Cool J, Public Enemy, Queen Latifah, EPMD, Big Daddy Kane, Eric B. & Rakim, N.W.A., Boogie Down Productions, Salt-n-Pepa, and Biz Markie.

Today, when hip hop culture is over 40 years old, calling this period "new school" (approx. 1984–1992) may seem strange. At the time, however, the second-generation artists believed that they were taking hip hop in a new direction—away from boasting and party lyrics and towards greater diversity in themes and styles. Arguably, the new school's more aggressive orientation might have been inspired by the battle between Busy Bee and Kool Moe Dee (see Chapter 4), but it can also be viewed as a response to the Sugar Hill Records model that had watered down the tradition to one element: rapping (see Chapter 5).

In 1983, Run-D.M.C. released a traditional boasting rap, "Sucker MC." Unlike the old-school model from which they developed their style, they offered listeners a more aggressive delivery with a back-to-basics rock sensibility and renewed attention on the DJ (Jam Master Jay) in the music-making process. The artists themselves identified their work as "new school" and "**hardcore**"; as D.M.C. states in "King of Rock" (1984), "It's all brand new, never ever old school. . . . Like we said before, we rock hardcore."

Nevertheless, what is "new" in hip hop changes very rapidly. Therefore, the term "golden era" identifies this period best in that it addresses the changes that took place after both the b-beat party period (ca. 1973–1983) and the old-school rap commercial era (ca. 1979–1983) and marks the crossover phenomenon that will establish rap music as a musical genre that is different from R&B and rock and roll. Golden era artists were overwhelmingly based in New York City; in fact, artists emerging from Queens, in particular Queensbridge (the Juice Crew members, such as Roxanne Shanté, Big Daddy Kane, and Biz Markie) and Hollis (Run-D.M.C., Def Jam co-founder Russell "Rush" Simmons, and LL Cool J), stimulated much of that initial change from the old-school ways of doing rap music.

Lyricists from other regions within New York and New Jersey—including Public Enemy's Chuck D (Long Island), KRS-One (South Bronx), Rakim (Long Island), and Queen Latifah (East Orange)—inaugurated the complex phrasing, delivery style, and themes that continue today in contemporary hip hop. Some rappers of the golden era grew up in inner-city communities, while others were raised in the suburbs, and various regions throughout the United States; this is especially important as the tough, streetwise ethos came to the fore with the emergence of Run-D.M.C. and Public Enemy, who had group members that grew up in middle-class neighborhoods. The broad and diverse range of hip hop styles and lyrical content reveal the range of diverse experiences and worldviews that characterize the multiple and changing voices in African American communities.

Golden era rap is characterized by skeletal beats, electric guitar riffs and samples from hard-rock or soul tracks, tough "dis" raps, and heavy commercialization of a street style that was largely ignored in the party lyrics of most old-school MCs. The notion of a hip hop culture began to transform. No longer would the four elements—DJing, MCing, breaking (b-boying), and graffiti—be connected to each other. In fact, by the end of the era, producers had replaced DJs, and breaking and graffiti were treated as old fads that had passed. Also, the local element disappeared: unlike old-school MCs who earned their fame through live performances and audience-judged lyrical battles, this new generation of MC-rappers garnered fame through radio play, record sales, and a new format—music videos.

New-School Innovations

Many new-school/golden era rappers retained aspects of the old-school party styles—themes of "rockin' the house" and boasting—to which they introduced new themes. Some told humorous stories of adolescent life in the suburbs. Others addressed social-political issues, expounding aggressively on the social ills that adversely affected the critical mass of African Americans, most still living in inner-city communities. New-school rappers also introduced new musical styles, fusing musical elements from rock, pop, R&B, jazz, and gospel, that launched the crossover of hip hop into the mainstream.

A Survey of New-School Styles and Themes (1980s–1990s)

By the mid-'80s, rap music began to make its mark as a musical genre. A **genre** is a category of artistic, musical, or literary composition characterized by a particular style, form, or content. Rap music developed numerous styles and themes.

Rap-Rock Fusion: The Emergence of Run-D.M.C. and the Beastie Boys

Run-D.M.C. are widely credited as the architects of the mainstream hip hop music revolution in the mid-1980s. The first thing they purposely changed was the flashy, fancy dress style of the old-school stars. They modeled their look after the street hustlers in Queens. Originally, this meant wearing Adidas with no laces, tracksuits, Stetson hats, and huge gold chains.

Commercial rap of the old school was inspired by the block party with beats that were funky (often taken from disco records). Old-school rap was more about the groove than the delivery of the rhymes. Run-D.M.C. expanded their rap, making it tough yet spare by adapting the sound and attitude of hard rock. The production is built on Jam Master Jay's scratching and minimalistic, drum-machine beats and Eddie Martinez's hard-hitting, rock-guitar-style solos that complement the hip hop aesthetic. Additionally, Run and D.M.C. changed the delivery style of the rhymes. Instead of delivering melodic raps in the style of the Sugarhill Gang, Spoonie G, or the Sequence, or sounding like cheerful party revelers Kurtis Blow and Melle Mel, Run and D.M.C. gave us a tough, shout-like rapping style.

Run-D.M.C. fused rock with rap music in the song "Rock Box" (1984), which was also the first video by rap artists to get regular rotation on the mostly white lineup on MTV. In 1986, the group collaborated with Aerosmith to create the first hip hop crossover hit, "Walk This Way." The song is largely a rap cover with vocal accents provided by Aerosmith's lead singer Steven Tyler. The loud, hard-rock sound of "Rock Box," "King of Rock," and "Walk This Way" appealed to tastes of MTV fans and changed the direction of MTV programming.

Run-D.M.C., 1986.

Source: *Photo © Ebet Roberts*

⬡ Listening Guide

Listening to Run-D.M.C.

"ROCK BOX"

COMPOSED BY Darryl McDaniels/
J. K. Simmons/Joseph Simmons/
Larry Smith

Appears on *Run-D.M.C.*, 1984, Profile
Records PCD-1202; peaked at no. 53
on *Billboard* 200 and no. 14 on
Billboard R&B Albums.

"Rock Box," the third single from Run-D.M.C.'s debut album, is a classic example of the group's collaboration with producer Rick Rubin. It offers their joint vision of **rap-rock fusion**, which incorporates the hard-rock sounds in vogue in the mid-1980s with a new, aggressive rap style. The track is characterized by a bare-bones approach similar to that of contemporary hard-rock groups such as Def Leppard and Billy Squier. The hard-rock sound is matched by a pioneering style in the vocal arrangement that reflects a hard, street aesthetic. Run and D.M.C. shifted rap's lyrical delivery away from the singsong style of the old-school superstars towards a new-school style that highlighted a streetwise toughness and menacing antagonism in the vocals. The aggressive rap vocals that the group delivers in "Rock Box" are placed over a repeated electric guitar riff, with minimalistic drum machines and a variety of synthesized sounds interjected throughout.

One of the primary indicators of the "rock" style is a number of short guitar solos, leading up to an extended guitar solo at the end. Studio guitarist Eddie Martinez plays in a theatrical hard-rock style similar to guitarists like Eddie Van Halen. The dramatic character of Martinez's solos is further accentuated by the use of **stop time**, an interruption of the rhythmic pattern punctuated with strongly accented rhythms and rests, to draw attention to key moments in the guitar solos or to set up an instrumental breakdown. The theatrical '80s rock vibe that "Rock Box" affects is further accented by many of the studio production techniques that give the song its new-school defining sound: **gated drums** that enable a strong and prominent presence of drums in the mix; reverb-saturated guitars; and vocals with added echo effects that give this studio recording the feel of a grandiose arena concert.

While "Rock Box" pulls heavily from these defining characteristics of '80s hard rock, the song also contains a number of elements that affirm the group's status as the new leaders of rap music. D.M.C. and Run execute their raps aggressively, as one may expect from a hard-rock or heavy-metal band, but they do not replicate the falsetto singing or guttural growling that defined the vocals of hard-rock bands at the time. Rather, the vocalists shout their rap lyrics in strongly accented rhythmic patterns and often rap important rhymes at the end of lines together; entire sections of this dual vocal technique appear throughout the song. The holler-like raps that take place throughout the song, beginning from 0:00 with an echoing, call-and-response effect, "Run, Run, Run . . ."—immediately followed by a prototypical "dis" to all those "sucker MCs" that rap with no style or originality and boast of lyrical prowess—are elements that draw on hip hop MC techniques not typical in the hard-rock tradition.

The instrumental arrangement of "Rock Box," while prominently incorporating the guitar sounds and studio production techniques of '80s rock, also contains a number of unique elements that set this song apart from the mainstream hard-rock music of its day. The looping of the group's signature bell sound via digital sampling throughout the song mimics the sound that a DJ might create by backspinning a sample from a record. Additionally, while the drums may sound like typical '80s hard-rock "gated" drums made popular by Phil Collins in 1981, they were in fact programmed by Jam Master Jay on a drum machine rather than played by a live drummer in the studio. "Gating reverb" is when the audio engineer limits the number of reverberations on a sound and cuts it off abruptly as opposed to allowing it to naturally fade out. On this recording, Jam Master Jay uses a drum machine to cut off the tail of the snare and bass drums' sounds. The sound effect makes an impressive, synthetic drum "pop" that was popular in 1980s rock.

The group sets itself apart from the "Rock" in "Rock Box" in other ways as well, boasting that "our DJ's better than all these bands" and incorporating a turntable solo by Jam Master Jay. Run-D.M.C. further position themselves apart from many of the negative clichés of hard-rock music by denouncing the hedonism of drug culture ("we don't drop dimes") and consumer culture ("Calvin Klein's no friend of mine") that were firmly associated with the hard-rock acts of their day.

Run-D.M.C. effectively fused many of the signature sonic elements of the hard-rock style with their own unique set of hip hop sounds. This fusion not only blended rap and rock but also provided a critique of many of the cultural elements associated with hard rock. Run-D.M.C. set themselves apart both sonically and culturally from the hard-rock music that figured so prominently into the soundscape of "Rock Box," while simultaneously incorporating key sounds of this rock music that helped them appeal to a commercial audience.

Continued

Listening Guide

Listening to Run-D.M.C. **Continued**

0:00	"Run [Run], D.M.C. . . ."	Introductory shout-outs announcing the group's name enter with echo effects, followed by a brief segment of the song's main guitar riff and a couple of pronounced drum pops.
0:04	"Rock . . . For you . . ."	The Run-D.M.C. signature bell sound is added to the mix. This sound was likely played on a keyboard synthesizer and duplicated using an electronic sampler.
0:11		The bass guitar kicks off the song's introductory riff; electric guitar enters and plays a full iteration of the riff. Digital snare drum sequence begins in $\frac{4}{4}$ time.
0:23		The guitarist plays a solo fill, in a hard-rock style that resembles the period's most fashionable rock guitarists, such as Eddie Van Halen.
0:32	"For all you . . ."	Run begins the first verse, and the main riff plays uninterrupted. Run and D.M.C. alternate lines and interject duo vocal sections throughout.
0:47	"Because we're wheelin' . . ."	The guitar punctuates the verse with a solo similar to what has been heard in the introduction added to the song's main riff. This type of solo gesture returns periodically during verses throughout the song.
1:11		Stop-time break interrupts the established main riff, with a short hard-rock guitar solo.
1:29	"Because the rhymes I say sharp as a nail . . ."	The band drops out; only bells and drums remain. Run continues as the primary vocalist.
1:36	"Took a test to become an MC and didn't fail . . ."	D.M.C. takes over lead vocal duties.
1:39	"I couldn't wait to demonstrate . . ."	The main riff returns.
1:54	"Burst into the party . . ."	Run takes over lead vocals. Solo guitar punctuations return here.
2:03	"So listen to this because it can't be missed . . ."	D.M.C. returns to lead vocals.
2:09	"You can do anything that you want to . . ."	The guitarist ceases playing prominent lead lines. The band returns to vamping on the groove.

2:32	"So move your butt to the cut . . ."	Run and D.M.C. rap together, and continue either alternating lines or rapping together until the end of the song. Solo guitar returns here.
2:46	"Side to side, back and forth . . ."	The guitarist again ceases soloing. The band returns to vamping on the main riff.
3:01	"Our DJ's better than all these bands"	The band stops. Jam Master Jay, the group's DJ, scratches a record, punch-phrasing in drum sounds.
3:05		The bells return, this time with synthesizer hits and bass drum kicks.
3:15	"We've got all the lines . . ."	Stop-time feel returns with guitar and drums. The bell sounds and synthesizer hits continue.
3:25	"Calvin Klein's no friend of mine . . ."	The drum groove returns. The main guitar riff is still absent.
3:34		One iteration of the main riff is played, and then ceases.
3:39	"Jay . . ."	The previous stop-time pattern returns.
3:58		The main riff returns and an extended guitar solo begins. Name shout-outs and other vocal interjections can be heard shouted over the solo.
4:27	"Don't stop . . ."	Stop time returns. The guitarist continues soloing.
4:36	"Don't stop . . ."	The song's main riff returns. The guitarist continues soloing over this and vocal shout-outs continue; "Krush Groove" and "Bass," etc., can be heard.
4:56		Stop time returns and the song begins to fade out, with the guitarist still soloing. Shouted vocals can still be heard on top of the riff and solo.

Boasting was still part of Run-D.M.C.'s lyrical themes, but the group also took on grittier realities of urban life or cultural relevance. Listen to the commentary in the video "King of Rock," addressing the fact that African American contributions to rock and roll have been ignored. The music, the attitude, the words, and the themes together marked a turning point for rap. Years after the release of Run-D.M.C.'s 1984 debut, the group signaled a cultural and musical change for the music, ushering it into its accepted form.

A trio of white rappers from Brooklyn, New York, also contributed to the rock-rap sound and the crossing over of rap music into the mainstream. The Beastie Boys began as a punk rock band that learned about hip hop by hearing Afrika Bambaataa

The Beastie Boys salute their fans, 1987.

Source: *Photo © Ebet Roberts*

and other old-school artists performing at downtown punk clubs. Initially the Beastie Boys imitated their African American counterparts, especially in terms of fashion and posturing, but soon afterwards they integrated an almost exaggerated, "white" sensibility in delivering their rhymes, such as overstressed, nasal diction and a tough Brooklyn accent that ultimately earned them the reputation as the clown princes of hip hop. Their style did not mock or parody the culture so much as acknowledge that they were white kids performing an African American art form. When they signed with Def Jam records, they appeared in the rap music film *Krush Groove* (1985), performing an early single, "She's On It," and toured with Run-D.M.C. The group had an African American following up until their crossover hit "Fight for Your Right (to Party)" in 1986. This single garnered lots of attention on MTV and pop radio stations across the country, and their next album *Licensed to Ill* was one of the fastest-selling records for Columbia Records. Their rock-fusion approach brought them an alternative-rock identity that persisted into the new millennium. Though they lost their African American fan base, they remain important contributors to the tradition.

Response Rap/Dis Rap: Putting Beef on Wax

During this era, rap artists attempted to gain an edge on their competition by exchanging insults about their appearance, character, personality, material possessions, physical attributes, lack of lyrical skills, and other personal qualities or activities following the model Kool Moe Dee provided in 1981 (see Chapter 4). These attacks were performed in the studio by up-and-coming rappers challenging established recording artists; the listening audience waited patiently beside their radios for a response.

According to many rap critics and scholars, including rap journalist Laura Jamison and ethnomusicologist Cheryl Keyes, female rappers introduced the African American oral tradition of signifyin' to old-school hip hop. In Chapter 4, we defined signifyin' as the exchange of indirect insults during verbal dueling or a way of subtly implying messages intended as insults.

UTFO released "Roxanne, Roxanne" in 1984, which drew a flurry of responses to the group's rather sexist criticism of a young lady who rejected their romantic overtures. Among the many responses to the song, two became quintessential. The first "Roxanne" to get her rap on the radio was 14-year-old Queens native Lolita "Roxanne Shanté" Gooden, who disparaged each member of UTFO one by one. Working with producer Marley Marl, Roxanne Shanté applied the same logic that drives ritual dueling to produce the hit underground sensation "Roxanne's Revenge" (1984). Her **response rap**, or **dis rap**, created a new model for unknown rappers to lyrically challenge established rap musicians in an MC-type battle in the recording studio. The other dis rap came from Adelaida "The Real Roxanne" Martinez, who was the inspiration for the song and had appeared in the video for "Roxanne, Roxanne." UTFO members invited Martinez into the studio to record "The Real Roxanne" (1985) in an attempt to shut down Shanté's dis rap success.

There are stylistic differences between the two Roxannes' delivery styles, rhymes, and musical production. The Real Roxanne's production followed the electro–hip hop style of UTFO, and she delivered smooth rhymes with a melodic tinge. On the vanguard of the "new" style, the teenaged Roxanne Shanté rapped some vicious lines of disrespect, curse words included, in a tough, raspy, but recognizably youthful tone of voice that rivaled the aggressive and audacious delivery styles of contemporaries like LL Cool J and Run-D.M.C.

Roxanne Shanté, 1990.
Source: Photo © Ebet Roberts

Unlike battles in the old-school tradition, this battle was no longer live onstage and no immediate audience was present to proclaim a winner. Recall from Chapter 4, the famous battle between Busy Bee and Kool Moe Dee in 1981 that transformed the battle's structure to include direct insults. At this event, Kool Moe Dee brought the battle closer to the African American verbal art forms of signifyin' and ritual dueling. The new generation took it to the next level, by recording their dis in the studio and playing it on the radio. The Roxanne response records changed the format in which MCs could battle.

Following the success of Roxanne Shanté, younger rappers employed the same tactic. For example, Steady B attempted to knock down the very famous rap artist LL Cool J with his humorous rap threat "I'll Take Your Radio" (1985) that mocks the established rapper's hit "Can't Live Without My Radio" (1984). Steady B's attack is pale by modern standards, but it is a strategy that up-and-coming artists would employ over and over again.

Another battle that erupted during this period was between the Queens- and South Bronx–based rappers. It began when MC Shan of Queensbridge released "The Bridge" (1985) to celebrate all the pre-commercial DJs and MCs from Queens. He was part of the Juice Crew, the Queensbridge artists' collaborative that included Marley Marl, Roxanne Shanté, Big Daddy Kane, Biz Markie, and Kool G Rap. KRS-One (Bronx) interpreted "The Bridge" as a dis against the South Bronx's history and claim of hip hop's origins, so he released a response record called "South Bronx" (1986). MC Shan responded with "Kill That Noise" (1987), only to be bested by KRS-One with the dis to end the battle, "The Bridge Is Over" (1987). In listening to these four songs, note especially how KRS-One speeds up the delivery style and incorporates a Jamaican patois in "The Bridge Is Over" as if to remind us that hip hop is rooted in a Jamaican mobile-DJ, party tradition, a heritage that is not shared by the Queens rappers, who—KRS-One suggests—appropriated it from the South Bronx.

The dis rap tradition raises interesting questions about the authenticity of its performers. To what extent are these records self-promoting vehicles and to what extent do they reflect genuine hatred between artists? At this time, in almost every case, these battles were metaphorically vehement and nonphysical. In fact, no real violence ever arose from this tradition until the gangsta era of the 1990s and the beef that changed the rap world: Tupac versus Notorious B.I.G. (see Chapter 8).

Rap Ballads

Although love as a theme appeared in old-school rap tunes—such as Spoonie G's "Love Rap"(1980) or "One Love" (1986) by electro–hip hop stars Whodini—the golden era superstar LL Cool J was the first to popularize the style. The earlier models might have had "love" as their inspiration, but they fell short in terms of revealing a sense of romance. Spoonie's love rap is a tale about greedy women more than romance, and Whodini's romantic verses ["I guess it's the way I smile, when I hear your name/It's the little things that you do, that mean so much/It's the care that you put, into every touch" . . .] get lost in the hard, staccato cadence and the techno-funky beat.

Releasing his first hits, "I Can't Live Without My Radio" and "Rock the Bells," in 1985, 17-year-old LL Cool J was originally known for his hard-hitting, streetwise, and virulent rhymes. However, his mainstream breakthrough single "I Need Love" (1987) introduced fans to a vulnerable, romantic rapper in search of true love and monogamy and brought him a teen-idol appeal: "Romance sheer delight how sweet/I gotta find me a girl to make my life complete/You can scratch my back, we'll get cozy and huddle/I'll lay down my jacket so you can walk over a puddle." LL Cool J recites his lines softly and smoothly over a simple, romantic melody played on a Yamaha keyboard. He foregoes the tough, staccato delivery style favored in that time period to set a romantic mood that is not found in his predecessors' work.

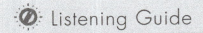

Listening to LL Cool J

"I NEED LOVE"

COMPOSED BY Bobby Erving/Darryl Pierce/David Pierce/Dwayne "Muffla" Simon/James Todd Smith

PERFORMED BY LL Cool J

Appears on *Bigger and Deffer*, 1987, Def Jam Recordings FC 40793; peaked at no. 1 on R&B Charts and no. 14 on Top 100.

While hip hop fans and critics might choose "Rock the Bells" as one of the most important LL Cool J songs of the golden era, "I Need Love" is a significant rap song for a number of reasons: it represents a departure from LL's normally aggressive delivery; it strays away from the rock sensibility of rap music in that period; and, most importantly, it provides an example of tenderness that other rap artists would later emulate, effectively making "I Need Love" the first successful crossover rap ballad. Other artists, such as Spoonie G and Whodini, created love-themed raps in the 1980s, but neither of these conveyed an audible sense of romance. This song was not only a pioneering moment in shaping the themes and delivery styles appropriate for rap artists, it also proved that a formula differing from established tropes could be commercially viable, as this song peaked in the *Billboard* Top 20.

Party motifs and hard-rock sounds were a key part of golden era rap music, and the young LL Cool J's music was no different. Songs like "I Can't Live Without My Radio" or "Rock the Bells" (both 1985) were primarily characterized by a

LL Cool J onstage.
Source: *Photo © Ebet Roberts*

Continued

Listening to LL Cool J Continued

minimalistic, loud, and bare-bones approach to production, with the street-tough MC's rhymes shouted in a loud, aggressive voice. "I Need Love," however, showcases a more intimate side of LL—who raps in a soft, affected manner—rather than the brash brand of machismo he was famous for at the time. He reveals to his female listeners that he is lonely and vulnerable, a reformed playboy who is ready for a monogamous relationship. What makes this love song particularly successful is that he is reaching out to all young ladies—not a specific woman—to find the woman who will reveal herself to him, love him, and relieve his loneliness.

To create the romantic mood and give the song a softer feel, LL Cool J raps over lush layers of synthesized keyboards. The softer drum machines are programmed to accentuate the hi-hat more than the kick and snare drums. The placement of keyboard sounds changes from the verses to the choruses, with a countermelody added when less activity is taking place in the rap's lyrics. Towards the song's four-minute mark, LL increases the rhythmic activity in his rap and delivers his rhymes in an increasingly impassioned way as the accompaniment similarly adds layers and rhythmic activity. This climax is followed immediately by a breakdown, in which LL pleads, rather than raps, his final words before the song fades out. These shifts reflect the dynamism that appears throughout many of his early recordings, but in a very different context: LL is not expressing how tough he is through the song's lyrics and accompaniment, but rather he is expressing how passionate a lover he is through the peaks and valleys of this song's musical and emotional activity. With his contemporaries usually boasting of their sexual and romantic prowess, his expressions of amorous passivity were new to rap, especially when he softly says, "If you wanna give it [love—not just sex] to me girl make yourself seen/I'll be waiting." "I Need Love" served to reposition this artist, transforming him from a tough rapper into a crossover teen idol. It redefined the thematic and sonic material that was permissible for rappers, popularizing the rap ballad as a subgenre.

0:00		Introductory keyboard line plays; the sound is similar to a celesta, a keyboard instrument that features steel bars like a xylophone to produce a shimmering, ringing sound.
0:10	"When I'm alone in my room . . ."	Vocals and hi-hat enter; the song remains very subdued.
0:21	"There I was giggling . . ."	Drum-machine bass drum, claps, and snare sounds enter along with the left-hand keyboard playing bass notes. The song's texture thickens.
1:05	"I need love . . ."	The chorus enters. A new synthesized keyboard sound begins, contrasting with the earlier electric piano sound. This added hollow, synthetic sound provides a countermelody to the melody played by the original celesta sound.

1:25		A brief snare drum fill occupies the place between the interlude/chorus and the next verse.
1:27	"Romance, sheer delight, how sweet . . ."	The verse texture returns here; everything but the lyrics remains the same.
1:46	"I could go on forever . . ."	The hi-hat break here builds rhythmic intensity.
1:48	"But where you at . . ."	The tension created by this hi-hat break is released; the verse returns to its original feel.
2:08	"When I find you . . ."	A snare break begins, building to the chorus.
2:10	"I need love"	The countermelody returns with the chorus.
2:30		A hi-hat fill begins here, transitioning to the next verse.
2:32	"I wanna kiss and hug you . . ."	The verse texture returns here.
2:51	"I love you more than a man . . ."	The snare break here builds rhythmic intensity.
2:53	"I watch the sun rise . . ."	The tension created is released; the verse returns to its original feel.
3:14	"I swear to you, this is something . . ."	Another hi-hat break leads to the next chorus.
3:15	"I need love . . ."	The countermelody returns with the chorus.
3:34		There is a hi-hat break here to transition from the chorus to the next verse.
3:37	"See what I mean . . ."	The original texture returns and the verse feel continues.
3:57	"From the slightest touch . . ."	There is a snare drum break here, leading to the next section of the song, which begins increasing rhythmic and dynamic activity.
3:59	"Of your hand . . ."	The instrumental texture gradually becomes denser and louder as the rhythmic and emotional activity in LL's rap intensifies: the keyboards are doubling in octaves now, and the drum sounds are more active here, building to the chorus.
4:21	"I need love"	The countermelody returns with the chorus.
4:43	"Girl, listen to me . . ."	The instruments break down here: the keys are doubled in octaves and there is less drum activity. LL speaks the song's final words, rather than rapping them, slowing the song's rhythmic activity.
5:05		The full instrumental texture returns; LL has finished with his vocals now. The song fades out.

Feminist Themes

Women of the new school introduced new themes and interpretative approaches to hip hop that distinguished their voices from those of their male counterparts. Women rappers like the two Roxannes, as we have noted, reintroduced verbal dueling/ritual insults into a battle-like structure called **dis raps**, **answer raps**, or **response raps**. However, as Queen Latifah observed, the major record labels did not financially support their female rappers in the same way they supported the men—in terms of salary, promotion, videos, and concert tours.

Female rappers have addressed a wide range of issues, including partying, relationships, social and political issues, and sexuality. Women rappers have responded to their position as subjects and objects, challenging the social norms of female sex roles in hip hop. They have also asserted control, power, and authority over themselves and their sexuality. In the process they have transformed hip hop into a platform for female empowerment that challenges the stereotypes perpetuated by male rappers. Through their dialogues, women have raised an awareness of a range of social and political issues that affect women. They also have transformed hip hop into an empowering agent by defining themselves with confidence and an attitude, in songs like Salt-n-Pepa's "Tramp," MC Lyte's "Paper Thin," and Yo-Yo's "Girl, Don't Be No Fool." The female rappers' records sometimes reflect the macho style and aggressive delivery of male rappers (e.g., Boss's "Deeper"). Women's rap also includes an Afrocentric, black feminist (or womanist) ideology to empower black women (Queen Latifah's "U.N.I.T.Y. (Who You Calling a Bitch?)" and Salt-n-Pepa's "Blacks' Magic").

By the end of the '80s, female rappers were making music videos that layered the lyrical content with meaningful visual content. For example, Queen Latifah's video for "Ladies First" (1989) begins with a slide show of important women in African American history that sets the viewer-listener up for Latifah's narrative about sisterhood and women's rapping prowess. The video also features British rapper Monie Love, a collaboration that arguably speaks to the pan-African connectivity or African-diasporic agenda of this work. Visual elements in the video that complement the lyrics of the song include anti-apartheid, pro-pan-African imagery, expressed in the still photographs and video footage of South Africa; Afrocentric clothing; and the sequence showing Latifah knocking down masculine figurines and replacing them with soul fist statuettes on a battlefield strategy board.

 Listening Guide

Listening to Queen Latifah

"LADIES FIRST"

COMPOSED BY Dana "Queen Latifah" Owens, Shane "The Doctor" Faber, Mark "DJ Mark the 45 King" James, Lakim Shabazz, and Anthony "Apache" Peaks

Queen Latifah's "Ladies First" is a prime example of her **womanist** brand of rap music. Latifah and her British partner Monie Love demonstrate that women rappers can "flow" and need to be taken as seriously as their male counterparts, while destroying sexist "stereotypes—they got to go." Latifah delivers her

PERFORMED BY Queen Latifah (vocals), Monie Love (vocals), Mark "DJ Mark the 45 King" James (producer/mixer), Shane "The Doctor" Faber (bass guitar/ engineer), and Paul C. (engineer)

Appears on *All Hail the Queen*, 1989, Tommy Boy TB 1022; peaked at no. 5 on *Billboard* Rap Charts.

rhymes assertively throughout the song but doesn't shout as was typical among male rappers in the late '80s. While Love's delivery is softer and more relaxed than Latifah's, her rhymes have the same intensity and are equally formidable in the challenge they issue to male MCs and rap music listeners. These women are not asking, they are *showing* listeners (consumers), colleagues (predominantly African American male rappers), and record executives (predominantly white, male, industry decision makers) that Latifah was not getting the same publicity and touring support that her male counterparts received. On the album, this song is a straightforward rap song, a fairly traditional boast (see Chapter 4) with a feminist twist, whereas the video is very politically charged in its imagery, unifying all African and African-descended peoples, and adds R&B elements with an all-female chorus singing in harmony, "Oooo, Ladies First, Ladies First, Ladies First."

The intensity is heightened by the song's soundscape. Much of the production credit goes to DJ Mark the 45 King, who manipulated funk samples from 7th Wonder's "Daisy Lady" and Kool & the Gang's "Good Times" in order to give the track its polyphonic, polyrhythmic feel. DJ Mark the 45 King used these tracks along with a drum machine in the studio to create a multilayered soundscape taking cues from the sound style created by the Bomb Squad on Public Enemy's recordings but redesigned in complexity that favors repetitive, melodic interludes. There are fewer samples in "Ladies First" than in typical Public Enemy tracks of the same period, but they are layered in similar ways. For example, the short, held saxophone blast from "Good Times" is combined with the song's main bass groove created from "Daisy Lady." It is further enhanced by "The Doctor" playing the song's bass line on bass guitar in the studio and spoken-word samples that are layered on top of one another and punch-phrased in a variety of configurations throughout. There is also one appearance of an unidentified vocal sample of a man's voice saying "Yeah, there's going to be some changes in here," that adds another layer of texture to these samples and serves as an interlude between verses.

DJ Mark the 45 King uses punch-phrasing extensively. For instance, throughout many of the verses, the drum machine and bass guitar continue playing the song's groove while samples are punch-phrased in at key moments (usually on the

Continued

☼ Listening Guide

Listening to Queen Latifah Continued

first beat of a phrase), creating a stop-time effect. Brief excerpts of the samples are also added at key moments in order to heighten the rhythmic intensity, usually with the sample played in its full form afterwards. Just as adding punch-phrased samples to the mix alters the texture of the song's groove, subtracting elements from the arrangement also creates musical interest. In the song's break-down that appears at 3:25, gradual addition or subtraction of portions of these samples creates textural shifts in the same way that punch-phrasing is used to create a stop-time feel or to build towards another section.

Queen Latifah and Monie Love's intense verbal delivery, DJ Mark the 45 King's use of samples and studio production techniques, and the contributions made by the rest of Latifah's Flavor Unit crew equaled the work of the hardcore male artists of the day without any evidence of mere masculine imitation. With this song, Queen Latifah set the stage for the female MC to be a success in the mostly "man's world" of rap music in the golden era of hip hop.

0:00		The introduction begins, sampled from 7th Wonder's "Daisy Lady," with guitar, bass, drums, and horns; a second sample of a saxophone from Kool & the Gang's "Good Times" also appears alongside a studio-added drum machine on this track.
0:17	"The ladies will kick it . . ."	Queen Latifah begins her first verse. The song's texture is sparse, consisting only of the programmed drum machine and the sample of the saxophone note.
0:24	"Now it's time to rhyme . . ."	All instruments stop for Latifah's one-bar rhyme break.
0:27	"A sister dope enough . . ."	A drum fill is played, and the samples return.
0:29	"Ay, yo, let me take it from here . . ."	Monie Love enters with her first verse. Here the samples are punch-phrased in over the drum machine. This punch-phrasing creates a stop-time feel.
0:50	"Yes, there's gonna be some changes . . ."	Instrumental interlude of the song's original samples with an unidentified vocal sample: "Yes, there's gonna be some changes . . ."
0:54	"Believe me when I say . . ."	Monie Love returns, rapping over the stop-time feel from earlier.
1:12	"I break into a lyrical freestyle . . ."	Queen Latifah returns; the stop-time feel continues.

1:27	"Into reverse . . ."	Queen Latifah and Monie Love engage in a brief, one-bar-long call-and-response figure over a break in the music.
1:29		Latifah utters the song's tagline. The instrumental groove begins here and plays out, abandoning the stop-time feel.
1:48		This groove breaks down to the drum machines with the 7th Wonder sample punch-phrased in periodically. The sample of the single saxophone note continues in its regular pattern.
1:56		The "Daisy Lady" sample plays out again, with its main groove returning here.
2:04	"You say that the ladies couldn't make it . . ."	Queen Latifah returns for another verse, with a stop-time feel throughout.
2:12	"I'm divine, and my mind . . ."	There is a one-bar break in the instrumental samples. Latifah fills in this break with a rap.
2:15	"A female rapper . . ."	The main groove returns here, ending the stop-time feel.
2:19	"My sista . . ."	Monie interjects in Latifah's verse and Latifah verbally surrenders the mic to Monie during this break.
2:22	"Yo, praise me not . . ."	Monie Love begins her next verse, with the stop-time feel returning here.
2:32	"To enable you . . ."	Monie continues; the groove plays out here.
2:40	"I wish for you to bring me to . . ."	The stop-time feel returns here.
2:58	"Contact, and in fact . . ."	Queen Latifah returns here, with the stop-time feel continuing.
3:08	"The next man . . ."	The main groove returns.
3:15	"The title of this recital . . ."	Repeated punch phrases build to the tagline and instrumental break.
3:17		The instrumental groove returns here.
3:26		The song breaks down: bass and guitar are removed, with the drum machine and horn samples remaining.
3:35		One horn sample is removed, with only drum machines and the sax squeal remaining.
3:46		The guitar and bass return and the song fades out.

This section on feminist themes has thus far focused on women's contributions to rap's lyrical content; however, listening to their musical productions (e.g., Queen Latifah's "Ladies First" and "U.N.I.T.Y. (Who You Calling a Bitch?)" or Salt-n-Pepa's "Blacks' Magic") underscores that women were on the vanguard of R&B-rap fusion before it became standardized in the late 1990s. In fact, the women rappers of the old school were incorporating sung choruses into their rap songs a decade earlier, for example on the Sequence's "Funky You Up," Sylvia [Robinson]'s "It's Good to Be the Queen," and Sylvia Robinson's collaboration with Melle Mel on "Jesse" (see Chapter 4).

Novelty/Humorous Rap

Rap artists constantly are on the lookout for an angle to make their material fresh and new, so it will stand out and attract an audience. Humor has been a part of the hip hop tradition from the earliest time, even before the more pointed political and social satire. It could be revealed in the form of jocular-insulting dance moves, lampooning graffiti cartoons and messages, playful musical choices by the DJ, or witty remarks by the MC. "Novel" can be synonymous with unique, original, and innovative, as in the invention of beatboxing (see below); however, "novelty" sometimes carries the more pejorative connotation of a lack of seriousness or importance, as in, "It's just a novelty." For this reason, novelty and humorous rap is not always taken as seriously as more hardcore styles.

A new vocal style that evolved in the mid-'80s was **beatboxing**, the vocal imitation of percussion instruments. Doug E. Fresh's "La Di Da Di" (1985) was among the first to incorporate these rhythmic vocal effects. In many ways, beatboxing was the human version of what Grandmaster Flash did when he converted a Vox drum machine to allow him to add more percussion to a musical mix; however, the style also harks back to earlier African American human-percussive art forms such as scatting (Jazz Age vocalizations imitating sounds of instruments) and hambone (body percussion; slapping hands to other parts of the body).

Beatboxing became the signature of Darren "Buff the Human Beat Box" Robinson of the comic hip hop group the Fat Boys. Originally known as the Disco 3, these Brooklyn rappers (Mark "Prince Markie Dee" Morales, Damon "Kool Rock-Ski" Wimbley, and Darren "Buff the Human Beat Box" Robinson) won a talent contest at Radio City Music Hall in 1983 thanks in part to Robinson's talent for vocally creating hip hop rhythms and a variety of sound effects. The trio changed their name and recorded a series of good-time party anthems and songs humorously exploiting their weight. Old-school superstar Kurtis Blow produced their first few records. The Fat Boys re-created the talent contest that brought them such good fortune in the film *Krush Groove* (1985), but this time at the old-school South Bronx hotspot, Sal Abbatiello's club Disco Fever. The lyrics to "Pump It Up—Let's Get Funky" (1985) perpetuate the distinction between the old school and the new school, with a tip of the hat to the first generation (Grandmaster Flash and Kurtis Blow) and to the young Turks breaking new ground (Run-D.M.C.).

Moving away from New York, Philadelphians DJ Jazzy Jeff (Townes) and the Fresh Prince (Will Smith) added a humorous suburban perspective with songs like

"Girls Ain't Nothing but Trouble" (1986) and "Parents Just Don't Understand" (1988). They also helped make rap music popular on top 40 radio stations. DJ Jazzy Jeff and the Fresh Prince got together in 1986, when they performed together at a house party after years of separately pursuing hip hop careers around the Philadelphia area. Later that year, they performed at the New Music Seminar, where Townes placed first in the DJ competition, which helped them land a record deal with Jive Records. The duo never pretended to be "street." They rapped about what they knew: suburban life and middle-class values. The popularity of the duo and their humorous videos helped launch Will Smith's acting career with the NBC sitcom *The Fresh Prince of Bel-Air* in 1990 and then in Hollywood movies.

Freestyle: a.k.a. Latino Hip Hop

Latinos were considerably less visible in the commercial rap music period between 1979 and 1984. Many of the old schoolers (DJ Charlie Chase and MC Whipper Whip of the Fantastic Five) did not continue to record after the new styles emerged in the mid-'80s. That is not to say that they disappeared. Instead, Latino hip hoppers created a new brand of hip hop music: freestyle. **Latino freestyle** should not be confused with the improvisational, rapping verbal art form that is called "freestyle." Latino freestyle is an electronic dance music that had its greatest crossover popularity between 1984 and 1992. Its sound relies heavily on electronic drums, bass, and synthesizers in the tradition of Bambaataa's electro-funk style of the early 1980s. Unlike its contemporary cousin, rap, the lyrics are sung in English and usually by female vocalists. Themes address matters of the heart, teen love and loss, invoking some of the heartbreaking drama in the *telenovela* tradition.

Freestyle emerged out of the Bronx in the mid-1980s and expanded into Miami. Some of the crossover sensations included the Cover Girls, Exposé, and Lisa Lisa and Cult Jam, but rap fans outside of New York got their first glimpse of freestyle in the film *Krush Groove* (1985). The film featured Cuban-Brooklyn songstress Nayobe performing her 1984 hit "Please Don't Go" in the audition sequence with Rick Rubin, Run-D.M.C., and Dr. Jekyll & Mr. Hyde. Nayobe sings a tale about a young woman trying to prevent her lover from committing a revenge murder and begs him to choose their love and not his foolish pride:

> The only thing we have that we can call our own
> Is this sweet love that we share
> But if you leave tonight you may not come home
> And that's just one thought I can't bear
> Let's run away from here, to some place far away
> 'Cause if we stay our love won't last another day.

The rhythm is a fusion of Bambaataa's genre-defining style and an Afro-Cuban musical sensibility. With this song, the general themes and soundscape of Latino freestyle were established. The trend peaked in the latter half of the 1980s, and by 1992 much of the fan base had moved on to newer trends in pop music.

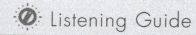

Listening to Nayobe

"PLEASE DON'T GO"

COMPOSED BY Andy "Panda" Tripoli

PERFORMED BY Nayobe

PRODUCERS INCLUDE Andy "Panda" Tripoli, Chuck Ange, Herbie Jr., Fred McFarlane (keyboards), Luie Rivera (percussion), Bashiri Johnson (percussion)

Appears on *Please Don't Go*, 1984, Fever Records SF 802.

Nayobe's "Please Don't Go" contains the blend of pop "diva" vocals, electro-funk instrumentation (Afrika Bambaataa's brand of hip hop music), and elements reminiscent of Latin music that characterize the Latin freestyle genre. This song gives an interesting window into other styles of hip hop that were evolving at the same time as the rap sounds that came to represent the majority of mainstream hip hop culture.

Throughout "Please Don't Go," Nayobe sings in the style of an '80s pop diva born from the soul-singing aesthetic, including emotionally charged, long held notes that highlight the extremities of her vocal range, and heartfelt glissando wails. Her voice embodies a pleading quality that is the theme of the song: choose me and our love over your gang and the need for blood vengeance. The introduction to "Please Don't Go"—with its **rubato** piano that expressively alters the rhythm and tempo, and its heavily ornamented singing—is reminiscent of the introduction to Gloria Gaynor's disco hit "I Will Survive" and countless other dance-pop anthems using a formula that includes a dramatic rubato introduction followed by an upbeat dance groove that continues for the rest of the song.

The sonic palette for most of "Please Don't Go" consists of electronic drum machines and layers of synthesized keyboard sounds, including a repeated melody played by synthesized marimba, which are defining characteristics of the electro-funk sound in hip hop pioneered by Afrika Bambaata. This recording served as a template for much of the freestyle that followed, as well as for other electronic dance music.

One of the most important elements of freestyle is its association with Latino dance music. In addition to the pop-diva and electro-funk sounds that permeate this song, "Please Don't Go" incorporates sounds that give it a Latin feel throughout. It is interesting to note that the piano and hand drums are the only acoustic instruments present in the arrangement. These two sounds are perhaps the most important elements creating the sense that this is a "Latin" dance track. Most of the percussion that appears throughout the song locks firmly into the 16th-note rhythmic groove that characterizes this song's electro-funk influence.

However, the conga drums are a sound associated with much Latin dance music, even though for the majority of the song the congas are not played as they would be in that context.

The acoustic piano functions similarly throughout. While the rhythms in the piano part are not "Latin" patterns per se, they mimic a Latin sound. The accompaniment feels similar to an Afro-Cuban **montuno** rhythm at times, and at others, short repeated figures give a rhythmic sense reminiscent of Latin piano stylings. Throughout the piano solo, the pianist employs a number of formulaic Latin jazz expressions that further cultivate a Latin feel in the absence of any actual Latin rhythmic patterns: repeated staccato rhythmic gestures; piano voicings spread throughout multiple octaves; the use of the extremely high range of the piano; and a **"locked-hands"** style of playing, where both hands play the same rhythms as though they are locked together. The synthesized marimba melody that appears throughout resembles a slowed-down version of a Latin-style **arpeggiated** piano melody, one that outlines the most important notes in the chord, spread from top down.

"Please Don't Go" is a fascinating example of the combination of pop sensibilities, electro-funk, and elements pulled from Latin dance music to create the characteristic feel of Latin freestyle music. Blending these elements solidifies "Please Don't Go" as a prime example of the freestyle sound.

0:00	"Sweet, sweet love . . ."	Piano and vocals enter. The introduction is slow rubato and ends with an extended piano flourish that holds as a cue for the rest of the band.
0:22		The drum machine enters, beginning the song's main groove.
0:24		Bass, keyboards, and synthesized marimba sounds enter, playing the song's main hook.
0:32		Congas and synthesized string stabs enter.
0:40		Sustained strings enter with lock-hand piano.
0:56		The piano, playing a gesture similar to a montuno accompaniment pattern, takes the lead.
1:03	"There's something scary . . ."	Repeated piano gestures in a high octave and synth hits enter. During the verses the congas are not present. The verses reflect a typical electro-funk style.
1:19	"Not much will come from . . ."	Synthesizer stabs return and the pianist plays blues-influenced gestures.
1:28	"I'm begging you, please . . ."	Sustained synthesized strings return for the pre-chorus.

Continued

⊘ Listening Guide

Listening to Nayobe **Continued**

1:33	"Please don't go . . ."	All instruments except percussion and synth string leads enter, playing the main groove for the chorus. Lock-hand piano can be heard playing short rhythmic motifs.
1:52		Instrumental interlude: congas return, sustained strings and piano are prominent.
2:07		Synthesizer hits and rhythmic piano gestures are prominent.
2:13		Drum fill leads into verse.
2:15	"The only thing . . ."	Verse texture returns with rhythmic piano gestures.
2:32	"Let's run away . . ."	The simulated montuno pattern returns.
2:39	"Don't throw our love aside . . ."	Sustained strings return with the pre-chorus.
2:47	"Please don't go . . ."	The chorus returns.
3:06		The instrumental break is extended with a staccato, Latin-influenced piano solo. There are octave tremolos (rapid alternations between two notes) punctuating the ends of the piano solo's bluesy lines.
3:27		An Afro-Cuban, Latinized-piano repeated rhythmic and melodic motif enters; the melody descends from high to low in steps.
3:35		The pianist plays more repeated blues motifs.
3:36		The pianist glissandos into a lock-hand pattern, another technique typical of Afro-Cuban, Latinized piano.
3:44		Lock-hand gestures that are spread over several octaves enter. The song begins to fade out here, alternating bluesy and lock-hand gestures until the song ends.

Hardcore Rap

Rap music acquired a more aggressive edge and a raw or hard aesthetic in the late 1980s. Rhymes of social and political commentary as well as graphic portrayals of inner-city life, gang life, criminal activity, violence, and abusive treatment of women mark this hardcore style. The idea of "hardcore" came as early as 1984 with the aggressive posturing and shouting-delivery performance styles of Run-D.M.C. and LL Cool J. However, most hip hop fans and scholars alike associate "hardcore" with groups that came in the latter half of the decade, such as Public Enemy, Boogie Down Productions, Ice-T, and N.W.A. Hardcore will be further examined in the following chapters, but a brief summary and examples are provided here to help contextualize our discussion of the various styles that developed during the golden era of hip hop.

Eric B. and Rakim's "Eric B. Is President" reminded listeners that the DJ was at one time the star—a novel notion in the mid-1980s because commercial rap from 1979 to 1983 mostly used studio bands and not a DJ to create the accompaniment for the rapper. "Eric B. Is President" is an ode to Eric B. that showcases his DJing skills and Rakim's formidable rhyming talent. For example, in the first verse of Rakim's rap, the listener encounters his use of internal rhyme (or middle rhyme): "biting me, fighting me, inviting me to rhyme. . . ." Rakim is credited with expanding the storytelling sophistication of rapping in this era. He demonstrates his skills on "My Melody" (1987). As opposed to shouting out the rhymes, Rakim offers his listeners a smooth-talking recitative. The duo also moved away from party anthems and the hard-rock style popular at the time. Most importantly, in his lyrics for "Follow the Leader" (1988), Rakim incorporated the Five Percent Nation ideology that would become more prevalent in the 1990s. "Follow the Leader" also ushered in the sonic qualities that would define the "hardcore rap" sound with strong lyrical delivery and smart lyrics rhymed alongside aggressive, minor-key arrangements (note the piano and strings), polysonic beats, and various sound effects.

Hardcore rap music is more serious in terms of its lyrical content and its sonic compositions, as well as the performers' clothing styles. East Coast rappers were the first to popularize social and political commentary in hip hop, sometimes called **message**, **conscious**, or **nationalist rap**, such as Public Enemy's song of awareness and empowerment "Fight the Power" (1989; see Chapter 7). Afrocentric rap led by Native Tongues artists and Five Percent Nation rappers made important strides by placing greater emphasis on African heritage and cultural pride, in performances such as the Jungle Brothers' "What's Going On" or Brand Nubian's "I'm Black and I'm Proud" (1998; see Chapter 7). Arguably, feminist raps address issues of unification, raised consciousness, and Afrocentricity, such as Queen Latifah's "U.N.I.T.Y." (1989; see earlier discussion and Chapter 8). West Coast rappers were the first to popularize the gangbanging street style that became known as "gangsta rap" in the early '90s; for example, Ice-T's "Squeeze the Trigger" (1987) and N.W.A.'s "Straight Outta Compton" (1988; see Chapter 8). However, the innovator of this style was Philadelphia native Schoolly D, who self-produced records as early as 1984.

Dirty/Booty Rap

The X-rated style, also known as dirty rap or booty rap, tells the tales of sexual encounters in the manner of a dirty limerick or dirty joke. This style was pioneered by the Miami-based group 2 Live Crew with sexually explicit songs like "Throw the D" that came from their first studio recording in 1986. Their more popular X-rated offerings, like "Put Her in the Buck," "Me So Horny," and "Hoochie Mama," received more national attention in 1989. Another pioneer of X-rated lyricism came from a West Coast teenager named Too $hort who was selling his dirty rap mixtapes to friends as early as 1985. Beyond the sexually explicit narratives, the Miami dirty rappers performed their stories over fast, minimalistic, electronic, booty-shaking bass music that was very different from the trends coming out of the East Coast.

Rap: Just a Fad?

With its first crossover peak in 1986, many industry leaders and mainstream listeners thought rap music would have a lifespan similar to the disco fad of the '70s, that is, three to five years. In fact, rap music's physical counterpart, breakdancing, was declared dead by the mid-'80s and rap was sure to follow, as it too was being exploited on film and radio. Critics assumed rap music would fade once mainstream consumers grew bored with it. However, unlike breakdancing, rap music had a viable product: vinyl records and later CDs. Sales of rap music remained strong, and increasingly the record industry recognized a rich vein of current and future income.

In June 1988, the National Association of Recording Arts and Sciences (NARAS) officially announced a new Grammy Award category for rap. The rationale at the time was that the genre had proven its market durability and demonstrated commercial staying power. In the words of Mike Greene, president of NARAS: "Rap last year was *an urban black music form*, and over the last year it has evolved into something more than that. It has matured into several kinds of music, with several kinds of artists doing it. We felt there was enough product coming out to justify a rap category" (quoted in *The "Vibe" History of Hip Hop*; emphasis added). Greene's statement exposes the industry's capitalistic values, which disconnect culture from commerce. Furthermore, Greene articulates a more biased perspective: when rap was just an "urban black music form," it did not warrant NARAS recognition; however, with its market growth and geographic expansions into new social sectors (i.e., the mass white audience), NARAS deemed it worthy of its own Grammy category.

As a result of this perceived bias, rap artists boycotted the Grammys that year. DJ Jazzy Jeff and the Fresh Prince gained critical acclaim for winning the first-ever Grammy in the rap category for their song "Parents Just Don't Understand," but they chose to skip the official Grammy ceremonies and instead attended the boycott hosted by *Yo! MTV Raps* along with Public Enemy, Run-D.M.C., and other artists and celebrities sympathetic to their cause. In the broadcast of the boycott, Fresh Prince explained that they did not want "a quiet win" but rather "we wanted a loud win." Despite the diversity of rap as a musical genre, this sense of unity among the rap artists as African Americans demonstrates that they felt they must band together to earn the real respect of the music industry.

With NARAS's stamp of approval, rap music was eagerly embraced by the mainstream music industry, offering more options for marketing and promotion to a wider range of consumers, as well as regular placement in record retail outlets, TV, film soundtracks, and music and culture magazines. With the mainstream's acceptance, was rap music getting too soft? Too pop? A kind of standardization began to take place, focusing on the pop market and winning formulas, as in MC Hammer's "U Can't Touch This" (1989), Vanilla Ice's "Ice Ice Baby" (1990), Young MC's "Busta Move" (1988), and P.M. Dawn's "Set Adrift on Memory Bliss" (1991). Also, in the mid-'90s, rap artists began teaming up with R&B and funk artists and producers, and some employed the R&B verse-chorus and funk song structure to try to gain increased popularity on the charts. This R&B-rap fusion gave rise to what some call "neo-soul" or "hip hop soul." Meanwhile, the underground rappers were getting harder and edgier in their explicit descriptions of gang life and street activities and questioning pop rap stars' authenticity.

As mainstream acceptance led rap music to soften its sound to appeal to least-common-denominator tastes, it stands to reason that this might have been one of the incentives for the underground rap music scene to get harder and grittier. The other major influence on hip hop was an element of hardcore that incorporated what Ice-T called "G-style" or "gangsta style" perpetuating the street sensibility, ghetto origins, and ideas about "blackness." By the early '90s it would become an established style the mainstream media called "gangsta rap," and the artists themselves would change our ideas about what "real" rap music should be.

CHAPTER SUMMARY

New-school rap (ca. 1984–1992) was marked by rap's first mainstream success. It was a period of stylistic diversity in rap, beginning with the success of "Walk This Way" by Run-D.M.C. and Aerosmith, the first rap-rock fusion. The Beastie Boys were the first successful all-white rap group, who self-consciously adapted this African American style to express their own experiences. Women arose as both creators and performers of rap, articulating issues of self-empowerment, such as in Queen Latifah's "U.N.I.T.Y. (Who You Calling a Bitch?)". The Fat Boys were major proponents of novelty/humorous rap, playing off both their physical size and Darren "Buff the Human Beat Box" Robinson's ability to vocally reproduce intricate drum patterns. More commercially oriented rappers arose, both in the Latino freestyle movement and also among mainstream radio stars like DJ Jazzy Jeff and the Fresh Prince. Finally, hardcore, socially conscious rap came to the fore in the early '90s, predicting a return to rap's inner-city roots.

STUDY QUESTIONS

1. Identify innovations in the following new-school styles:

   De La Soul "Potholes in My Lawn"

   LL Cool J "I Need Love"

   Fat Boys "Jailhouse Rap"

2. Identify new lyrical themes in new-school hip hop:

   Queen Latifah "Ladies First"

   Public Enemy "Fight the Power"

   N.W.A. "Straight Outta Compton"

3. What strategies did record companies employ to broaden the consumer base for hip hop beyond the African American community? Use the following songs in your answer:

   Run-D.M.C. "Rock Box"

   Beastie Boys "Fight for Your Right to Party"

4. Describe the ways in which new-school rap artists became popular and built their reputation. How did it differ from the old-school era?

KEY TERMS

Beatboxing

Dis raps/answer raps/response raps

Genre

Hardcore

Latino freestyle

Message/conscious/ nationalist rap

New school/golden era/third wave

Rap-rock fusion

CHAPTER 7

HARDCORE: "MESSAGE RAP" AND "GANGSTA RAP"

Learning Objectives

When you have successfully completed this chapter, you will be able to:

- Discuss the emergence of hardcore styles at the end of the golden era of rap music.
- Identify messages of the black nationalist movement reborn in rap music.
- Discuss the social roots of gangsta and X-rated rap and relate these forms to African American folk traditions.

Hardcore Rap

Following the near bankruptcy of New York City in the 1970s, the '80s brought further hardships for inner-city America. The conservative policies of the Reagan administration, structural changes in the urban economy, the continuing rise in unemployment and poverty, the continued proliferation of drugs (especially crack cocaine), a rise in crime, an intensification of police repression, and the continuing migration of middle-class African Americans to the suburbs made the situation worse for the urban populations throughout the country.

By the late 1980s, rap music had become a public forum for social and political commentary as well as the expression of inner-city rage and resistance. The hardcore style known as message rap in the late 1980s, as heard in the socially conscious and political lyrics of Public Enemy and KRS-One of Boogie Down Productions, was one of the first manifestations of this political anger. It foreshadowed the street-reality raps of Schoolly D, Ice-T, and N.W.A. that opened the door for **gangsta rap** to commercial appeal throughout the 1990s. The various hardcore styles were distinct from the crossover rap of the mid-'80s and challenged the pop-rap of the late '80s with abrasive beats, street-sonic effects, and a more deliberate, aggressive delivery of provocative lyrics.

Flashback: "The Message" That Almost Didn't Happen

Several factors led to the arrival of message and gangsta rap in the latter years of the golden era, but none was as musically influential as the old-school tune "The Message," released in the summer of 1982 and credited to Grandmaster Flash and the Furious Five. Ed "Duke Bootee" Fletcher, a session musician and producer for Sugar Hill Records, developed most of the lyrics of "The Message." His intention was to recite them accompanied by a West African–influenced track that he was working on, following the tradition of political poets such as H. Rap Brown and the Last Poets. Sylvia Robinson, the head of Sugar Hill Records, liked the concept and especially the verse "It's like a jungle sometimes," but she wanted to switch the track to something more commercial.

Robinson took the track to the Furious Five, but they were doubtful the song would be popular. The music that had emerged from the South Bronx community in the 1970s and throughout the commercial era of the early 1980s was party rap—music to escape the harsh realities of daily living. However, Fletcher and more importantly Robinson were both adamant that the song would be successful. Melle Mel eventually came on board, adapting a few lines he had used on the song "Super-rappin.'" Even though it was released as a Grandmaster Flash and the Furious Five song, only Melle Mel performed on the actual recording; Rahiem appears on the video lip-syncing to Duke Bootee's rhymes. In addition to breaking new lyrical territory, "The Message" was also one of the first records to use bass synthesizer instead of a live bass player as in the previous Sugar Hill sessions. The song reached number 4 on the R&B chart and number 62 on the pop chart and changed the possibility of rap music themes forever.

The song was a perfect response to the hard times that inner-city youth were facing during the '80s. As Melle Mel later commented, "At that time anybody could have said that . . . half the people in America probably wanted to say that" (quoted in Ogg 1999: 69). Grandmaster Flash and the Furious Five followed up with socially conscious songs such as "New York, New York" (1983) and "White Lines (Don't Do It)" (1983), as well as Melle Mel and Duke Bootee's "The Message II (Survival)" (1982) and Grandmaster Melle Mel's "Jesse" (1984; see Chapter 4).

Perhaps even more importantly, "The Message" was not the first message, conscious, or reality rap. Other songs with this message orientation include Kurtis Blow's "The Breaks," "Hard Times," and "Tough" (1980); and Brother D and Collective Effort's "How We Gonna Make the Black Nation Rise?" (1980). Brother D and Collective Effort articulated explicitly a rap that is profoundly nationalist and more politically proactive than any others of the period. They were highly critical of the "party-people" orientation of old-school rappers and their fans. Their lyrics are fierce and demand unity and political action, but they did not have the commercial success to reach a larger audience.

Kurtis Blow, on the other hand, was the biggest-selling rapper of his day. "The Breaks" exposed the stresses of ghetto living:

And the IRS says they want to chat
And you can't explain why you claimed your cat
And Ma Bell sends you a whopping bill
With eighteen phone calls to Brazil
And you borrowed money from the mob
And yesterday you lost your job
Well, these are the breaks.

Nevertheless, this rap did not achieve the impact of a "message" rap song. As journalist Tom Terrell observed, "From the exuberance of Kurtis Blow's intro to the mad percussion/booty-shakin' bass/palm slapping/party-people-chanting slow fade, 'The Breaks' is seven minutes and forty-six seconds of the greatest party you never went to" (1999: 47). The party atmosphere of the record obscured its provocative lyrics.

Nonetheless, "The Breaks" and the new school's edgier musical ethic moved rap music in a totally new direction in the late '80s. As this hardcore style was coming into its own, hip hop artists began to embrace the ideas of socially conscious, black nationalist icons of the past—musicians and rhetoricians alike—and they began to represent these ideas lyrically, visually, and through social action.

Lyrical Referencing: Sister Souljah

We have discussed how black nationalist poets of the 1960s–1970s, such as Gil Scott-Heron ("The Revolution Will Not Be Televised"; 1970) and the Last Poets ("Niggers Are Scared of the Revolution"; 1970), told lyrical narratives over drummed rhythms that embodied the concept of Black Power musically (see Chapter 4). The works of the Last Poets, Gil Scott-Heron, Sonia Sanchez, and other Black Arts Movement artists resonated with the emergent political rap movement some 20 years later and encouraged rap fans to reconsider the state of African America in the late 1980s and early 1990s.

Direct allusions to these political poets can be heard in Sister Souljah's "African Scaredy Katz in a One-Exit Maze" (1992). This song is modeled after the Last Poets' "Niggers Are Scared of the Revolution" and similarly combines politically charged street poetry with African percussion and jazzy riffs. Souljah's song begins with a prologue reminiscent of the dramatic monologues used by R&B artists in the 1960s and 1970s, which is performed by a gospel-like orator over natural sounds of the outdoors and drumming. The lengthy recitative prefaces Souljah's politically charged rap that critiques the complacent, apolitical behavior of African American youth in a post–black nationalist revolutionary era.

Visual References and Message Rap

Similar to the soul music performers promoting the ideology of Black Power (see Chapter 4), message rappers promoted their messages not only through the lyrics but also through their dress and other visual referencing. Just as wearing very thick gold chains, Kangol hats, name-brand clothes such as Adidas, and Gazelle glasses marked rap's golden era fashion sense, message rappers also understood the importance of their stage dress to market their ideas. Public Enemy took their black garb style from the Black Panthers to advocate national black unity and activism, while Afrocentric rappers like Queen Latifah and the Jungle Brothers preferred African-derived clothing to encourage self-pride and an identification with Africa.

Visual imagery also played a key role in the promotion of hardcore rap. Boogie Down Productions took a more provocative approach in designing their first two album covers. For example, on the second album cover, *By All Means Necessary* (1988), KRS-One positioned himself looking from behind a window curtain while gripping an Uzi, referencing a photograph of Malcolm X posed with his rifle two decades before. Similarly, Public Enemy conveyed important visual commentary with their logo: a b-boy in a Kangol-style fedora, arms crossed behind the scope of a rifle, suggesting that young African American men are treated as if they were Public Enemy Number One.

Political Empowerment: Public Enemy

Academicians, journalists, and fans often treat Public Enemy (a.k.a. P.E.) as the definitive example of hip hop's political potential. This group was more successful than Brother D and Collective Effort in flavoring their raps with revolutionary, nationalistic ideas. They motivated young people to action like nothing had since the Black Power movement of the 1960s. Frontman Chuck D claims that P.E. is rock 'n' roll simply played a lot faster, maintaining the hard-rock musical ethic pioneered by Run-D.M.C. (see Chapter 6) and reclaiming rock 'n' roll as a black popular musical form that had been appropriated by the white majority since the 1950s.

While P.E. members were reverential of Run-D.M.C., they did not feel these golden era all-stars took the music far enough in terms of lyrical content and musical production. Public Enemy helped redefine the new hardcore sound: harder aggressive beats, syncopated rhythms, new street-sonic arrangements, and political (even radical) lyrics that made listeners question the state of African American affairs and social justice in the United States. They rewrote the rules of what rap music could do and also proved to be commercially successful, selling records even though they did not get much radio play.

Their first album, *Yo! Bum Rush the Show* (1987), demanded that listeners pay attention to social issues, using lyrical and musical content that

Public Enemy, 1991. L. to r.: Terminator X, Flavor Flav, Chuck D.
Source: © Ebet Roberts

honored past leaders of the civil rights and black pride movements. However, their second album, *It Takes a Nation of Millions to Hold Us Back* (1988), shifted towards a proactive, radical black nationalism. For example, the song "Bring the Noise" promoted current black Muslim Louis Farrakhan as the leader of the ongoing movement for civil rights' actualization. By the release of their third album *Fear of a Black Planet* (1990), Public Enemy was truly an artistic source of information calling for political activism; as Chuck D described their music, they were "a Black CNN." Flavor Flav's "911 Is a Joke" attacks the poor emergency service response time in black neighborhoods; "Burn Hollywood Burn" confronts Hollywood's racist past and current perpetuation of racist stereotypes; and "Fight the Power" urges listeners to confront injustice just as the leaders of the civil rights movement did in the '60s.

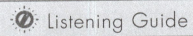 Listening Guide

Listening to Public Enemy

"BURN HOLLYWOOD BURN"

COMPOSED BY Carlton "Chuck D" Ridenhour, Eric "Vietnam" Sadler, Keith Shocklee, Antonio "Big Daddy Kane" Hardy, and O'Shea "Ice Cube" Jackson

PERFORMED BY Chuck D, Big Daddy Kane, Ice Cube, Sister Souljah, Flavor Flav, and the Bomb Squad

Appears on *Fear of a Black Planet*, 1990, Def Jam 314 523 446-2.

Public Enemy's "Burn Hollywood Burn" is a prime example of their hardcore, nation-conscious rap music. This song is unique among the group's recordings because it features rappers who are not members of Public Enemy: Ice Cube, a gangsta rapper who was a former member of N.W.A., and Big Daddy Kane, famous for his pimp persona, as well as the identifiable feminist, nation-conscious voice of Sister Souljah shouting the call to action in the chorus. These artists adapted their rap personas to fit into Public Enemy's sound style and social critique. Simultaneously, they manipulated and subverted stereotypes about warring rap musicians, unifying them, first and foremost, as black artists.

Right at the beginning of this song, the listener is disarmed. Unlike typical rap recordings that begin with a melodic, instrumental introduction, this tune opens with the lyrical terrorism of Chuck D's booming voice. His opening line, "Burn Hollywood burn! I smell a riot goin' on," connects a contemporary call to protest against Hollywood's historically negative representation of African Americans in film with the civil unrest and arson of the late 1960s. Chuck D is referring to Sly and the Family Stone's 1971 album *There's a Riot Goin' On*, which reflected that darker period with a darker funk. Chuck D's voice is frenetic and his agitation lends urgency to his subject matter.

Continued

Listening Guide

Listening to Public Enemy **Continued**

His colleagues propel his argument and encourage listeners to take action—to "burn" the mainstream film industry metaphorically, as will be depicted at the conclusion of the song in the dramatization of the three rappers walking out of a movie theater.

Ice Cube's and Big Daddy Kane's verses blend their styles over the heavily layered Bomb Squad soundscape. Ice Cube delivers his rhymes ferociously, rapping about a real-life scenario of being pursued by police in Los Angeles for being a young black male. He concludes that the only real solution for him is "don't fight the power, [*gunshot sound*] the motherfucker," providing a picture, and to some extent a justification, of the street violence Chuck D referred to in his verse. Kane has a more subdued delivery and takes a longer thematic view, looking at the history of degradation in Hollywood portrayals of African Americans. He points out that black people were typically "butlers and maids, slaves or hoes" in early films and notes that they continue to be cast in these roles. Sister Souljah raps the song's chorus, the three words "Burn Hollywood burn," with an anger and intensity that matches both the urgency of Chuck D's verse and the malice of Ice Cube's. The ease with which these very different rappers (a nation-conscious hardcore rapper; a gangsta; a pimp; and a nation-conscious, feminist rapper) are able to speak to the same problems of black representation in their respective verses reveals a convergence of rap music both sonically and thematically around pertinent social issues.

The members of the group explore problems and in the end propose a solution to Hollywood's predictable racism in two minidramas that conclude the recording. In the first, a white casting director tries to enlist a black actor, portrayed by Flavor Flav, to play a "controversial Negro." Flavor Flav imagines that he means a militant black figure like Huey P. Newton or H. Rap Brown, but in reality the part is a servant who "chuckles a little bit and sings." The second drama places Chuck D, Ice Cube, and Big Daddy Kane at a cinema. Chuck D declares that he doesn't want to spend his hard-earned money on a film like *Steel Magnolias*, but the other two insist that everything will be fine. As they wait for the film to begin, an announcer reveals that the feature will be *Driving Miss Daisy*. All three grumble. Chuck D leads them out of the theater, and they decide to go to Big Daddy Kane's house to watch *Black Caesar* (1973) instead.

To "burn Hollywood" here is to boycott films that feature blacks in stereotypical roles. *Black Caesar* as a cinematic alternative to *Driving Miss Daisy* is an interesting blaxploitation film choice because it was a black-centered film with a black hero that was written and directed by Larry Cohen, a white screenwriter and director. The rappers could have very easily selected *Sweet*

Sweetback's Baadasssss Song (1971), which was written, produced, and directed by a black artist and activist, Melvin Van Peebles. Their choice of Cohen's work serves as a teaching moment explaining that being pro-black does not mean being anti-white. While these alternatives exist, ultimately the artists' views are summed up by Ice Cube's "Fuck Hollywood"—a statement that references his 1988 proclamation against the L.A. police. These two routines are sharpened by exaggerated, cheesy "white guy" voices in the roles of the casting director and the movie announcer, who are hyperbolically patronizing to the point of satire. These "industry" voices were mixed to sound as though they were sampled into the song, in contrast to the crisp, clear sounds of the in-studio rappers, to increase the sense of separation.

The lyrical and thematic anxiety that permeates "Burn Hollywood Burn" operates aurally throughout the track as well. Public Enemy's production team, the Bomb Squad, craft another of their signature frenetic soundscapes, supporting the urgency of the rappers' verses. The song's tempo is fast and consists of a number of very short samples (typically less than five seconds long) layered upon one another. The song is primarily built on material from three samples, with the main groove excerpted from Badder Than Evil's "Hot Wheels (The Chase)" (1973), which consists of bass, drums, and guitar. Some additional drum machines were added to this sample in the studio to highlight important elements of the beat and enhance the rhythm present in the original. This production technique was not typical. Most golden-era producers did not go beyond supplanting the drums from the source material.

The song's verses are interspersed with a periodically punch-phrased horn-section sample from a remixed version of James Brown's "Give It Up or Turnit A Loose" (1986, remix), which returns on the first "Burn" of each iteration of Sister Souljah's chorus. The chorus also contains the sound of a whistle and some extraneous crowd noises from Herman Kelly's "Dance to the Drummer's Beat" (1978).

Other samples are more generic in nature and difficult to trace to specific source recordings. Throughout the verses and the chorus, a siren—one of the group's signature sounds—appears. During the movie theater skit, a short fanfare sample is punch-phrased repeatedly, conjuring the anticipatory feeling of a movie's opening credits. This sample is reminiscent of composer Alfred Newman's introductory brass fanfare used in all 20th Century Fox films, but sounds closer to Scott Bradley's theme music for *Tom and Jerry* cartoons (beginning at ca. 00:00-00:02), given the strength of the strings. These two samples are significant as they relate to this song's narrative: the sirens represent the chaos in the streets that Chuck D brought up in his verse, and the introductory movie-industry fanfare sample serves as a cinematic element in the movie theater skit regarding proprietorship and power. The heavy layering of the numerous brief samples that appear throughout the track amplify the

Continued

Listening Guide

Listening to Public Enemy Continued

sense of chaos that characterizes "Burn Hollywood Burn," while the sudden stops in the verses dramatize important lyrical moments as the bottom drops out of the Bomb Squad's sonic rollercoaster.

"Burn Hollywood Burn" is saturated with urgency—about the representation of black life in the media and about the grim realities of daily life on the streets—and it reminds listeners that civil rights, equality, and fair representation are yet to be realized. This song shows off Public Enemy's musical and lyrical styles and offers a shining example of how a group of rappers with varying personas can collaborate to achieve a congruent artistic vision.

0:00	"Burn Hollywood burn . . ."	The song begins abruptly, with no introduction before the lyrics enter. Chuck D raps over a very short sample of Badder Than Evil's "Hot Wheels (The Chase)" that is repeatedly iterated via digital sampler. This sample continues throughout the song with the addition of the signature Public Enemy sound of a siren. Horn hits from a remixed version of James Brown's "Give It Up or Turnit A Loose" appear throughout, punctuating key moments in the verses. There is also a drum machine present, accentuating the strong pulses of the drums on the recording.
0:07	"But it'll take a Black one . . ."	The layered samples break here for one measure, to highlight Chuck D's lyric.
0:09	"Get me the hell away from this TV . . ."	The verse texture returns as Chuck D continues his verse.
0:16	"Head out . . ."	The samples break again, timed with these words.
0:17	"So I'd rather . . ."	The verse texture returns as Chuck D continues his verse.
0:32	"The joke is over . . ."	The samples break again, timed with these words.
0:34	"Burn Hollywood Burn . . ."	Sister Souljah enters, rapping the chorus lyrics. The "Hot Wheels" sample continues, and samples of whistles, a crowd, and a brief excerpt of keyboards are added from Herman Kelly's "Dance to the Drummer's Beat." The "Give It Up or Turnit A Loose" horns are punch-phrased on the first "Burn" of each iteration of the song's tagline. The drum machine is more active here, incorporating more cymbal sounds than before.
0:50	"Ice Cube is down with the P.E. . . ."	Ice Cube begins his verse, with a return of the sonic texture from the previous verse.

1:07	"As I walk the streets . . ."	Big Daddy Kane takes over from Ice Cube. The verse texture remains the same.
1:14	"Slaves and hoes . . ."	The samples break again, timed with these words. The main groove returns immediately after.
1:30	"Even if now she got a perm . . ."	The samples break again, timed with these words.
1:40	"Burn Hollywood Burn . . ."	The chorus is repeated with the same sonic accompaniment.
1:57	"Now we're considering you for a part . . ."	The verse returns with a scene in which a white casting director offers a black actor, Flavor Flav, a stereotypical part in a movie.
2:13	"Hey, hey, hey . . ."	A dramatic scene begins here over the continuing verse groove. Chuck D is talking to Ice Cube and Big Daddy Kane about going to a movie.
2:29	"Ladies and gentlemen, to-day's feature presentation is *Driving Miss Daisy* . . ."	An exaggerated, cheesy white announcer introduces the movie presentation with a sample of what appears to be the *Tom and Jerry* cartoon title-reel music punch-phrased repeatedly throughout. The rappers grumble after the film title is announced.
2:38	"Yo, I'm outta here . . ."	The main verse groove returns here. The skit continues as the rappers leave the movie.
2:46	"Fuck Hollywood!"	The samples exit, and the song ends with Ice Cube exclaiming, "Fuck Hollywood!"

Public Enemy's work drew on an African aesthetic of layered and distorted sounds and multiple simultaneous rhythms (polyrhythms; see Chapter 4). Using "Bring the Noise" as just one example, listeners can hear how their production team, the Bomb Squad (Hank Shocklee, Keith Shocklee, Bill Stephney, Kerwin "Sleek" Young, Gary G-Wiz, and Eric "Vietnam" Sadler), created the chaotic polysonic and polyrhythmic production: mixing a plethora of sounds not traditionally considered musical with sampled beats was a distinct move away from the typical rap track Def Jam record producers were making at that time. Public Enemy's tracks were typically performed at a faster tempo than those of other rap groups; for example, the Bomb Squad increased the tempo in this song up to P.E.'s typical 109 beats per minute (bpm), compared to Run-D.M.C.'s typical 89 bpm. In the later years of hardcore's "incubation" period, producers like Dr. Dre and DJ Screw slowed down the tempo considerably, moving away from the dance function of the music. P.E. supported the party orientation of rap music of the day but also demonstrated that rap lyrics could be taken seriously and serve the community that created them.

From Cultural Movement to Political Movement to Popular Movement

Public Enemy's agenda is one of political dissent that attempts to incorporate the voices of displaced, marginalized, exploited, and oppressed people regardless of color—but who are overwhelmingly still African American, in this country. However, their effect has been broader: their musical productions and powerful delivery also appeal to a young, middle-class, mainstream audience. Early in their recording career, Public Enemy's hardcore, proactive music could be taken out of context. The song "Bring the Noise" originally appeared on the soundtrack to the Generation X-ploitation film *Less Than Zero* (1987), a film based on a novel about wealthy, privileged Beverly Hills slackers. Chuck D's lyrics speak to African American listeners in particular: "Farrakhan's a prophet and I think you ought to listen to what he can say to you. What you ought to do is follow for now." This poignant activist message was lost as white middle-class youth appropriated the aggressive tone and hard-hitting beats as a voice of dissent for their generation to create a music of rebellion that punk and heavy metal never achieved.

On the release of their second album *It Takes a Nation of Millions to Hold Us Back* (1988), P.E. responded to their popularity among white listeners. Take for example the song "Party for Your Right to Fight," a song that responds to the Beastie Boys' "Fight for Your Right to Party." The Beastie Boys' "Fight for Your Right to Party" was a party anthem for frat houses across the nation. Public Enemy's response pays homage to the Black Panther Party, reminding listeners that this is the *same* party that fought for civil rights, and that radical ideas are still needed for blacks to achieve power, equality, and a better future. By sharing a similar title to the Beastie Boys' chart topper, Public Enemy turn the "party" (have a good time) message of the original to one promoting the Party (i.e., Black Panther/political empowerment), for both the African American and white audiences listening to their records. P.E. made a concerted effort to incorporate white listeners into the movement by collaborating with heavy-metal act Anthrax on a re-recording of "Bring the Noise" in 1991, hybridizing metal with rap.

Hardcore, Too: From Gangsta Style to Gangsta Rap

During the late '80s/early '90s, rap music projected a critical voice that confronted the standardized education system's distorted histories, demanded justice, and urged social action. Rap music responded to society's marginalization of a youthful, black, and predominately male underclass, but it came to accent misery as entertainment and pander to a consumer culture. Audience members were also held accountable for focusing on what rap stars possessed and not on the steps they took to become famous and skilled artists. Chuck D explains, "part of making music is to sell out. Not keep your tapes on a shelf . . ." (quoted in PBS's *The History of Rock and Roll*). The idea is to get your message out there to be heard. However, it is difficult to gauge exactly *how* those messages are being heard.

Earliest Gangsta Style

Prior to the commercialization of "gangsta rap," Schoolly D debuted the prototypical gangsta rap track "Gangsta Boogie" in 1984 on his own label. He continued making self-produced rap songs, including the song that brought him fame, the single "P.S.K. What Does It Mean?" (1985). The track immortalized his Philadelphia crew, the Parkside Killers, also known as the 5-2 Crew, which stands for their West Philly neighborhood, Parkside Avenue and 52nd Street. Schoolly D tells a tale, built around a simple drumbeat, about metaphorically beating down a rapper who tried to steal his style, and about entertaining himself with a woman who turns out to be a prostitute. Lyrically, his boastful, thuggish machismo remains relevant to the gangsta pop-rap style of the second millennium generation, such as 50 Cent or Yung Joc.

Think Like a Gangsta

DJ Scott La Rock and MC KRS-One joined forces to form Boogie Down Productions (BDP) and came to rap fans' attention with a clever dis rap, "South Bronx" (1986), that verbally assaults MC Shan and his 1987 B-side hit single "The Bridge" (1986; see Chapter 6). On this recording, and its follow-up "The Bridge Is Over" (1987), KRS-One adopted a menacing tone, taking on the voice of a street tough and using Jamaican patois as a way to reflect his cultural heritage. Continuing this trend of aggressive, street sensibility, Boogie Down Productions' debut album cover as well as the lyrics of the title song on *Criminal Minded* (1987) suggested that they were supporting criminal activities and violence. However, KRS-One explained the concept of the album to Brian Coleman: "The purpose of the album was to attract a thug-type audience, so we could teach them later on. . . . We wanted to make intelligence a cool thing" (2007: 86). It can be argued that the image represents urban American survival tactics; that is, self-preservation through various means including acts of aggression. It was a message to other MCs to think twice about battling BDP, and it was a message to corporate America that Boogie Down Productions were going to stick it to mainstream rap clichés.

For example, the lyrics for the song "Criminal Minded" describe an MC competition using gangbanging language and imagery. KRS-One brags about his verbal skills, clever lyricism, and general toughness in conquering a competitor, but his lyrics are delivered in a harder and more aggressive style than Run-D.M.C.'s similar boastful tune "Sucker MCs" (1984). BDP brought street-gang themes to the fore with "9mm Goes Bang" (1987), a Jamaican patois–inflected rap that provides a reality report about surviving the mean streets of the city with the aid of a gun.

In 1987, DJ Scott La Rock was shot and killed mediating between a member of BDP and some neighborhood toughs. The murder had a profound effect on KRS-One and his approach to his own hardcore persona and messages. He released *By All Means Necessary* (1988) the following year, calling himself "the Teacher." His reality rhymes become less morally ambiguous and he rapped ardently about issues facing the black community. As gangsta rap in the 1990s trumped all the other hardcore styles, KRS-One united East Coast rap artists to form the Stop the Violence Movement that included MC Lyte, Kool Moe Dee, Doug E. Fresh, D-Nice, Heavy D, members of Public Enemy and Stetsasonic, and DJ Scott La Rock in spirit. Together they recorded "Self Destruction" (1989), a song that challenged the normative acceptance of black-on-black violence by young African American males. As Kool Moe Dee rapped: "How could you gang-bang?/I never ever ran from the Ku Klux Klan/and I shouldn't have to run from a Black man."

The L.A. Gangsta Rap Scene

On the West Coast, an East Coast transplant, Tracy Marrow, better known as Ice-T, began formulating his brand of gangsta-style rap music. As a youth, Marrow memorized the rhymes of the pimp-poet Iceberg Slim, from whom he took his name. Ice-T admits to having lived a lifestyle that included stealing, gangbanging, and hanging out with drug dealers; however, he originally represented himself as a breakdancing party rapper at the local clubs. His friends encouraged him to rap about the lives they led in L.A. and not follow the party-rap trend.

In the early '80s, Ice-T was introduced to Afrika Bambaataa, who indoctrinated Ice-T in the philosophy of nonviolence. He connected Ice-T to Afrika Islam, a member of the Zulu Nation and formerly known as the Son of Afrika Bambaataa. Afrika Islam as well as the NY-City Spin Masters (DJ Hen Gee and DJ Evil E) and together they formed the Rhyme Syndicate, a management company that produced Ice-T's first album. Mexican American rapper Kid Frost was also a prominent member. Ice-T performed a gangsta-life rap duet called "Killer" featuring Henry G (a.k.a. Hen G, Hen Gee) and David Storrs in the 1985 rap-exploitation film *Rappin'*. The song is a street narrative about thugs paying the price for their lifestyle. It is rhymed to a simple drum machine beat and synthesizer bass-line, and lacks the production that would truly bring him prominence in the industry. Up until that time, artists on the East Coast dominated hardcore rap. After the release of Ice-T's first album, that East Coast domination began to shift or, at the very least, be contested by West Coast rappers. Ice-T's debut album, *Rhyme Pays*, was hard-hitting and influenced the emergence of gangsta-lyric themes before the commercialized gangsta rap arose in the 1990s.

In "6 'N the Mornin'," Ice-T portrays a felon in the tradition of outlaw folk heroes or the "**baadman**" (see Chapter 4) and raps candidly about the horrors of the urban ghetto and the neighborhood's troubled relationship with the L.A. police department. Ice-T also brought heavy-metal influences to rap; for example, the title song "Rhyme Pays" begins with a biographical rhymed monologue that links Ice-T's heritage to New York, his true roots, then shifts into the rap tune performed to the hard-rock classic "War Pigs" by Black Sabbath. Ice-T also rejects status symbols ("I don't like Gucci, Fila, Louie or Fendi/Those are fads and I ain't trendy"), unlike his pro-commodification, gangsta-rapping successors of the bling-bling 1990s that celebrate their "ice," Cristal Champagne, "Benjamins," and other material possessions.

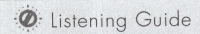
Listening Guide

Listening to Ice-T

"RHYME PAYS"

COMPOSED BY Dave Storrs and Ice-T

PERFORMED BY Ice-T (vocals), DJ Evil E (scratch art),

PRODUCER/MIXER Afrika Islam

ENGINEER Jim Lyons

Appears on *Rhyme Pays*, 1987, Sire Records 1-25602.

As the first track on Ice-T's debut album of the same name, "Rhyme Pays" introduced Ice-T's unique brand of West Coast gangsta-style rap. Ice-T brought a different kind of hardcore persona to a scene primarily dominated by East Coast artists, and he adopted the gangsta style pioneered by Schoolly D of Philadelphia. While "6 'N the Mornin'" remains a gangsta classic in its description of L.A. ghetto life, it was heavily modeled on Schoolly D's style; even the cadence and delivery of the opening line "6 'n the mornin', police at my door/Fresh Adidas squeak across the bathroom floor ..." matches almost identically Schoolly D's delivery of the opening lines to "P.S.K. What Does It Mean?" (1986): "P.S.K., we're makin' that green/People always say, "What the hell does that mean?" With "Rhyme Pays," Ice-T crafted his own sound signature that set him apart from his East Coast contemporaries. As the first rap album to be given a "parental advisory" label, *Rhyme Pays* also brought hip hop into a new era of raw sounds and controversial themes.

Ice-T's vocal delivery corresponds to his hardcore persona: his strongly accented syllables and menacing intensity set the stage for generations of hardcore and gangsta rappers to follow. Ice-T uses a mid-vocal-range monotone through most of the song. However, he occasionally switches to a high-pitched or sing-song rhyme style as a way of taunting and mocking any challengers who would attempt to take him on in a battle of rhymes or, as the listener might presume, in a street battle.

"Rhyme Pays" is, of course, a clever pun that further accentuates this aggressive, gangsta persona. Rather than "crime" paying, "rhyme" is Ice-T's outlaw occupation of choice, an illicit trade given the negative reception for his style of rap. The song's introduction portrays Ice-T as a sort of mythical character through an introductory dramatic monologue presented over a studio re-creation of "Tubular Bells, Part 1," which was made famous as the theme music for the 1973 horror film *The Exorcist*. The eerie mood established by this soundtrack music is intensified by sounds of wings and calls of what may be crows or other flying creatures with ominous associations.

Continued

Listening Guide

Listening to Ice-T Continued

These sounds continue once "Rhyme Pays" begins, and then a sample of a heavy-metal guitar riff from Black Sabbath's "War Pigs" (1970) is added, which is arguably one of the darkest tracks from the group generally considered to be the pioneers of heavy-metal music. The use of "War Pigs" is a precursor to the metal-rap fusion that became mainstream in the '90s. This sample provides the primary musical material for "Rhyme Pays" and is punch-phrased in throughout the verses on top of a repeated drum machine pattern. The arrangement is sparse—the Black Sabbath sample and drum machine provide a stark texture that is heavy, threatening, and, at times, mechanical. "Rhyme Pays" makes the rap-rock fusion of Run-D.M.C.'s cover of boogie-rockers Aerosmith's "Walk This Way" sound almost lighthearted.

As opposed to being played live in the studio by a session guitarist, this riff is sampled from a vinyl record by DJ Evil E. While not quite "horror core," it contains frequent shout-outs to Evil E, including a clever reference to Evil E "cutting" the record like the iconic serial killer Jason Voorhees—the fictional character from the *Friday the 13th* slasher film series—that add to that bleak, "unholy" eeriness. The guitar riff primarily consists of two notes excerpted from the "War Pigs" guitar riff, but Evil E allows the "War Pigs" riff to play in its entirety at key moments, usually interspersed with punctuated fills programmed on the drum machine. DJ Evil E, an East Coast transplant, demonstrates mastery of his craft in two fascinating turntable solos. The first (beginning at 4:39) consists of a number of baby scratches that set up punch phrases of the guitar riff over the drum machine pattern. The second solo features a blending of drum fills from the Sabbath recording (which do not appear elsewhere in "Rhyme Pays") with original fills played on the drum machine.

While this recording is intentionally cold and menacing, like the heavy-metal record that it samples, DJ Evil E's use of the drum machine evidences very real musicianship. Many of the drum fills are indistinguishable from what a live metal drummer might have done in the same musical situation, even though the main drum pattern—not a syncopated groove, but a cold, mechanical pulse similar to what one finds in some of the heaviest metal—evokes a kind of mechanical sonic alienation. In addition to the mood set by the "War Pigs" sample and drum machine programming, there are a number of other production effects, such as the use of delay and echo effects on the drum machine and vocal parts, that further contribute to this song's eerie, cinematic feel.

Ice-T's debut provided listeners with a taste of the West Coast gangsta style to come: heavy, threatening, and alienating. Yet it is not without a sense of self-awareness and critique, lost in much gangsta rap to follow. In its sounds and themes, "Rhyme Pays" can be seen as a hardcore bridge between earlier golden era rap music and the gangster rap of the 1990s.

0:00		The introductory sample, from Mike Oldfield's "Tubular Bells, Part 1" enters, and continues to play throughout the introduction.
0:07	"A child was born . . ."	Ice-T enters, telling his story of mythical proportions (orphaned, East Coast origins) with dramatic synthesizer and booming bass drum hits sounding throughout.
0:31	"But no matter . . ."	Heavily reverberated snare drum sounds begin with a sample manipulated to sound like the fluttering and caws of crows.
1:01	"With one intention . . ."	A synthesized choir sound enters over the "Tubular Bells" sample, and additional layers of synthesizers continue to be added throughout.
1:38	"On his never-ending journey . . ."	The final synthesizer chord is held. Ice-T's final words are processed with delay and echo effects to heighten his pronunciation of his name.
1:45		A drum machine fill segues from the spoken introduction into "Rhyme Pays."
1:48	"Magnificent rhymer . . ."	The "Rhyme Pays" lyrics begin, with a sample of the guitar riff from Black Sabbath's "War Pigs" punched in throughout the verse. A drum machine is playing a pattern that remains mostly consistent throughout the verse, occasionally adding fills or dropping out at key moments to build intensity.
2:00	"Your girl tried to jock me . . ."	A drum fill enters here, providing an extra rhythmic drive to highlight Ice-T's sing-song, taunting delivery.
2:03	"Always adventurous . . ."	The drum pattern and punch-phrased guitar riff return.
2:09	"Fila, Louis, or Fendi . . ."	Ice-T again incorporates a sing-song style into his delivery.
2:15	"Ice got the beef . . ."	The instruments drop out for one bar while Ice-T takes a vocal break.
2:18	"Bust a move . . ."	The drum pattern and punch-phrased guitar riff return.
2:25	"Was that the Ice . . ."	Ice-T imitates a female voice, then returns to his previous rap voice for "And then they see me. . . ." The instrumental samples have again dropped out for this vocal break.
2:28	"Rhyme pays"	Ice-T utters the song's tagline and the Black Sabbath riff plays in full twice with drum machine fills between iterations.
2:38	"Moves must be busted . . ."	A drum fill transitions into the next verse. The drum pattern and punch-phrased guitar riff return.
2:51	"Look at her lips . . ."	The instruments drop out for one bar while Ice-T takes a vocal break.

Continued

Listening Guide

Listening to Ice-T **Continued**

2:53	"Body that smells . . ."	The punch-phrased guitar returns once.
3:00	"Tie that freak outside . . ."	The instruments drop out for one bar while Ice-T takes a vocal break, this time with an altered vocal style using a high-pitched delivery.
3:03	"Because my jam . . ."	The drum pattern and punch-phrased guitar riff return.
3:10	"And I ain't lyin' . . ."	There is a drum break and Ice-T raps a modified version of the song's tagline.
3:13		The full iteration of the Black Sabbath riff returns with the drum machine fills and crow calls from before added. Ice-T's rhyme delivery alludes to Slick Rick's London-accented, sing-song style: "And I ain't lyin' rhyme do pay me!"
3:22	"I'm notorious . . ."	Ice-T begins his next verse. The drum pattern and punch-phrased guitar riff return; this time the rhythmic activity of the punch-phrasing intensifies during the course of the verse.
3:36	"It not to be banned . . ."	A drum fill enters, while vocals continue, building rhythmic energy. This returns immediately to the verse instrumentation. The punch-phrasing intensifies.
3:50	"Talkin' that gangsta shit . . ."	The instruments drop out for one bar while Ice-T takes a vocal break.
3:53	"Oh, I better chill out . . ."	The drum pattern and punch-phrased guitar riff return.
4:01	"Live for another day, rhyme pays . . ."	A drum fill, scratching, and the song's tagline enter.
4:03		Rather than allowing the record to play out the main Black Sabbath riff after the tagline as before, DJ Evil E repeatedly baby-scratches and punch-phrases this riff back in. The drum machine plays a fill-like pattern throughout these scratches and punch phrases, building in intensity.
4:13	"The front stage area . . ."	Ice-T begins his next verse. The drum pattern and punch-phrased guitar riff return.
4:21	"And Evil agitates the records . . ."	Evil E does some baby-scratching and punch-phrasing here, while Ice-T is talking about his DJ.
4:25	"My boy cuts like Jason . . ."	Drum machine fills enter here, building rhythmic intensity.
4:28	"That Evil is the great . . ."	The drum pattern with punch-phrasing continues in the manner of the previous verses.

4:35	"I'm bout to get off this mic . . ."	The instruments drop out for one bar while Ice-T takes a vocal break. Ice-T drops out so his DJ can take a solo.
4:38	"Kick it . . ."	DJ Evil E baby-scratches and punch-phrases the Black Sabbath guitar riff in rhythmically over the drum machine groove, adding rhythmic activity throughout his solo.
4:58	"Like me if you wanna . . ."	Ice-T begins his next verse. The drum pattern and punch-phrased guitar riff return.
5:08	"Like granite, I planned it . . ."	Two bars of drum fills here build rhythmic activity.
5:13	"Damn, shut up . . ."	The punch-phrased guitar returns once.
5:16	"Maybe you're just jealous . . ."	The instruments drop out for one bar while Ice-T takes a vocal break.
5:18	"But you're down with me . . ."	The drum pattern and punch-phrased guitar riff return.
5:25	"But right now . . ."	The instruments drop out for one bar while Ice-T takes a vocal break, setting Evil E up to take another solo.
5:28		Drum machine fills enter, interspersed with the drum fills from the "War Pigs" recording.
5:38	"Rhyme pays . . ."	The tagline here kicks off the next verse, rather than an instrumental break. The drum pattern and punch-phrased guitar riff return.
5:51	"Some young MC . . ."	Drum fills here create additional rhythmic activity.
5:54	"But there will always be . . ."	The drum pattern and punch-phrased guitar riff return.
5:56	"But I'm just caught in a battle . . ."	The instruments drop out for one bar while Ice-T takes a vocal break.
5:58	"Inevitable situation . . ."	The drum pattern and punch-phrased guitar riff return.
6:03	"Syllables jumble . . ."	Ice-T's sing-song delivery from earlier in the song returns.
6:16	"Damn, there I go . . ."	The instruments drop out for one bar while Ice-T takes a vocal break. The heavy-metal guitar lick and crow sounds return.
6:18		The full Black Sabbath riff returns with the drum machine and crow samples. This riff is reiterated twice, with baby scratches between and after each repetition.

N.W.A. (l. to r.): DJ Yella, Dr. Dre, Eazy-E, and MC Ren, 1991.
Source: © SuperStock/Alamy

Ice-T's next recording *Power* (1988) presents with brutal honesty and in first-person format the lives of L.A. gang members, pimps, and hustlers. In the song "I'm Your Pusher," Ice-T uses drug dealing as a metaphor for rapping success; that is, pushing "dope" records as opposed to drugs and getting high off the music and achieving gangsta-like success through entertainment as a result. Unfortunately, it was a metaphor that many media critics missed. Ice-T has always been vehemently outspoken in his opposition to drugs and the gangsta life. The raps he performed in the early days of "gangsta rap" delivered anti-crime messages, and the criminals he portrayed ended up dead or behind bars. However, critics often branded him as pro-violence and promoting drug use.

In 1992, Ice-T became the lead vocalist for his own heavy-metal group, Body Count, marking his work as the precursor to **rap-metal** (also called **nu-metal** or **rapcore**) in the late '90s. With Body Count, Ice-T recorded the controversial song "Cop Killer." The song was a revenge tale, coming out a year after the acquittal of Los Angeles police officers who were involved in the beating of Rodney King. The event gained national publicity because it revealed the brutal treatment that African Americans received from the local police. Eventually, after much controversy, the group removed the song from their album.

With the national success of Ice-T's music, the group N.W.A. (Niggas With Attitude) found a ready-made audience for gangsta-themed rap. Eazy-E formed N.W.A. in March 1987, collaborating with party-rap DJs Andre "Dr. Dre" Young and Antoine "DJ Yella" Carraby and rappers Lorenzo "MC Ren" Patterson and O'Shea "Ice Cube" Jackson. They released a debut album *N.W.A and the Posse* in 1987, but their groundbreaking album *Straight Outta Compton* (1988) transformed gangsta-style rap and reached double-platinum sales without the assistance of radio play.

Straight Outta Compton is not the first "gangsta rap" album, but the album's sensibility defined the style more so than the music of Schoolly D or Ice-T. Unlike the gangsta-tinged lyrics of Ice-T, most of the album's songs record episodes of Southern Californian wild nights, inebriated debauchery, easy women, and the strife between ghetto residents and corrupt police. The title track, "Straight Outta Compton," fulfills a goal set out by Eazy-E to celebrate their neighborhood and put Compton on the map. However, a song like "F—— Tha Police" carries the same sentiment to protect yourself against the unlawful lawmen of the LAPD that the Black Panther Party for Self-Defense espoused in the 1960s—perhaps even better than anything coming out of the East Coast.

Unlike the gangsta themes in the work of Ice-T or BDP, N.W.A.'s insistent claims of reality do not deal with the consequences of "gangsta" activities. The power of Ice Cube's lyrics made the exaggerations resonate with American youth and introduced the rest of the country to the "New Wild West" (in the words of Kool Moe Dee's 1988 rap), although some consumers were seduced by a romantic vision of outlaw empowerment and sexual prowess. As music journalist Cheo Hodari Coker observes:

> It was one thing to see KRS-One holding an Uzi on the cover of Criminal Minded and talking about gunplay in "9mm Goes Bang." He sounded like a rapper, boasting about a new type of dick. Ice Cube was different. He sounded like a gangster, the hardest one rap and street life had ever produced. (1999: 258)

Ice Cube may have "sounded like a gangster," but he and most of the N.W.A. crew were not members of any L.A. gang. Although Ice Cube wrote some of his band-mates' raps, each member had a distinct delivery and character. *Straight Outta Compton* remains an essential landmark, one of hip hop's greatest albums and the most significant in changing the direction of rap in the '90s—making "gangsta rap" as marketable and reproducible as the pop-friendly party rap against which N.W.A. and others were reacting. In the next few years, gangsta rap had to juggle the reporting of street realities with the "studio gangsters" taking advantage of the gangsta-styles' crossover appeal to shock-hungry, middle-class teenagers. Much of the music degenerated into cheap exploitation and empty cliché.

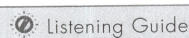 Listening Guide

Listening to N.W.A.

"STRAIGHT OUTTA COMPTON"

COMPOSED BY O'Shea "Ice Cube" Jackson, Andre "Dr. Dre" Young, Eric "Eazy-E" Wright, Lorenzo "MC Ren" Patterson, and Antoine "DJ Yella" Carraby

PERFORMED BY Dr. Dre (vocals/production), Eazy-E (vocals), Ice Cube (vocals), MC Ren (vocals), and DJ Yella (productions/scratch art)

ENGINEERED BY Donovan Sound

Appears on *Straight Outta Compton*, 1988, Ruthless Records, Priority Records SL 57102.

"Straight Outta Compton" was the lead single from N.W.A.'s debut album of the same name and served to introduce rap listeners to the group's West Coast perspective. This classic album organized the principles behind the gangsta rap sound and aesthetic in a way that earlier albums by artists such as Schoolly D or Ice-T did not. N.W.A.'s hardcore approach amped up the sound, lyrical content, and aesthetic of gangsta rap into one rife with violence or, perhaps more menacing, the threat of violence, demonstrating what the song's opening line heralds as "the strength of street knowledge." Each MC delivers his rhymes with unwavering intensity over soundscapes that are every bit as relentless and rhythmically intricate. The group members' gangsta personas align with a moral compass forged in the bleak realities facing those from Compton and other inner-city communities like it.

Continued

Listening Guide

Listening to N.W.A. **Continued**

Each verse is peppered with references to firearms, homicides, sexual violence, and threats, expressed to a degree practically unknown in rap before this time, particularly in terms of the song's graphic nature. These rhymes do not come across as metaphor. The three MCs draw the images convincingly, each bringing a signature sound and style of delivery to the table, maintaining an aggressive, threatening approach, but with increasing urgency matched by pitch. Ice Cube's voice is deep, remaining predominantly in his lower vocal register, and his consonants are explosive; he begins the song with an intensity that might convince the listener that he actually has "a crime record like Charles Manson." Ice Cube's voice sounds agitated; yet he preserves an unparalleled rhythmic flow, delivering his rhymes with ease. MC Ren, rapping the song's second verse in a voice that lies solidly in the middle range of the male vocal spectrum, has a slightly more subdued delivery than Ice Cube. Nonetheless, his lyrics are as violently themed as the previous verse. Eazy-E raps the song's third verse, maintaining a steady, high-pitched, nasal delivery that is nearly an octave higher than MC Ren's. Eazy-E's verse is the culmination of the gradual build in pitch that takes place during the song's verses, and he spits his rhymes with perhaps the greatest level of intensity of the three rappers. His treble voice cuts through the mix all the more sharply because of his vocal articulations.

The introduction of these three unmistakable MCs is underscored by the vocal breaks in the middle of the song that introduce MC Ren and Eazy-E and by Ice Cube stating his own name near the beginning of his verse. As these vocal breaks serve to introduce the group's MCs, so do the song's spoken-word intro and outro—these vocal bookends position the new group as bringing "street knowledge" and celebrating the West Coast's new sound and ethos, "Damn, that shit was dope!" Note that the last line was replaced on the video as "That's the way it goes in the city of Compton, boy!" which emphasizes narrative of place over stylistic delivery.

As the MCs of N.W.A. deliver aggressive, streetwise sounds on this track, the production team of DJ Yella and Dr. Dre provide a sound collage befitting the braggadocio and violence of the narrative. Yella and Dre previously worked together with electro-funk group the World Class Wreckin' Cru, and their familiarity with contemporary production techniques enabled them to create hardcore, funky sounds that are full of detail yet deceptively simple.

Yella and Dre flawlessly stitched together a number of samples that echoed the sound of their East Coast hardcore counterpoint, Public Enemy's Bomb Squad, while creating a new hardcore variation. They layered multiple samples throughout this song. The verses' main drum groove is taken from a drum break in the Winstons' gospel instrumental, "Amen, Brother" (1969), which has its kick and snare drums heightened and an added 16th-note high pattern provided by a drum machine that propels the original laid-back groove to a new level of relentless frenzy. This main loop is overlaid with other samples, described in the table. The layering becomes more complex at the song's musical tag, which follows the vocal tag of "Straight Outta Compton" at the end of each verse and serves the function that a chorus might in a typical verse-chorus-verse-chorus song form. Funkadelic's "You'll Like It Too" (1981) drives the main drum groove, again enhanced with a drum machine. It has several samples layered atop, outlined with timings in the table.

The layers of sounds in "Straight Outta Compton" are sutured seamlessly, sounding as though they naturally belong together. This is a testament to how smoothly DJ Yella and Dr. Dre were able to manipulate their source material to create a new set of sounds. The infectious multilayered main groove combined with the song's chaotic musical tag interspersed throughout demonstrate musically what the group's MCs deliver vocally: infectious flows interwoven with an overwrought emphasis on violence permeates the track's most melodic hooks and danceable grooves.

0:00	"You are now about to witness . . ."	Dr. Dre speaks the song's introduction.
0:04		The song's main groove begins, drawn primarily from the Winstons' "Amen, Brother" drum break with added drum machines accentuating the snare and kick drum and an added 16th-note hi-hat pattern. James Brown's screams from "Funky Drummer" are punch-phrased in the background.
0:13	"Straight outta Compton . . ."	Ice Cube enters with the song's first verse. A saxophone blast from "Amen, Brother" enters at the beginning of each musical phrase, altered in both pitch and speed. A guitar riff sampled from Dezo Daz's "It's My Turn" is looped repeatedly. A copy of Bob James's "Take Me to the Mardi Gras" is being **chirp-scratched** rhythmically (producing bird-like scratching sounds) in the background and a tom-tom sound from this record is cut in at the end of each percussive scratch sequence. These scratches are brought to the forefront of the mix periodically during the verses, but tend to remain in the background.
0:53	"AK-47 is the tool . . ."	A gun sound effect is punched in to accentuate the song's lyrics.
1:18	"I'm comin' straight outta Compton . . ."	The main groove breaks for a moment here. Five samples appear in quick succession along with a synthesizer accompaniment (at 1:20): a tire squeal from the Gap Band's "Burn Rubber on Me";

Continued

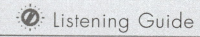

Listening Guide

Listening to N.W.A. **Continued**

		a scream from Wilson Pickett's "Get Me Back On Time, Engine #9" is scratched and punch-phrased in; the vocal phrase "City of Compton" sampled from Ronnie Hudson and the Street People's "West Coast Poplock" is slowed down, scratched, and punch-phrased twice; another sample, "Yo, Compton" from Dezo Daz's "It's My Turn" is punch-phrased; and, finally, all are layered atop the fifth sample, the introductory drum break from Funkadelic's "You'll Like It Too." This rapid-fire succession of samples that makes up the musical tag after the song's vocal tagline is iterated once each time it appears. A **transformer scratch** (tapping the cross-fader to chop up the long scratch sound into smaller pieces) appears at the end of this section. The high pitch suggests that it may be from "Burn Rubber on Me."
1:26	"Yo, Ren . . ."	Eazy-E appears, introducing MC Ren's verse.
1:27	"Straight outta Compton . . ."	MC Ren enters with his first verse. The verse groove returns. There are group vocals on significant rhymes at the end of some lines.
2:33	"Straight outta Compton . . ."	The tagline and its accompanying musical materials return with synthesizer accompaniment (at 2:36).
2:41		The instrumental groove from the verse plays as an interlude here.
2:50	"Eazy is his name . . ."	The groove breaks here as Dr. Dre introduces Eazy-E.
2:51	"Straight outta Compton . . ."	Eazy-E begins his verse. The verse groove returns. There are group vocals on significant rhymes at the end of some lines.
3:48	"Straight outta Compton . . ."	The tagline and its accompanying musical materials return (synthesizer at 3:50).
3:55		The verse groove returns here and vamps several times.
4:14	"Damn, that shit was dope!"	The music stops and MC Ren ends the song with this final line.

Rap Music as a Conduit for Political Culture

As early as 1982's "The Message," Melle Mel let the world know that ghetto living could sometimes be "like a jungle." Although it was different from the commercial old-school hip hop that was in vogue, it evoked the nation-conscious and street-reporting roots of rap better than anything before. The social consciousness and ghetto reality initially popularized by "The Message" was gradually emerging as a crucial element of the new-school rap as urban youth continued to reconstruct their social and political identities. It was in the best tradition of what KRS-One would describe as "edutainment." "The Message" expressed a communal sense of oppression made relevant to other African American, inner-city residents. Later rap artists like Public Enemy, Boogie Down Productions, Paris, Brand Nubian, and X Clan attempted to provide a more explicitly political and cultural analysis of urban African American life without compromise.

Black nationalism appears in various forms in rap music. Entertainment was the reason for rap's being, but entertainment could be couched in black nationalism and could become Afrocentric and transformative. Rappers articulate political, cultural, or economic elements in their music. Errol Henderson (1996) articulated three ways black nationalism appears in new-school rap:

1. **A common agenda:** Black nationalism offers itself as an appropriate vehicle for the realization of black aspirations. Artists such as Public Enemy, Paris, Boogie Down Productions (post second album), KRS-One, and Sister Souljah recognized a convergence of political purpose, objectives, and goals. They were guided by the teachings of Nation of Islam, Malcolm X, Stokely Carmichael, and the political activism of the Black Panthers; these rap artists, or "**raptivists**," following P.E. publicist Harry Allen's lead, aimed to help make African Americans self-sufficient and to encourage them to learn their history and acknowledge their past.

2. **A common sense of oppression:** Another brand of black nationalism arose in reaction to feelings of disenfranchisement from the African American middle class and the civil rights–era leaders. This was first articulated by Grandmaster Flash and the Furious Five's "The Message" but is also relevant in the works of Boogie Down Productions (especially their first album), N.W.A., Eazy-E, Geto Boys, and Compton's Most Wanted. This kind of black nationalism, however, disregards the diversity within the black community, especially around issues of class, gender, and cultural identification.

3. **A common cultural perspective:** This form of black nationalism suggests that African Americans should, as a people, have a common agenda because they have been historically subjugated as a group into a caste in the United States. Notice here that although a commonality of oppression is recognized, it is not primary for this African-centered nationalism. As a concept, culture is inclusive; it incorporates gender, class, and other diverse components of society within its construct. This third type of expression of black nationalism in rap would be best expressed in Afrocentric and Five Percent Nation rap.

Afrocentric Rap

Afrocentric rappers identify Africa as the source for black ideals, practices, and social order, and they express their African heritage through beats, lyrics, and Afrocentric dress and other images. Artists include the Jungle Brothers, A Tribe Called Quest, Queen Latifah, De La Soul, and X Clan. They are also often affiliated with the Native Tongues rap collective that came together in response to the growing popularity of gangsta rap. Afrocentric music-making drew rhythms and samples from soul and jazz, influencing the emergence of another subgenre, **jazz-rap fusion**.

Based in New York, the Native Tongues came into importance in the late '80s to the early '90s. The Jungle Brothers (the JBs—a subtle homage to the Godfather of Soul and Black Power musician James Brown; see Chapter 4) and Afrika Bambaataa (see Chapters 2 and 5) led the movement in order to support and promote each other's projects. The Native Tongues encouraged their members to create raps with positive Afrocentric messages and good beats, without ignoring the gritty realities of street life. They hoped to preserve rap's humor and good-time atmosphere, while supporting lyrics that promoted tolerance rather than violence. De La Soul was the next rap group to join, followed by A Tribe Called Quest. Bambaataa made it known that he had helped to form the group but otherwise remained in the background and watched the younger MCs make the music. Queen Latifah and Monie Love joined, followed by Five Percent Nation rappers Brand Nubian.

The Native Tongues were not alone in presenting a cultural nationalist approach to the politically charged Afrocentrism espoused by many East Coast rappers. Two Atlanta art students founded the Secret Society to affirm that not all expression in black America occurs in metropolitan centers. They positioned the American South as the intersection between black America and Africa. The Secret Society changed their name to Arrested Development, releasing the album *3 Years, 5 Months and 2 Days in the Life of* . . . in 1992. The album brought socially conscious rap with a southern sensibility to the mainstream with hits such as "Tennessee." In this song, the protagonist wrestles with the problems in the African American community and "the importance of history/why people be in the mess that they be." Their rhetoric survives in works of other southern rappers, such as Outkast (in particular, "Rosa Parks") and the rural orientation of Louisville's Nappy Roots.

Five Percent Rappers

The **Five Percent Nation** (a.k.a. the Nation of Gods and Earths) is a splinter group of the Nation of Islam founded by Clarence 13X in 1963. The doctrine of the Five Percent Nation is based on concepts of black nationalism and principles associated with the Nation of Islam. The Five Percent Nation espouses the philosophy that 85 percent of the world's population is uncivilized, 10 percent are rich slave owners, and 5 percent are the poor, righteous teachers whose mission is to spread awareness. Their teachings are partly based on a Supreme Alphabet and a Supreme Mathematics that work in conjunction with one another. They are systems that connect letters and numbers to concepts that are key to understanding one's relationship to the universe and carry spiritual messages of guidance. For example, Felicia M. Miyakawa (2005) observed the ways Five Percent artists embed hidden meanings in their lyrics, such as the expanded acronym "*I Self Lord Am Master*" in Brand Nubian's "Drop the Bomb" (1990); or in the form of mathematics when Wise Intelligent wishes "peace" in the line "16-5-1-3-5 coincide freak wise" on the Poor Righteous Teachers' "Allies" (1996), where "p" is the 16th letter in the alphabet, "e" is the 5th, and so on.

The Five Percent doctrine hinges on the identity of God, or Allah; adherents believe that each black man is divine and is in fact a god, and that black people are the original people of Earth and the mothers and fathers of civilization. Some Five Percent rappers, such as the Wu-Tang Clan, Brand Nubian, and the Poor Righteous

Teachers, find hip hop music an important vehicle to spread their doctrine. For example, in the Wu-Tang Clan's "Wu-Revolution" (1997), the crew promotes the belief of "each one, teach one" according to one's individual knowledge. Brand Nubian rap about their goal, which is to teach righteousness, in their lyrics for "Allah and Justice" (1992). It should be noted that some Five Percenters, such as Busta Rhymes, live by the doctrine but do not rap about it.

Consideration of Black Nationalism and Rap Music: Wasn't Old School also "Message Rap"?

Black nationalism in hip hop did not emerge exclusively from the lyrics of early rap music. In the early days of hip hop (ca. 1970s), this nationalism developed from the collective ethos of the South Bronx party community that spawned the new musical genre. The terrain of hip hop was the urban wasteland of the South Bronx; youth gangs were encased in what could only be described as a war zone. After the Black Power movement, the Vietnam War, and the FBI Counterintelligence Program against positive black community organizations such as the Black Panther Party, gangs were almost alone as an institution in the inner-city neighborhoods offering consistency (more so than stability), protection, and ways to survive the environment.

The largest of these African American gangs in the Bronx was the Black Spades. Its youthful leader Afrika Bambaataa transformed the Black Spades into the Zulu Nation and turned his party people on to black nationalism through action: positive creativity, vision, and healing through hip hop's four elements (see Chapter 2). Lyrically, however, the MCs' messages did not articulate the ideology as it is articulated in the conscious, political, and Afrocentric or even gangsta-centered rap lyrics of the new school. Nevertheless, the old-school party culture is couched in the philosophy of black empowerment by way of black nationalism. In this respect, the very framework of the hip hop community fostered and allowed to flourish a collective nationalist practice, and later, through the Zulu Nation, expanded to one of unity. This occurred because hip hop culture was incubated in the community's house parties, public parks, community housing projects, and local jams.

Gangstas and Stock Characters from Folklore: Two Types of Hustlers

As you recall from Chapter 4, there are two types of hustlers who originate in African American folklore and have been revived by rap artists: the trickster and the badman (or baadman). The trickster lives by his wits and is constantly scheming and manipulating others. A West African example of the character occurs as a spider in the Liberian folktale "The Wax Doll," while the African American tradition has many examples, including the well-known "tar baby" stories. In most variants of the tar baby tale, the troublemaking Brer Rabbit has to be taught a lesson for his misbehavior. The animals in his community create a doll made of tar and turpentine to entrap him. Brer Rabbit greets the tar figure on the first meeting. He argues with the nonresponsive, ill-mannered tar baby and slaps and kicks the doll until all his limbs are stuck in the sticky muck. He must devise an escape from the clutches of his captors. He convinces them to toss him into the briar patch as if that would be a worse punishment, but in actuality, it is the place where he was raised, and he makes his escape to cause havoc another day.

A contemporary rap example of the trickster occurs in Hammer's "Somethin' 'Bout the Goldie in Me" (1993). Hammer (formerly MC Hammer) released this song when he was trying to remain current and palatable to the gangsta rap trend. The Goldie character's name was taken from the lead in the blaxploitation film *The Mack* (1973; see below). The trickster-narrator of this rap is a ghetto hustler who lives more by his wits than his gun. Hammer disses the studio gangsta rappers in the industry who criticized him for making pop-rap despite his history growing up in the poorest regions of Oakland. He mocks the "wannabes" who "have been watchin' too much TV" for their claims that their raps are more authentic than his. This narrative echoes sentiments expressed by Ice-T in "Rhyme Pays" a few years earlier but failed commercially to re-establish Hammer as a ghetto survivor.

While the trickster survives through cunning, the badman/baadman rules by force and intimidation. He (and sometimes she) feels justified in "beating" the system, making ends meet illegally or outside conventional paths, which often are not available to people living on the edge of society. In Chapter 4, we discussed how Melle Mel's treatment of Jesse Jackson as a "baadman" portrayed him as a hero who was fighting a racist sociopolitical structure. However, in gangsta rap, the baadman is transformed into the drug dealer or modern-day gangster as depicted in N.W.A.'s "Straight Outta Compton" (1988). The baadman narrators in gangsta rap either promoted thug life or used the tactics of a gangsta to make right urban social ills. After 1987 and through the 1990s, the pimp, hustler, thug, and gangster were often the "heroes" in rap music. As West Coast "gangsta" became the dominant style of rap music, the other regions in the United States followed suit. However, unlike the toasting tradition (see Chapter 4), the rapper often performs the rap using the first-person voice—as if it were his experience.

Male performers usually dramatize the criminal lifestyle of "the hustler" and paint vivid scenarios of the violent, often misogynistic, illegal street culture of the disadvantaged and impoverished, but women rappers like Boss, Yo-Yo, Lil' Kim, and Foxxy Brown did not lag behind. The baadman is not typically attributed to a female character; in fact, Jerry H. Bryant argues a "baadwoman" type does not exist outside of characters acting out of jealousy, such as Frankie killing Johnny in the traditional African American ballad, as opposed to baad temperament.

On the other hand, the African American folk character Annie Christmas is an equally baad female counterpoint. Langston Hughes and Arna Bontemps recount the tale of Annie Christmas in their folktale collection, describing her as tremendous, strong, a hard drinker, and tough enough to scare the gruffest of men: "The tough keelboatmen, terrors of the river in other days, stood in awe of her and there wasn't a stevedore who didn't jump when Annie snapped her fingers. She could lick a dozen of them with one arm tied behind her back and they knew it." However, she was not without feminine charms: "Then every once in a while, Annie would get into a feminine mood. When this happened she was really seductive and enticing in a super sort of way" (1958: 223). Annie Christmas is equally menacing and intimidating as the baadman but provides a feminine perspective that would inform characters in the blues and rap traditions.

Popular Culture Media Images in Gangsta and X-rated Rap: Blaxploitation and Gangster Films

Gangsta rap artists also tapped into another pop-cultural media form from their youth: the **blaxploitation films** of the 1970s. These films celebrated strong black men who often used violence to achieve noble ends; they were known as "blaxploitation" films because they exploited common stereotypes of ghetto behavior, from drug use to gun violence. This film genre also drew on traditional figures from African American folklore. Folklore plays a direct role at least in one case, Rudy Ray Moore in *Dolemite*, who performs several toasts: "I'm gonna let 'em know that Dolemite is back on the scene. I'm gonna let 'em know that Dolemite is my name, and fuckin' up motha fuckas is my game."

The characters and themes of blaxploitation films were resources for a generation of rappers to draw from. Many of these artists were audience members when the films were popular in the 1970s. However, they also drew from other pop-cultural heroes and anti-heroes: *The Godfather*, *Scarface*, and Hong Kong martial art films, such as the Wu-Tang series. Some artists' personae drew directly from these characters: Snoop Dogg refers to himself as "Dolomite" and used the *Godfather* film logo for his *Dogfather* album; Geto Boys rapper Scarface derived his alter ego from the infamous gangster; and, as was mentioned already, MC Hammer refers to himself as Goldie from the 1973 film *The Mack* in the song "Somethin' 'Bout the Goldie in Me" (1994). Rappers also drew on various mobster images celebrating the Sicilian Mafia as a departure from the more usual street-thug imagery.

CHAPTER SUMMARY

This chapter traced the development of hardcore and gangsta rap. Both of these genres used graphic, sometimes violent, imagery and language to portray the hard realities of ghetto life and the need for young African Americans to fight back against oppression, lack of opportunity, poverty, and racism. Performers like Ice-T and N.W.A. asserted a strong message that included celebrating the past achievements of the civil rights and Black Panther movements. The gangsta image developed as an outgrowth of African American folklore and popular culture, including the popular blaxploitation and Mafia-themed movies of the '70s. The gangsta movement brought rap to a new level of popularity and notoriety—raising new controversies in both the African American and mainstream communities, as we shall see in Chapter 8.

STUDY QUESTIONS

1. Who were the old-school rappers that established social commentary in the hip hop tradition?

2. How is the concept of black nationalism manifested in conscious rap?

   Brand Nubian "I'm Black and I'm Proud" (1998)

   Brand Nubian "Love vs. Hate" (1998)

   Common (Sense) "Retrospect for Life" (1997)

   X Clan "Fire & Earth (100% Natural)" (1992)

3. What features are common to conscious rap and soul music?

4. How can you distinguish the various styles of conscious rap?

   Public Enemy "I Don't Wanna Be Called Yo Nigga" (1991)

   Brand Nubian "Meaning of the 5%" (1993)

   Queen Latifah "Latifah's Law" (1989)

   Arrested Development "Tennessee" (1992)

5. What social conditions are associated with the emergence of gangsta?

6. What characters from African American folklore are also found in rap lyrics?

7. What popular media genre influenced the narrative and images in many gangsta rap songs of the 1990s?

KEY TERMS

baadman/
baadwoman

Blaxploitation film

Chirp-scratched

Five Percent Nation

Gangsta rap

Jazz-rap fusion

Rap-metal (also,
nu-metal or rapcore)

Raptivist

Transformer scratch

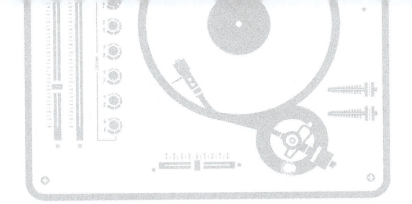

CHAPTER 8

HARDCORE II: GANGSTA IN THE '90s AND RESPONSES FROM WITHIN THE RAP COMMUNITY

Learning Objectives

When you have successfully completed this chapter, you will be able to discuss:

- Issues of authenticity in rap.
- How hardcore rap music has been represented and exploited.
- The censorship campaign against rap music in the early '90s.
- How women are represented in hip hop and how they represent themselves.
- The ways white rappers have participated in rap music.

Keeping It Real? Issues Underscoring the Representation and Exploitation of Rap

New-school rappers, in particular the pantheon of hardcore artists that emerged in the late '80s and early '90s, broadened the parameters of rap's lyricism and the accompanying soundscape by loosening the treatment of the rhymed couplet as well as the rhythmic placement of lyrics, reciting fully developed narratives that freely incorporated street slang and expletives, and creating musical collages with sampling technology and other studio innovations. In the era of hardcore rap, the narrative frame quickly shifted as rap songs with positive messages became less sellable and harsh street tales situated in America's ghettos and celebrations of thug life and hustling dominated the scene.

Before gangsta rap developed as a subgenre, g-style, "reality" raps, such as Ice-T's "6 'N the Mornin'" (1987) and Slick Rick's "The Moment I Feared" (1988), revealed a gritty trustworthiness about survival, street life, and consequences for living *the life*. Underground scenes from other regions emerged, providing similar narratives but from a perspective that was unmistakably not New York City. Those artists, with the help of major-label marketing executives, pushed this storytelling to the extreme, as the growing numbers of mainstream rap music consumers knew little about the inner city, poverty, and racial discrimination.

Controversy arose and debates ensued, promoting censorship on one side while inspiring underground music scenes to respond by celebrating a shared African cultural heritage that reinvented classical black popular musics such as jazz, R&B, and gospel. While "keepin' it real" became hip hop's credo in the 1990s, sustaining reality proved more complicated. Yet many artists faced this challenge head-on and sought solutions without killing the genre.

Harsh Messages of Gangsta and X-rated Rappers

While gangs had always existed, the crack cocaine epidemic made it worse and changed the direction of hardcore music. Rappers continued to report on issues concerning the ghetto, but more attention shifted toward explicit details of street violence, the crack trade, and other realities of the urban poor. Unlike the old-school ideology that seemed to exclaim, "Escapism will help us deal with the bad elements of the ghetto," the new-school, West Coast ideology demanded, "We are not going to ignore these bad elements in the ghetto anymore." N.W.A.'s "F—— Tha Police" (1988) woke up the world to the gang violence and turmoil of the West Coast and challenged police brutality unlike any social protest song before it (see Chapter 7).

The era following the release of N.W.A.'s *Straight Outta Compton* (1988) can be perceived as an incubation period for gangsta rap (1988–1992). More rappers fell under the category of "gangsta" rappers describing the chaotic, rough, and seedy side of inner-city life using graphic language laced with expletives. For example, the Geto Boys' song "City Under Siege" (1990) recounts a survival tale from the perspective of a thug trying to live in Houston's ghetto. Bushwick Bill of the Geto Boys admits that he did not live the life but it was the life around him, and he uses a first-person voice as a narrative choice to make the story more meaningful to his listeners.

Sometimes rappers' lyrics exploit and dramatize ghetto-life experiences, glorifying drugs, violence, criminal acts, and misogynistic and X-rated behavior. In Chapters 4 and 7, we examined the ways the toasting tradition and the stock folk character of the baadman informs the narrative structure in modern rap, as in Scarface's "Jesse James" (1994). This song is formatted much like the traditional toast (a story about an antiauthority figure) but performed in the first person; however, this outlaw is a historic criminal who terrorized the western frontier of the 19th century. As an inspiration, Jesse James is not an outlaw character who is fighting against society's racism, as was the case in Melle Mel's "Jesse" (1984). Scarface, speaking as Jesse James, coldly describes his actions:

> Snuck up behind him, had his hands in his pocket
> Took my pistol out, unlocked it
> Pulled the hammer back and—cocked it
> And left his shit all on the carpet
> I seen a (murder, murder) I pin-pointed my target
> I'm making my way up out the building
> I got the nigga that I came here to get, notify his children

That they old man done fell up out the game
Because I came to this muthafucka
and killed his ass just like Jesse James

This is not a song that asks listeners to think like a criminal in order to obtain justice, but rather offers listeners a portrait of an unapologetic, cold-blooded murderer. There is a cinematic quality to this song in that it sets up scenes much like the critically acclaimed 1986 film *Henry: Portrait of a Serial Killer*. As in the film, the narrative is presented intelligently and artistically despite its revolting topic. Unlike the slasher film genre it closely resembles, the focus is not on building suspense or following the terror felt by the victim but on portraying the murderous logic of a criminal mind.

The album cover for N.W.A.'s third album *Efil4zaggin* continues to present images of unfair, brutal police behavior, but the songs describe a kind of hedonistic, self-indulgent depravity, pandering to the fantasies of a new Wild, Wild West in which listeners can participate without having to set foot in Compton, South Chicago, or other American ghettos. A kind of tug-of-war emerged between expressions about the hardships of ghetto life and narratives that deliver tales consumers wanted to hear. During this "incubation period" of gangsta rap, some rappers demonstrated a bipolar commitment to street reporting on one end of the spectrum and glamorizing the gangsta or thug life on the other.

Take for example Tupac "2Pac" Amaru Shakur. Unlike some other rappers, who came from middle-class backgrounds, 2Pac was raised in the ghetto, the son of a Black Panther, Afeni Shakur. 2Pac raised awareness of the plight of unwed mothers in songs like "Keep Ya Head Up" (1993), which begins by honoring Afrocentric beauty that goes beyond the superficial ("Some say the blacker the berry, the sweeter the juice/ I say the darker the flesh then the deeper the roots") followed by some very pro-female or feminist-sympathetic rhetoric. The song is comparable to the sociopolitical, pro-Afrocentric lyrics in Arrested Development's "Mama's Always On Stage" (1992) and Queen Latifah's "The Evil That Men Do" (1989). However, on the same album 2Pac produced party anthems with misogynistic lyrics associated with gangsta rap; for example, "I Get Around" (1993), which is a no-holds-barred assault on the gold-digging, scheming, and conniving women that pursued him after he became famous.

2Pac's use of "thug life" in his work represents his fascination with poverty and crime and the ways in which it relates to the urban poor, especially the African American poor. Furthermore, much like the gangsta rap that produced lyrical themes that existed on a continuum with reality rap on one end and exploitative sensationalism on the other, the "thug" has the potential to represent the thug-entrepreneur who works with the illegal economies available in order to lead a better life and the thug-activist who raises awareness

Tupac Shakur.
Source: © AF archive/Alamy

of the social injustices *on behalf of the community*. Many could not see any alternative for supporting themselves beyond the thug life; for example, Ice Cube's "A Bird in the Hand" (1991) explains the logic to pursue thug entrepreneurship:

> Fresh out of school 'cause I was a high school grad
> gots to get a job 'cause I was a high school dad
> Wish I got paid like I was rappin' to the nation
> but that's not likely, so here's my application
> Pass it to the man at AT&T
> 'Cause when I was in school I got the A.E.E.
> But there's no S.E. for this youngsta
> I didn't have no money so now I have to hunch the
> Back like a slave, that's what be happenin'
> but whitey says there's no room for the African
> Always knew that I would boycott, jeez
> but welcome to McDonalds can I take your order please
> Gotta sell ya food that might give you cancer
> 'cause my baby doesn't take no for an answer
> Now I pay taxes that you never give me back
> what about diapers, bottles, and Similac
> Do I gotta go sell me a whole lotta crack
> for decent shelter and clothes on my back?

2Pac claims that if he had had an interested father, maybe things would have been different and he might have led a different life; instead, his father figures were thugs, gangstas, pimps, and junkies. He embraced the thug life but, interestingly enough, never had a criminal record or did any time in jail until he became famous.

X-rated Rap/Miami Bass

Another style that grew in popularity during this period was a rap music that focused solely on sexy lyrics with an accompaniment that emphasized a deep, driving bass. Musically, Afrika Bambaataa's electro-funk masterpiece "Planet Rock" (1982) and the techno and house scenes coming out of Detroit and Chicago, respectively, were the inspirations for DJs and producers to experiment with drum machines, synthesizers, and bass-heavy grooves. This brand of rap music was not gangsta but was often included in that category in the early '90s because of the slew of obscenities incorporated into the lyrics. However, this style—often referred to as X-rated rap, booty rap, or dirty rap—was largely a party music that did not take itself seriously. It had its origins in Miami, Florida.

The pioneers of the genre were 2 Live Crew, who were also one of the leading groups of the groove-heavy Miami bass sound, releasing sexually explicit lyrics as early as 1986 with "Throw the 'D'," which garnered a female response by Anquette, "Throw the P," in the tradition established by the Roxannes in New York around the same time (see Chapter 6). Some of their lyrical inspirations came from the sexy comedy routines of Richard Pryor, Redd Foxx, and Rudy Ray Moore of *Dolemite* fame.

Too $hort of Oakland, California, also falls into this category. He claims that he built his career on the word "bitch," arguing with those who object to this word that it is the term he hears women use to refer to each other. Some representative works include "All My Bitches Are Gone" (1993) and "Cocktails" (1995). 2 Live Crew put out "D.K. Almighty" (1989) and "Put Her in the Buck" (1989). Most X-rated rap was simply bawdy party rap designed to keep the party rolling, and it has been criticized for not having much musical or lyrical depth. However, the gritty, funky sound of bass music began to spread throughout the South and established the foundation for the southern sound that would drive the new millennium's pop rap scene.

Controversy with Gangsta and X-rated Rap

Despite the global success of rap music, controversy arose in the early 1990s. The news media fervently reported on concert violence, obscene lyrics, pornographic behavior onstage, and sexually explicit music videos, as these topics were bound to grab headlines. Yet they did not report on rap artists lyrically challenging the gangsta rap trend, the various benefit rap concerts, or the Stop the Violence Movement spearheaded by KRS-One, which raised $400,000 for the National Urban League through the song "Self Destruction" (1989). The West Coast artists did not lag behind, with the release of the single "We're All in the Same Gang" (1991) by the West Coast Rap All-Stars (featuring Ice-T, MC Hammer, Tone-Loc, N.W.A., and Young MC, among others). The media veered away from covering socially conscious and Afrocentric rap in favor of the more controversial and titillating "gangsta rap" subgenre growing in the early '90s, within which X-rated rap was often subsumed. In the sensationalism, non-gangsta rap artists fell by the wayside while one-dimensional studio "gangstas" were signing six-figure album deals—dragging rap music to a narrower perspective.

Rappers' portrayals of gangstas, thugs, pushers, pimps, and sex kittens—mixed with some artists' real-life brushes with the law—led the media and the public to question the moral value of all rap music and not just the gangsta-laden material. Commercial sponsors pressured radio stations across the country to stop playing rap because they feared that consumers would associate their products with this music. The Parents Music Resource Center (PMRC), the Anti-Defamation League, former civil rights advocates, politicians, and Christian ministers fueled the fires of fear.

Scholar Michael Eric Dyson analyzed the tactics used against rap music, citing two different types of attacks. *Censorship* sought to prevent the sale of "vulgar" music that offended the mainstream moral sensibility by suppressing the First Amendment. The second tactic, which he called *civil responsibility*, was more difficult to accomplish, in that it sought to oppose the expression of misogynistic, sexist, and self-deprecating sentiments and images in hip hop culture through protests, boycotts, and consciousness raising; for example, the East Coast artists who participated in the Stop the Violence Campaign or produced socially conscious songs, such as Public Enemy's "I Don't Wanna Be Called Yo Nigga" or Queen Latifah's "U.N.I.T.Y. (Who You Calling a Bitch?)." The debate within the rap community raged lyrically, but those outside the rap community made headway in controlling what artists could or could not recite in their music.

Parents Music Resource Center (PMRC)

In 1985 Tipper Gore, the wife of then senator Al Gore, founded the **Parents Music Resource Center**. At the time, the Gores had teenaged children and were "shocked" when they heard the type of music that their suburban, white daughters enjoyed. The PMRC's mission was to "inform" parents about the content of popular music and to provide a way for parents to identify potentially "obscene" music before buying a single or an album. The group's greatest triumph came when it lobbied successfully for a voluntary labeling system to identify explicit albums in 1990. The Recording Industry Association of America (RIAA) encouraged the labeling of the "Tipper Sticker," as it came to be known, on any album containing explicit lyrics, but it was up to the artist to apply it. The system was voluntary, but many stores would not carry albums without the sticker. Many artists also took to releasing "clean" and "dirty" versions of the same album, as a way supposedly to sidestep the issue. However, with the exception of parents, the reality was that no hip hop fan intentionally bought the clean version.

Charges of Obscenity and Censoring Hip Hop

The first spark of things to come occurred in 1987, when a Florida record-store clerk was charged with a felony for selling the album *The 2 Live Crew Is What We Are* by 2 Live Crew to a 14-year-old minor. He was later acquitted. It should be noted that 2 Live Crew had the foresight to produce a "clean version" that had most of the profanity and sexual references deleted so that younger fans could still buy their music, even though the clean version was not the album most kids sought.

In 1989, the group released *As Nasty as They Wanna Be*, which became a multiplatinum success. True to 2 Live Crew's style, this album was raunchy, sexually explicit, and full of immature humor. With limited airplay, the album reached the top 40 charts and sold over two million units, primarily on the strength of the clean version of the single "Me So Horny." As a result of the album's commercial success, the Crew were thrust into the limelight as First Amendment advocates and the three group members became the focus of a national campaign against obscene lyrics.

Jack Thompson, a high-profile attorney and antiporn activist, sent copies of the album's contents to every sheriff in the state of Florida, and Broward County Sheriff Nick Navarro brought the album to a federal judge in Ft. Lauderdale who declared the album to be obscene. Florida's governor at the

2 Live Crew onstage, from the *As Nasty as They Wannabe* tour, 1990.

Source: © Ebet Roberts

time, Bob Martinez, declined to get involved, maintaining that community standards were not a state issue but a local one. The judge's ruling meant that record stores selling the record in Broward County could be subject to prosecution. This was the first time in US history that a musical recording was ruled "obscene."

The ruling was also applied to the recitation of such lyrics in live performances. Members of 2 Live Crew were arrested in Broward County for reciting the obscene lyrics in concert at Club Futura, an adults-only venue in Hollywood, Florida. This is somewhat ironic since Broward County had adult venues where one could watch strippers or buy explicit sexual material on video or in print. At 2 Live Crew's trial, renowned scholar Henry Louis Gates Jr. testified on behalf of the Crew, citing their risqué humor as a part of a long-standing African American verbal art tradition called signifying (see Chapter 4). The US Supreme Court overturned the Broward County decision, maintaining that the lyrics were protected under the First Amendment [*Luke Records v. Navarro*, 960 F 2d (1992)]. The members of 2 Live Crew, Luther Campbell, Brother Marquis, Fresh Kid Ice, and DJ Mr. Mixx, were acquitted.

1994 Senate Hearings Against Gangsta Rap

On February 23, 1994, the Senate Subcommittee on Juvenile Justice—part of the Judiciary Committee of the United States Senate—met to "Examine the Effects of Violent and Demeaning Imagery in Popular Music on American Youth." These hearings focused on rap/hip hop music, addressing issues of censorship related to pornography and obscenity. Panelists including politicians, civil rights activists, journalists, music industry representatives, and scholars presented their various views on the positive qualities and negative effects of hip hop. The National Congress of Black Women took credit for requesting the hearings. Like many older civil rights organizations, this group was uncomfortable with the image it felt rap was promoting of black life as being dominated by sex, violence, and obscenity.

Both sides presented strong arguments for their positions. Some arguments made by the anti-rap forces were these:

- While some scholars have argued that rap's lyrics have roots in toasting and signifying traditions, "humorous" lyrics advocating violence against women in the form of rape or physical altercation should not be acceptable.
- Rap music has normalized the use of the N-word as well as expletives in pop music lyrics.
- Major labels, such as Time Warner, involved in producing rap music and benefiting financially from its popularity should also be held accountable.
- "Reality raps" that exaggerate ghetto life pander to the desires of the white-run record industry and the approximately 70 percent of consumers who are middle-class and not African American.

On the other hand, arguments made by the pro-rap forces included:

- Rap is a means of escaping from street life by talking about it, not living it.
- The issues of violence and obscenity do not concern African Americans exclusively, in that misogyny and violence are parts of American culture.

- Many African American leaders do not live in the "'hood" anymore and so have lost touch with urban life (nor do many commercially successful rappers, but that is another issue).
- There are worse things to protect "our" children from than naughty lyrics, such as the drugs and the guns readily available to inner-city kids.
- Bringing back jobs that can sustain a decent livelihood would be a more effective means of attacking rap than censoring it.
- Critics of rap are ignoring that entertainment often includes a willing suspension of disbelief.

The romantic poet Samuel Taylor Coleridge coined the term "suspension of disbelief." Coleridge believed that in lyrical art forms, broadly speaking, readers have "to transfer from our inward nature a human interest and a semblance of truth sufficient to procure for these shadows of imagination that willing suspension of disbelief for the moment." In other words, we as the audience must accept that the "theater on display"—whether it is a film, a play, or a gangsta rap narrative—is part of make-believe. It is important in terms of understanding that a character like the android in the Terminator films in the 1990s is not really Arnold Schwarzenegger, and it is not really Arnold committing all those acts of violence but a character he is portraying. Rap artists such as 2Pac, Bushwick Bill, and Ice Cube claim that, in their songs, they are sometimes observers of the environment and sometimes participants. The rapper shows the most graphic images of the street as if he or she is experiencing them firsthand. Consider the fact that all rappers have MC names—alter egos that are much like the characters of professional wrestlers or superhero comics: Tracy Morrow is not Ice-T; O'Shea Jackson is not Ice Cube; Will Smith is not the Fresh Prince; and Marshall Mathers is not Eminem.

The Emergence of G-Funk

Dr. Dre left N.W.A. and, assisted by businessman Marion "Suge" Knight, launched Death Row Records. He released the definitive gangsta rap album *The Chronic* in 1992; Snoop Dogg, a budding rapper from Long Beach, California, at the time, is the star of this album. *The Chronic* is a concept album—one that makes sense in a cinematic manner, in that song sequences follow a filmmaker's logic, moving from one scene to the next. It helped change the sound of hip hop. Dre took the best elements of Parliament-Funkadelic and added the eerie sound of a high-pitched synthesizer and other grittier gangsta elements. Arguably, Dre created the first "pop gangsta" album, taking a pop approach and wedding it to a ghetto sensibility that served as a model for others to imitate. This musical style came to be known as **G-Funk**.

The funky grooves of James Brown, Sly Stone, Kool & the Gang, and Parliament-Funkadelic had been moving the crowd since the old-school days, with the DJs putting their distinct stamp on tracks by manipulating and extending the break sections (see Chapter 4). When hip hop moved from the streets into the recording studios in the 1980s, funk continued to be a part of the production. G-Funk's piercing synthesizers, slow grooves, deep bass, fewer layers of sound, and liberal play with low and high frequencies reinterpreted the earlier funk format. After the success of Dr. Dre's

1992 album *The Chronic*, many new and established rap artists and producers copied his musical techniques, making G-Funk the most recognizable sound in rap for much of the early '90s. Furthermore, this was not a music focused on radio play but rather on the car-stereo consumer whose ride was equipped with massive subwoofers.

Dr. Dre's "Let Me Ride" (featuring RBX and Snoop Dogg) ushered in the new sound, looping two measures of Parliament's "Mothership Connection" (1975). In fact, the trio makes an assertion similar to the one made by Run-D.M.C. in the mid-'80s proclaiming the new-school sound. Dre tells his listeners that this is not Aerosmith, a subtle disapproving reference to Run-D.M.C. and their remake of Aerosmith's "Walk This Way" (1986; see Chapter 6). G-Funk is, in essence, the *newer*-school sound. Similarly, "F—— wit Dre Day" (featuring Snoop Dogg) samples George Clinton's "Atomic Dog" (1982) and is a song that both commemorates a master musician from hip hop culture's past and celebrates the new Wild, Wild West. Snoop also introduces the alternative pronunciation "Biotch" ("Bee-ahtch") that would be incorporated into the slang of hip hop fans worldwide in the 1990s and cross over into the mainstream as well. Finally, on an album in which the title itself celebrates self-indulgence, the song "The Roach" samples Parliament's "P-Funk." But, unlike in the Parliament song, Dre is not playing with the metaphor of getting high off the music. G-Funk transformed the images of poverty, social injustice, and male-on-male violence of 1988 Los Angeles into a stylish, malt-liquored city of decadent pleasure where every man has a harem of bikini-clad women at his disposal.

Followers of G-Funk

Warren G exploded out of the Long Beach rap scene in 1994 with the smash single "Regulate," a duet with vocalist and longtime friend Nate Dogg, which uses a sample from Michael McDonald's "I Keep Forgetting We're Not in Love Anymore." As teens, Warren G, Nate Dogg, and future superstar Snoop Dogg formed the group 213, named after their area code. Warren G played the group's demo that showcased Snoop Dogg for his half-brother Dr. Dre, and Dre invited all three to his studio, where Snoop Dogg collaborated heavily on the album *The Chronic*.

In 1993, with the guidance of Dr. Dre, Snoop Dogg released his debut album *Doggy Style* to a built-in audience following the success of *The Chronic*. Snoop confessed that he was a better MC-battler than writer until Dre taught him to write. Snoop introduced vocals that are more agile and melodic than anyone's at that time—a singing-rhyming style with new inflections.

Snoop Dogg's "Who Am I (What's My Name)?" is a song that immediately references the underground hit "F—— wit Dre Day" (1992), once again redoing funk impresario George Clinton's "Atomic Dog" (1982). For the most part, this song is a traditional boasting party rap in the old-school tradition, but with a gangsta rap twist. The line "Bow wow wow yippee yo yippee yay," which is part of the original sample, alerts the listener to the new Wild, Wild West metaphor thrust forward by this West Coast rapper. Though both tunes celebrate and romanticize gang violence, they were released at a time when gangs in Los Angeles had called a truce.

Death Row also signed 2Pac, and in 1996 he also applied the G-Funk tradition to his music in songs like "I Ain't Mad at Cha." It samples DeBarge's 1983 hit "A Dream" and is a song about forgiveness for all his old friends who turned on him once he became famous. Even non-gangsta rappers fell under the spell of G-Funk. Pop rappers made the R&B elements more evident in their music, forecasting the fusion of hip hop with R&B throughout the 1990s (a.k.a. hip hop soul or neo-soul).

G-Funky styles from the West Coast drove the musical sound in the early '90s, and R&B, pop, and East Coast rappers responded to the trend. Pop rap act DJ Jazzy Jeff and the Fresh Prince's track "I'm Looking for the One (to Be with Me)" (1993)—which drew on the S.O.S. Band's "Tell Me If You Still Care" (1983)—has a more prominent R&B sound than their previous work while still maintaining non-gangsta sensibilities. Hip hop artists began to team up with R&B artists and producers. They incorporated sung choruses and verses from R&B, and borrowed rhythmic patterns, guitar licks, and other musical features from both R&B and funk traditions. R&B artists also borrowed elements—rapping, hip hop beats, and slang—from the hip hop tradition.

Artists inspired by G-Funk truly managed a healthy marriage between R&B and rap. Some examples include Aaliyah's (featuring R. Kelly) "Down with the Clique" (1994); TLC's "Kick Your Game" (1994); Montell Jordan's "This Is How We Do It" (1995); Mase's (feat. Total) "What U Want" (1997); and Lauryn Hill's "Doo Wop" (1998). This union has been so successful that R&B-rap fusion styles have been referred to as "hip hop" since 2000, whether or not there is any rapping incorporated in a song. This is a bit of a misnomer in terms of what hip hop culture used to be; however, hip hop no longer "belongs" to a small community of artists in the South Bronx but rather to a "global community" of hip hop aficionados, a phenomenon that will be problematized and addressed in Chapter 9.

Furthermore while **R&B-rap fusion** became a style unto itself in the '90s, credit has to be given to many of the early women rap artists who included sing-song delivery in their rhymes, like the Sequence in 1979, or those who incorporated sung choruses in their work early in their careers, like Queen Latifah ("Ladies First," 1989) or Salt-n-Pepa ("Blacks' Magic," 1990) and super-producer Sylvia Robinson on Grandmaster Melle Mel and Duke Bootee's "Jesse" (1984).

Pop Rap Goes Hardcore

As we have noted earlier in this chapter, some rappers did live the gangster lifestyle, such as Ice-T, Tupac, and Snoop Dogg, and some were involved in the drug trade, such as Eazy-E and Notorious B.I.G. Still others who grew up in the "hood" were not criminals themselves but instead drew on others' experiences, sometimes using the first-person voice for added impact. Other rap artists made up or imagined the gangsta experience as a slew of wannabe, studio gangstas tried to break into the industry.

With the growing critical and commercial success of gangsta-themed rap, pop rappers' street credibility was called into question. The '90s brought forth what scholar Michael Dyson (1997) accurately calls "the art of Representin'," raising questions of ghetto authenticity expressed in the popular phrase "keepin' it *real*."

Pop rap stars like MC Hammer and Vanilla Ice tried to harden their image during this period. Both came out with a new gangsta-centered approach to their pop rap style; for example, Hammer dropped the "MC" from his name and released *The Funky Headhunter* in 1994. He tried to reassert his ghetto roots in the song "Oaktown," reminding fans and doubters that he was from a poor ghetto in Oakland, California ("representin' the West Coast"). His beats were funkier and darker in the G-Funk fashion of the day, and he reintroduced himself as a ghetto hustler in two ways: in the song "Somethin' 'Bout the Goldie in Me," which draws from the street-hustler character in the blaxploitation film *The Mack* (see Chapter 7), and in his new stage name taken from the film *Hammer* (1973).

In comparison to his earliest video of the colossal hit "Can't Touch This" from 1989, Hammer's look is harder in the video "Don't Stop" (1994). Viewers can easily observe the strong differences and physical changes to his image. The gold lamé parachute pants, neon colors, and humorous dance steps of his pop persona are replaced by black and white street clothing, bandannas and baseball caps, aggressive stomping on stage, and fewer smiles; yet the musical sound and dancing performances echo his past pop-star stage presence. Despite his Oakland-ghetto credibility, he was not successful in remaining relevant to hip hop fans, though with this album he became the first rap artist to achieve platinum record-sales status.

East Coast–West Coast Rivalry: Not Just Biggie and 2Pac

The rivalry between East and West Coast rappers developed over many years as each side declared its superiority as the most "authentic." As early as 1988, Public Enemy joined with Ice Cube's solo project to quell those differences between the East and West Coast styles. While some rap historians credit Tha Dogg Pound's 1995 single "New York, New York" as the dis rap that began the "beef" between the East and West Coasts, it is perhaps more telling that by 1993 the West Coast rap scene was outselling the East Coast rappers by three to one.

The East Coast establishment refused to acknowledge those styles emanating from the West and the South—such as the work of N.W.A., Compton's Most Wanted (Compton), Too $hort (Oakland), or the Geto Boys (Houston)—as legitimate forms of rap music. Nonetheless, the West's laid-back, Jeep-ready, G-Funk sound was beginning to appeal to more rap fans across the country. Dream Hampton observes that for two years the West Coast's "languid rhyme style and murderous mentality" (1999:342) enjoyed incredible success. However, during this two-year period when gangsta rap was developing, West Coast rap artists were not played on East Coast radio, even after the skyrocketing success of N.W.A.'s *Straight Outta Compton* (1988) or *Efil4zaggin* (1991) or Dr. Dre's *The Chronic* (1992).

In response to N.W.A.'s blistering street narratives on *Straight Outta Compton* (1988), Bronx rapper Tim Dog fired the first shots with his song "F—— Compton" (1991), which brought lots of attention to his album *Penicillin on Wax* although it did not become a major hit. Many rappers hailing from Compton and the

Los Angeles area responded vehemently. Dr. Dre and Snoop Dogg dissed Tim Dog twice on *The Chronic* (1992). First, on "F—— wit Dre Day," Snoop states:

> *Play with my bone, would ya Timmy*
> *It seems like you're good for makin' jokes about your jimmy*
> *. . . But fuck your mama, I'm talkin' about you and me*
> *Toe to toe, Tim M-U-T*
> *Your bark was loud, but your bite wasn't vicious*

Dre made Tim Dog the answer to a clue, suggesting that Tim Dog enjoyed homosexual acts, in a skit that parodied the popular 1970s game show *The $20,000 Pyramid* (renaming it the "The $20 Sack Pyramid"). Other West Coast artists also dissed Tim Dog; for example, Compton's DJ Quik on "Way 2 Fonky" (1992) and Compton's Most Wanted on "Who's Xxxxing Who?"(1992).

A spirit of aggressive competition has been integral to hip hop music from its inception. We began our discussion of hip hop culture by acknowledging the South Bronx youths' invention and unification of the four formative elements that were created in part to sublimate the violence plaguing the neighborhoods into a positive outlet (see Chapter 2). We listened to some of the earliest, old-school battle rhymes, such as the one between Busy Bee and Kool Moe Dee, and to the spirited rivalries in the golden era between the Bronx's Boogie Down Productions and the Queensbridge artist MC Shan, and even to the commercially successful battles between LL Cool J versus Kool Moe Dee, and UTFO versus Roxanne Shanté (see Chapters 4–6). Taking the battle off the stage and into the studio kept fans glued to their radios to catch the latest dis records. However, in the 1990s "battling" became a bloody mess. No longer were these battles concerned with lyrical virtuosity and style on record but rather with a distorted sense of reality and territorialism.

While the West Coast was enjoying domination of the hip hop music scene and eventually the mainstream music scene, a New York gangsta sensibility began to emerge on the East Coast. The Wu-Tang Clan out of Staten Island were the first to bring fans' attention back to the East. Their 1993 album *Enter the Wu-Tang* mapped out the blueprints for other hardcore rappers to follow much in the same way *The Chronic* did for the West. The members of the Wu-Tang Clan expanded gangsta style in a unique way, represented the streets on the East Coast, and laid the foundation for the Notorious B.I.G., Junior M.A.F.I.A., Nas, Mobb Deep, and Jay-Z to reintroduce New York hip hop in the gangsta era.

The Wu-Tang Clan followed the "gangsta style" of Ice Cube but added an East Coast, nationalist and political agenda. In "C.R.E.A.M. (Cash Rules Everything Around Me)" (1994), the rappers stress the importance of obtaining money, as opposed to spending it, and promote hard work, diligence, and creativity as the best way to earn it, as opposed to the drug trade. They were also not afraid to take risks early in their careers. For example, in 1996, the Wu-Tang Clan collaborated with other East Coast rappers on a compilation album *America Is Dying Slowly*, to promote HIV and AIDS awareness, and donated all proceeds to fight against AIDS in communities of color. Their contribution "America" echoes the album's title, enabling the Wu-Tang Clan to confront HIV and AIDS as it affects African Americans and dispelling notions that AIDS is "just" a gay man's disease.

A key figure in the growing East Coast gangsta movement was producer/record company executive/performer Sean "Puffy" Combs. Combs founded Bad Boy Entertainment in 1993 after losing his position as vice president of Uptown Records. Combs had garnered respect for his work with Mary J. Blige and for the music he had produced at Uptown. With Notorious B.I.G. (a.k.a. Biggie Smalls, Big Poppa) of Brooklyn, and his debut release *Ready to Die* (1994), Combs proved that Bad Boy could produce hits that sold nationally. The duo branded hip

Notorious B.I.G.

Source: © Moviestore collection Ltd/Alamy

hop with Bad Boy's aggressive promotion of conspicuous consumption and the luxurious life by way of their lyrics, sampling art, public appearances, and video.

Biggie came from a middle-to-working class neighborhood, but he was fascinated by the street game and subsequently dropped out of school to pursue it by selling drugs. Puffy was attracted to B.I.G.'s voice and ghetto-life credibility and found in him the face for Bad Boy. Puffy treated making records like making movies: he was the director to B.I.G.'s actor/storyteller. Like Wu-Tang before him, B.I.G. revitalized the East Coast rap scene and introduced a new delivery style that was as powerfully unique as Rakim a decade before or Snoop two years prior. His single "Juicy" (1994) was a familiar rags-to-riches tale where wealth is obtained through the underground economy. It is the story of the American dream but from a Brooklyn, ghetto perspective, smothered in authenticity since fans knew of B.I.G.'s drug-dealing past.

2Pac and B.I.G. began their careers around the same time and had been friends. However, these two rap icons' camaraderie transformed into a bitter rivalry that triggered an East Coast–West Coast feud that fueled deadly animosities in communities already crippled by excessive violence. That experience made it clear to observers that rap beefs sometimes have deadly consequences beyond the recording studio. According to Ice-T, 2Pac acted out his stories. He always challenged authority but never got into criminal trouble until after he became famous. A series of violent incidents culminated in a charge of sexual assault that was filed against 2Pac and his associates, who were said to have attacked a woman in a hotel room in November 1993. One day before the verdict in his trial, on November 30, 1994, 2Pac was shot five times outside the Quad Recording Studios in New York City. Police believed the attack was the result of a botched robbery attempt, but 2Pac disagreed. He believed that Sean "Puffy" Combs and Biggie were responsible for his shooting because they were working in the same studio recording with Junior M.A.F.I.A. that day.

Shakur began serving his prison sentence for sexual abuse at Clinton Correctional Facility on February 14, 1995, exactly one month before his album *Me Against the World* made its debut at number one on the *Billboard* 200 and stayed at the top of the charts for five weeks. Suge Knight—the head of Death Row Records—visited 2Pac in jail and offered to post the bail that 2Pac could not raise. In exchange, 2Pac signed a three-album contract with Death Row Records, with the money used to post bail considered an advance on future royalties. Commitments to cleaning up his act while in prison would soon be forgotten once 2Pac joined Death Row, arguably the closest he had come to joining a gang and behaving like a "gangsta."

This made good business sense as the rivalry brewing between two rap superstars like 2Pac and Notorious B.I.G. could address the potential and growing economic threat that East Coast artists, in particular those coming from the Bad Boy camp, posed to Death Row records. After his release on October 13, 1995, Knight flew 2Pac to Los Angeles and he recorded seven songs for *All Eyez on Me* before the day ended.

It did not help matters on the West Coast that Queens native Nas released *Illmatic*, which was treated at the time of its release in 1994 as an instant classic by fans and critics alike and remains one of the most significant contributions to rap recordings. "NY State of Mind," for example, reminded listeners of New York's important position and heritage in the rap game. The inclusion of a sample of golden era icon Rakim chanting "New York state of mind" (from Eric B. & Rakim's single "Mahogany") seemed to suggest to listeners that Nas might be the new Rakim, the *newer* school's master storyteller and lyricist—as if fans were hearing an audible passing of the torch, so to speak.

In response, in 1995 Tha Dogg Pound (Kurupt, Daz Dillinger, and Snoop Dogg) released an attack on New York with the single "New York, New York." It was broad in scope as far as rap battles are concerned, but it did create a kind of turf war in the vein of Bloods versus Crips, moving beyond the MC battles that have always defined a major aspect of this musical culture and continue to do so. Mobb Deep responded on behalf of "New York" with the release of "Shook Ones Pt. II" (1995), which contends that East Coast gangsta rap is "realer" by calling on its golden era Queensbridge heritage that West Coast rappers cannot claim.

During this time, B.I.G. was getting bigger and was named Lyricist of the Year at the 1995 Source Awards in New York. That same night, Suge Knight took a public swing at Combs and Bad Boy, stating "any artist who wanna be an artist . . . [and] not have producers all up in the videos . . . come to Death Row." The attack was a direct affront at Combs for his appearance in virtually every Bad Boy artist's videos. This waging "war" spoke more to two record companies vying for the favor of the rap music market and brand loyalty than it did to rap musicians' dislike for one another.

Escalating the animosity further, Death Row released 2Pac's brutal diatribe "Hit 'Em Up" (1996). In the song, 2Pac claims that B.I.G. stole his style and insinuates that B.I.G.'s wife is carrying his baby. It also targets Sean "Puffy" Combs, Mobb Deep, Lil' Kim and Junior M.A.F.I.A., Chino XL, and Bad Boy Records and New York as a whole. Performed and written by 2Pac and his clique, the Outlawz, the track uses the melody line of Junior M.A.F.I.A's big hit "Get Money" (1996) and Notorious B.I.G.'s chorus in "Player's Anthem" (1996). Some fans and critics felt that this song went too far with Shakur's claim that he had slept with Notorious B.I.G.'s wife, Faith Evans, suggesting that he is the real father of Biggie's kid. Many listeners and critics have also criticized it for further inciting violence in the 1990s East Coast–West Coast rap wars. None of the criticism affected 2Pac at all, and he seemed very proud of the song. He remarked that "Hit 'Em Up" was a "classic battle record," suggesting that these public and lyrical rumbles were not meant to stray from the recording studio, the video shoot, or publicity sound bites. However, Biggie discovered that perhaps 2Pac actually took this battle seriously, especially when he approached the stage alongside his entourage at the 1996 *Soul Train* Awards while B.I.G. performed. Notorious B.I.G. finally followed with a response rap of his own, "Who Shot Ya" (1996).

On September 6, 1996, in Las Vegas after a Mike Tyson fight, 2Pac, Suge Knight, and their entourage beat up Crip gang member Orlando Anderson in the MGM Grand Hotel, and it was captured on security videotape. Knight was affiliated with the Bloods, the notorious Los Angeles gang who were rivals of the Crips. It remains rumored that Bad Boy had affiliates in the Crips, which further suggests that the labels' rivalry was related to gang violence. Later that night, twelve shots were fired at Knight's vehicle while it was in transit to Knight's Club 662, and four of those bullets struck 2Pac. Seven days later 2Pac died from the wounds at the age of 25.

Fans were stunned by 2Pac's death because he had survived gunshot wounds in the recent past. B.I.G. expressed the same surprise on the last track of his posthumously released second album, *Life After Death*. B.I.G. delivered an 11-minute monologue that attempts to make sense of his supposed rivalry with Tupac, trying to settle this beef that he did not take seriously. As hateful as the verses might have sounded in the battle between 2Pac and B.I.G., they kept the fight framed in the hip hop way—taking it to the stage and studio. We must keep in mind that it was outsiders, not the hip hop artists themselves, who took it upon themselves to end the life of the two biggest rap acts of the 1990s. After 2Pac's public murder, B.I.G. knew that his life was also in danger. He intentionally visited Los Angeles a couple of months after 2Pac's death to put to rest the East Coast–West Coast rivalry by conducting interviews on L.A. radio stations and making public appearances. To what end? B.I.G. was shot after attending a *VIBE* magazine-sponsored party in Los Angeles on March 8, 1997. The "MC battle" ended in two murders, which remain unsolved. B.I.G.'s murder froze the

Jay-Z, left, and Mary J. Blige onstage, 2008.
Source: *Photo: D. Ross Cameron/The Oakland Tribune; © ZUMA Press, Inc./Alamy*

industry momentarily and no one toured in the other's territory. Following B.I.G.'s lead, Puffy made amends with Snoop publicly and later released *No Way Out* (1997), which brought him several hit songs—including one commemorating the Notorious B.I.G., "I'll Be Missing You." Puffy became the biggest artist on his own label.

Artistically, another one of B.I.G.'s protégés emerged as a dominant figure in the New York revival and remains an enduring hip hop mogul. In 1996 Jay-Z released *Reasonable Doubt*, which was compared to Queens rapper Nas's 1994 album *Illmatic* and sparked a rivalry between the two new, young heavyweight contenders. Jay-Z followed B.I.G.'s example, presenting himself as a smooth-operating, well-groomed professionalized gangsta, reciting raps without shouting or using a sharp-ended, staccato cadence. This style is featured in "Brooklyn's Finest," in which we get an endorsement by B.I.G. in the mock battle of skills between mentor and mentee. He also took risks. Produced by Mark 45 King, the song "Hard Knock Life (The Ghetto Anthem)" contains a driving sample that is signature Broadway: "It's a Hard Knock Life" from the musical *Annie*. Musical theater was an unlikely match for hardcore rap, but the juxtaposition of children's voices in the chorus balanced the tough street narrative with greater efficacy than Slick Rick's golden era classic, "Children's Story."

Responding to Gangsta Rap's Domination

While gangsta rap became *the* story and sound of hip hop in the early '90s, artists drew on other elements important to the lives and cultural traditions of African Americans to produce alternative styles. As we have observed with R&B, fusion styles allowed rappers to broaden the parameters of hip hop. In R&B-rap fusions, the two aesthetics were blended by wedding R&B melodies and singing styles with elements of rap, including "shout-outs," slang, sung and rapped choruses, and hip hop rhythms. Christian rappers followed a similar approach; they incorporated melody into the rap tradition by borrowing choruses from R&B and frequently applying the chorus-verse format. Christian themes and Christian rap opened the doors to making Christian music cool. Also in this period, a marriage between jazz and rap materialized. The rhythms of jazz-rap fusion remained within the aesthetics of hip hop but sampled liberally from cool jazz and hard bop recordings. Jazz-rap fusion connected African American music of the past with a modern African American music. Young rappers paid homage to musical pioneers and encouraged rap listeners to pay attention to this "old" music, much like the hardcore rappers on the East and West Coasts reintroduced the funk and soul of James Brown and George Clinton/Parliament.

Spiritual Themes

Spirituality and religion have always been central to African American community life. African Americans traditionally have relied on their belief in a God or a Supreme Being for inner strength to overcome hardships and struggle. Spirituality and religion also provide many rappers with inspiration for the content of their poems and narratives. Rappers have drawn from biblical scriptures and references, as well as the tenets of Islam, Five Percent Nation (see Chapter 7), and Rastafarianism. Thus, hip hop can blend sacred and secular themes.

MC Hammer's "Pray" (1990) integrated his Christian faith through a party anthem that was lyrically minimalistic and largely a boast about personal achievement with the assistance of prayer. It is enticing all the same with its excitable, spiritual-party chant, "That's word. We pray (pray, pray)/We got to pray/Just to make it today," rapped atop Prince's "When Doves Cry," which provides listeners an allusion to Christian symbolism and the dove of peace. Similarly, Brand Nubian praised Allah in a 1992 Five Percent Nation party anthem "Allah and Justice"—a song that introduced listeners to Five Percent tenets via party groove and chant: "Peace, to All-ah, and justice, and ju-stice, justice!/Peace, to All-ah, and juuhhhhstice!"

Lauryn Hill

One artist who was particularly successful in promulgating a religious message through her music was rapper Lauryn Hill, particularly on her 1998 debut solo album, *The Miseducation of Lauryn Hill*. A devout Methodist, Lauryn Hill demonstrates her lifelong commitment to God as the center of her life throughout this album—her personal journey into the joy and pain of her life.

According to Dina Bennett in her unpublished paper on Christian themes and Lauryn Hill, Hill has stated that God was her inspiration for creating *Miseducation*. Many of her words are based on biblical scripture and Rastafarian themes. For example, Hill employs toasting or praises in "To Zion," a song about the struggle of going through an unplanned pregnancy in the midst of public scrutiny. Hill uses biblical metaphor from the book of Luke to compare the birth of her son [David] Zion to the Christ child (Luke 1:28, 31):

> And the angel came in unto her, and said, Hail, thou that art highly favored, the Lord is with thee: blessed art thou among women.
> And, behold, thou shalt conceive in thy womb, and bring forth a son, and shalt call his name JESUS.

Even Hill's reference to Zion as the name for her child is based on the city of pre-Israelite Jerusalem (a.k.a. Zion), King David's royal city (I Kings 8:1):

> Then Solomon assembled the elders of Israel, and all the heads of the tribes, the chief

Lauryn Hill.
Source: Photo © Ebet Roberts

of the fathers of the children of Israel, unto King Solomon in Jerusalem, that they might bring up the ark of the covenant of the Lord out of the city of David, which is Zion.

Zion is also referred to in the Baptist hymn "We're Marching to Zion" as "the beautiful city of God":

We're marching to Zion, Beautiful, beautiful Zion;
We're marching upward to Zion, The beautiful city of God.

Hill incorporates the words of this standard Baptist hymn into the chorus of "To Zion":

Marching, marching, marching to Zion
Marching, marching . . .

Rastafarian Themes

Hill also alludes to the Zion referenced in Rastafarianism. Rastas believe that Zion or Mt. Zion is the geographic center and symbol of Rasta spirituality and is located in Ethiopia rather than Jerusalem. The Rastafarian movement proclaims that Haile Selassie I of Ethiopia represents a divine power whose domain is Zion and whose subjects are mainly black people, hence, a black god for the black man. Rastafarians believe in a divine existence:

I'm from Zion the people call heaven. From the foundation of Creation, I was not just born, I was what Him talking to. I was smuggled from my father's waist-line, emptied in the abscess of my mother's womb, and bursted forth upon this land as a mirror to reflect the divine qualities of Rastafari.
(Hearne and Nettleford: 1963)

Black Feminist Spirituality and Values

In recent years women rappers, through their music and their lyrics, have not only controlled the images and creative expression of women in the male-dominated hip hop industry but have also turned the image of the woman from object to subject. The religious metaphor of Lauryn Hill's lyrics in *Miseducation* reflects a feminist voice. Hill's socially conscious lyrics moved hip hop to higher ground and gave the hip hop world a new image of womanhood as being sultry and sophisticated as opposed to promiscuous.

Religious themes and metaphor in *Miseducation*'s lyrics express and embody the essence of Hill's humanity as a Christian. In her hit rap "Doo Wop (That Thing)," Hill raps a "warning" to all the ladies out there who are being taken advantage of by men who just want "that thing." Hill has encoded many biblical messages within this song's text:

Talking out your neck sayin' you're a Christian
A Muslim sleeping with the gin

> *Now that was the sin that did Jezebel in*
> *Who you gon' tell when the repercussions spin*

Hill's biblical references to being a Christian refer to women who profess their Christian or spiritual values and principles yet enter into situations that are in direct violation of them. Hill is talking about "saying one thing and doing another." Her reference to Jezebel is taken from the Old Testament book of First Kings, which tells the story of Queen Jezebel (wife of King Ahab of Israel) and her downfall as a result of her evildoing (I Kings 21:9–11):

> *And she wrote in the letters, saying, Proclaim a fast, and set Naboth on high among the people:*
> *And set two men, sons of Belial, before him to bear witness against him, saying, Thou didst blaspheme God and the king. And then carry him out, and stone him, that he may die.*
> *And the men of his city, even the elders and the nobles who were the inhabitants in his city, did as Jezebel had sent unto them, and as it was written in the letters which she had sent unto them.*

Because Jezebel sent forth an order to kill Naboth, a godly man, her wickedness caused her own downfall and death (I Kings 21:23): "And of Jezebel also spake the Lord, saying, The dogs shall eat Jezebel by the wall of Jezreel [because of her evildoing in conspiring to kill Naboth]." Likewise, Hill is warning ladies that they can cause their own downfall if they go against their own core beliefs and values.

Hill also preaches a message of self-confidence and self-respect for women, evident in these lines from verse one:

> *Girlfriend, let me break it down for you again*
> *You know I only say it 'cause I'm truly genuine*
> *Don't be a hardrock when you're really a gem*
> *Babygirl, respect is just a minimum*
> *Niggas fucked up and you still defending them*
> *Now Lauryn is only human*
> *Don't think I haven't been through the same predicament*
> *Let it sit inside your head like a million women in Philly, Penn.*

In a black feminist voice, Hill is saying that women should have a little respect for themselves. Even though their partners, or "niggas," messed up in terms of being disrespectful, irresponsible, and undependable, many women still defend the men in their lives at the expense of their own self-respect. Hill encourages black women (and women in general) to think about the October 1977 Million Woman March in Philadelphia, Pennsylvania, in which a million-plus women came together to celebrate their strength and commitment to family, community, God, self, and womanhood.

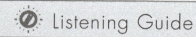

Listening Guide

Listening to Lauryn Hill

"DOO WOP (THAT THING)"

COMPOSED BY Lauryn Hill

PERFORMED BY Lauryn Hill (vocals, producer), James Poyser (keyboards and backup vocals), Lenesha Randolph (backup vocals), Jenni Fujita (backup vocals), Rasheem Pugh (backup vocals), Fundisha Johnson (backup vocals), Dean Frasier (saxophone), Everol Ray (trumpet), Nambo Robinson (trombone), Indigo Quartet (strings), DJ Supreme (DJ elements)

PRODUCER/MIXER Commissioner Gordon Williams

PROGRAMMERS Che Guevara and Vada Nobles

Appears on *The Miseducation of Lauryn Hill*, Ruffhouse Records C2 69035; peaked at no. 1 on Hot 100 and no. 1 on *Billboard* Rap Chart.

Lauryn Hill's "Doo Wop (That Thing)" simultaneously recalls classic doo-wop and soul music while presenting a modern hip hop sensibility. Its eclectic blend of musical styles is reminiscent of Hill's earlier recordings with the Fugees, who added Afro-Caribbean sounds to their brand of hip hop. Hill's use of classic soul styles and her incorporation of doo-wop harmonies into the song's arrangement allow her to draw on the past as a source of inspiration while engaging with current musical sounds and social issues.

In the song's lyrics, Hill comments on a variety of issues facing contemporary men and women. She warns women against being promiscuous ("that was the sin that did Jezebel in") and warns black women against following European standards of beauty ("hair weaves like Europeans, fake nails done by Koreans"). Though her words are didactic, she is not being judgmental; she makes clear that she has empathy, stating, "Now, Lauryn is only human/Don't think I haven't been through the same predicament." She cautions men against the perils of materialism and critiques the excessive value they place on decorative hubcaps and status-statement clothes and shoes ("with his rims and his Timbs"). She stresses that men need to take part in building a healthy domestic life with their families, commenting on child support and domestic violence. Hill's warning, "You better watch out," is fundamentally a sociocultural and political statement; she is warning her audience against what she sees as many of the spiritual dangers of contemporary culture. Hill's musical landscape may be seen as an extension of this social consciousness. By incorporating older musical styles, she suggests that a return to the musical and cultural values of the 1950s and 1960s would cure the ills that she mentions in her lyrics.

The contrast between classic soul and contemporary rap is underscored by the multitrack duet that Hill sings with herself (with supporting vocals from Lenesha Randolph) throughout the song. Her sung vocals over-dubbed on her rapped verses recall '60s soul singing, while her rapping over the sung chorus reinforces the song's contemporary setting. Her voice remains relaxed: the sung portions are harmonious and gently melismatic, and her rapped verses have a relaxed, low-key flow. This recalls the mellow sensibility of both doo-wop and soul music that she uses to color this song. The group harmony vocals consist primarily of repeated patterns, drawing on the doo-wop vocal style of the 1950s and early 1960s. The song's title calls attention to this approach and to the fact that these vocal stylings would likely be out of place in rap music of the late 1990s.

The vocal hook at the introduction of "Doo Wop" is an in-studio re-creation of a group vocal section from Brighter Side of Darkness's 1971 song "I'm a Loser," an obscure cut that emulated the doo-wop sound some 20 years after its initial popularity. By referencing a song that itself recalled an earlier style, Hill is showing how earlier musical styles are constantly recycled through contemporary reinterpretations. Like Brighter Side of Darkness, Hill re-creates a doo-wop feel through her use of some of the genre's signature sonic elements, interjecting an extended a cappella vocal section prior to the song's second chorus and emphasizing the multilayered polyphonic vocal textures throughout the song.

Hill's instrumental arrangements also use vintage African American musical styles that give the song its "retro" feel, honing in on the **neo-soul** trend of the 1990s led by Erykah Badu, D'Angelo, Angie Stone, Jill Scott, and Maxwell. The first instrumental figure is a signature doo-wop piano accompaniment pattern: repetitive piano chords playing an unadorned rhythm with a simple, repeated chord progression. Studio keyboardist James Poyser re-created this piano embellishment based on the 1971 song "Together Let's Find Love" by The 5th Dimension—another emulation of the doo-wop sound that was recorded after its initial heyday. The song's main groove, which first appears as a left-hand piano figure, has a more strongly accented rhythmic feel than would typically be expected of doo-wop piano. Its intense groove is more typical of the mellow hip hop feel that Hill maintains across many of her recordings than of doo-wop. In its contemporary sound that finds inspiration in earlier eras, Hill's work is similar to that of her neo-soul contemporaries and rap-R&B fusionists. In addition to these key rhythm section elements, a soul-revue-style horn section appears throughout the song, evoking soul music of the 1960s and '70s. The strings that appear during the song's vocal breakdown strengthen the smooth, soul-influenced feel of this track in a similar way to the doo-wop piano, serving as a reminder of vintage sounds from earlier eras.

In "Doo Wop (That Thing)," Hill employs older soul and current hip hop sounds to comment on the values of family and community while acknowledging the struggles of contemporary life. This blend of old and new evinces Hill's eclectic ideological positioning and musical aesthetic.

Continued

Listening Guide

Listening to Lauryn Hill **Continued**

0:00	"Yo, back in the boogie when cats . . ."	The song begins with a single finger snap. Doo-wop-style piano enters, borrowed from The 5th Dimension's "Let's Find Love" and re-created by a studio pianist. Group harmonies, re-created by studio vocalists from Brighter Side of Darkness's "I'm a Loser," also enter alongside Lauryn Hill's spoken introduction to the song.
0:07	"My men and my women . . ."	The left-hand piano enters, playing the song's main groove, with a more percussive hip hop feel.
0:17	"Feel real good, wave your hands in the air . . ."	The drums kick in, picking up on the song's main groove, played by drums, bass, and piano. A soul-revue-style horn section enters with "yeah, yeah" group vocals throughout.
0:28	"It's been three weeks since you were looking for your friend . . ."	The horns exit and the song's first verse begins; drums, bass, and doo-wop piano continue. Hill raps the first verse.
0:46	"If you did it then . . ."	There is a brief break in the groove and a bass fill.
0:49	"Talkin' out your neck . . ."	The groove returns here, with the full band playing.
1:07	"Baby girl . . ."	The horn section punctuates the groove with a rhythmic kick. Hill's overdubbed vocal, sung in a soul-influenced style, begins echoing the lyrics and improvising around her rapped verse.
1:26	"Come again . . ."	The soul-horn-section hits enter for the pre-chorus, with the band playing a different groove punctuated by Hill singing a duet with herself and additional harmony vocals.
1:35	"Guys, you know you better . . ."	The chorus begins here; harmony vocals and the soul horn section continue. The chorus is both rapped and sung by Hill overdubbed on top of herself, continuing her duet with herself.
1:55	"This second verse is dedicated to the men . . ."	This vocal break begins the second verse with a stop-time feel.
1:59	"Him and his men . . ."	The groove returns here, punctuated with group vocals at the end of lines, and some added extraneous vocal sounds.
2:04	"Let's not pretend . . ."	The doo-wop piano drops out, leaving the bass line (doubled on left-hand piano) and drums.

2:13	"Uh, uh, come again . . ."	There is a break and then the band returns to the pre-chorus; soul horns return and Hill's overdubbed soul singing reappears. These vocals build in anticipation of the coming chorus, with additional layers of voices.
2:43	Wordless vocal	In lieu of the expected chorus, an a cappella wordless vocal section begins, in a pseudo-doo-wop style. More female voices are added, and a male voice enters singing a bass part in counterpoint to the other independent lines.
2:50	Wordless vocal	Strings are added to the a cappella vocal section.
2:51	Wordless vocal	The band returns, playing the main groove, while the harmonized group wordless vocals continue.
3:03	"Girls, you know you better . . ."	The chorus that was delayed by the preceding a cappella section returns. The chorus remains the same, but the lyrics "guys" and "girls" are swapped from the first chorus.
3:22	"Guys, you know you better . . ."	The chorus repeats, this time with "guys" and "girls" returned to their original position in the lyrics.
3:40	"Some guys, some guys . . ."	Lauryn's voice is overdubbed, singing a harmony part with the melody. The song fades out.

Christian Rap

Christian artists have always used inspirational themes in their music. Younger, up-and-coming hip hop–generation artists pioneered another fusion style, **Christian rap**, to tap into a market that had yet to be fully integrated. Early Christian rappers usually borrowed elements from old-school rap and golden era rap, like DC Talk's pop rap "Word 2 the Father" (1995), but other rappers experimented with hardcore rap styles of the late '80s, like Sinnection's hardcore "Down Wit G.O.D." (1992).

In the mid-'90s, Christian rap strove to challenge gangsta rap and the groove-oriented G-Funk. Christian spiritual music and gangsta rap did blend rather successfully in works like "Before Redemption" (1995) by West Coast rappers Gospel Gangstaz on their first album *Gang Affiliated*. "Before Redemption" describes a ghetto—where God does not seem to exist—in search of salvation:

> What should I do?
> And who can I turn to?
> I got the feds on my back
> Cause they know I'm sellin' crack

I'm sick of bein' locked up in the cage
So tell me who got the key and is he down to set me free, G?
Cause any second from now, I might go crazy

Throughout the song, a significant plea, "Dear God, I wonder can ya save me?"—sampled from gangsta rap icon Snoop Dogg's "Murder Was the Case" (1994)—reminds the listener that the track is gangsta rap to the core yet offers an alternative perspective: searching for a life of peace, joy, hope, and happiness through Christ. The album collected tales about selling crack, drive-by shootings, and carjacking. The raps are laden with violent imagery and the pervasive use of the N-word, giving hardcore fans the Christian rap equivalent to Dr. Dre's *The Chronic*. Tik Tokk, Mr. Solo, and Chille Chill emulate the delivery styles of Ice Cube and Snoop Dogg; they opened the doors for the growing hardcore Christian rap post-2000.

Rap and Judaism

Jewish rap gives Jewish hip hop fans a connection to the secular world in a different way, by taking secular music and using it to educate listeners and celebrate Judaism. Remedy (born Ross Filler; Hebrew name, Reuven ben Menachem) is a white Jewish New Yorker who has worked closely with the Wu-Tang Clan. The Wu-Tang Clan used Remedy's "Never Again," a Holocaust-based track, on their 1998 release, *The Swarm*. Remedy then re-released the track on his own album, *The Genuine Article*. "Never Again" includes samples of the Israeli national anthem, "Hatikvah." The song provides a chilling look at Jewish heritage in a place where it is not often found—rap. This was a way for Remedy to memorialize Holocaust survivors, especially members of his own family.

Jazz-Rap Fusion

Common (originally Common Sense) was a highly influential Chicago rapper in the hardcore, underground scene of the 1990s. In the song "Resurrection" (1994), Common moved towards more socially conscious lyrics while continuing to demonstrate his sophisticated lyrical technique. "Resurrection" echoes the themes of Christian rap but speaks more to the rebirth of urban African American males, using Common as an example ("Cause of the malt liquor I fought niggaz/Now my speech and thoughts quicker . . ."). This performance also plays on the idea of resurrection, because, with this record, Common *resurrects* the flowing syncopations of jazz-rap fusion, drawing our attention to music of a shared African American cultural past: jazz, the classical music of African America.

Origins

Herbie Hancock's 1983 album *Future Shock* marked the first collaboration between hip hop and jazz with the song "Rockit." This single was one of the earliest popular songs to feature scratching and other DJ techniques, performed by old-school DJ Grandmixer D.ST. (DXT). "Rockit" introduced the crafts of **turntablism** and **scratch art** to a broader audience outside of a rap music context. Its music video received more airtime in the United States than the record did on the radio. While Michael Jackson's "Billy Jean" (1983) was the first video featuring an African American artist on MTV, this video was a close second, although you only catch glimpses of Hancock's hands playing the keyboards and a couple of face shots on a TV monitor in the background.

Jazz-Rap Fusion Movement in the 1990s

"Rockit" broke new ground, especially since scratching was the main feature of the song itself. However, no one at the time really followed Herbie Hancock's lead. In the 1980s in the United Kingdom, club DJs began playing funk-jazz, which they labeled "**acid jazz**." In the 1990s, they began experimenting with contemporary popular forms, mixing jazz and R&B recordings as well as using live musicians—percussion and horn players—over pre-recorded music to create a new form of danceable jazz. They later teamed up with hip hop artists to produce a new jazz sound called **new jack swing**, especially when funk, soul, and other R&B elements were incorporated.

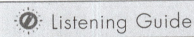 Listening Guide

Listening to Us3

"CANTALOOP (FLIP FANTASIA)"

MUSIC CREDITED TO Geoff Wilkinson, Mel Simpson, and Herbie Hancock, featuring samples from "Cantaloupe Island" as performed by Herbie Hancock, the introduction from *A Night in Birdland, Vol. 1* by Art Blakey Quintet, and additional samples from "Everything I Do Gonna Be Funky" by Lou Donaldson

LYRICS BY Rahsaan Kelly

PERFORMED BY Rahsaan, Gerard Presencer, Geoff Wilkinson, and Mel Simpson

Appears on *Hand on the Torch*, Blue Note Records 1993 CDP 0777 7 80883 2 5, released 1993.

"Cantaloop (Flip Fantasia)" is an excellent example of the production-driven jazz-rap fusion that Geoff Wilkinson achieved with the group Us3. This track is particularly successful in its combination of elements sampled from classic Blue Note jazz recordings with original studio material. The result is a cohesive dance track that both hearkens back to the golden age of Blue Note records in the 1950s and early '60s and provides a modern update that makes this music more accessible to a younger audience. When "Cantaloop" was recorded, interest in jazz had been growing thanks to new jazz studies programs in music schools and jazz performance programs in venues previously associated with classical music, such as the establishment of Jazz at Lincoln Center. This positioning of jazz as "high art" occurred in part through the success in both the jazz and classical worlds that Wynton Marsalis achieved as a trumpeter.

Perhaps the most striking elements of this recording are the ways in which samples from classic Blue Note jazz records and original studio material by Us3 are combined. It is particularly telling that they chose to include a sample

Continued

Listening Guide

Listening to Us3 Continued

of Pee Wee Marquette, the famous MC at Birdland, a New York jazz club known for presenting progressive jazz in the '50s. Marquette was well known for his unusual announcing style, which itself was a kind of predecessor of rapping. By choosing to start the piece with a sample in homage to Marquette, Us3 is making a clear connection between jazz and rap. Similarly, the selection of the Hancock instrumental as a basis for this piece shows how jazz riffs and rhythms are one of the inspirations for the repeated melodic hooks and danceable beats of contemporary rap.

The producers of "Cantaloop (Flip Fantasia)" enhance the samples from Hancock's original recording (titled "Cantaloupe Island") by adding new instrumentation to them. The track begins with a drum machine superimposed over the original recording that both accentuates the drum pattern of the Hancock excerpt and adds more notes, providing a more active groove for dancing. The drum machine kick drum pattern is considerably busier than the one on the original Hancock recording, and the superimposed tambourine sounds twice as often as the original ride cymbal pattern. While it is still possible to hear the original bass and drum parts, the new drum machine is placed more prominently than the sample in the mix. Similarly, additional layers of left-hand piano and bass (most likely played on keyboard synthesizers rather than acoustic piano or electric bass) further strengthen the low-end groove that is an essential element of a danceable song. The new piano and bass parts are, like the drum machine, foregrounded in "Cantaloop": they are louder than the corresponding parts in the original sample, and they are the only parts of the original **vamp** (the repeated musical phrase from the Hancock introduction sample) that remain during the rapped verses.

Even though the melody for "Cantaloupe Island" appears on the original Hancock recording, on "Cantaloop" it is performed by a live musician, trumpeter Gerard Presencer. This reflects a merging of hip hop and jazz performance practices: the technique of sampling existing recordings (a common hip hop production technique) and the common jazz practice of live musicians interpreting melodies and improvising over a rhythm section, in this case, a sampled rhythm section from a jazz recording. The blending of hip hop and jazz is also apparent during Presencer's solo section at the end of the song. Presencer's approach to this solo is reminiscent of Freddie Hubbard, who was the trumpet soloist on the original Hancock recording of "Cantaloupe Island." Presencer's use of short, punctuated rhythmic gestures and longer held notes interspersed by flurries of fast bebop lines creates a stop-and-go motion, similar to Hubbard's playing on the original recording.

While the verses of "Cantaloop" vamp on the melodic figure that serves as the introduction to "Cantaloupe Island," the chorus works with the "Cantaloupe Island" melody (played by Presencer). The chorus opens in a new key (D-flat) as it does on the Hancock recording, using a sample that is actually drawn from Hancock's piano solo rather than from a section accompanying the melody. The final four bars of the Hancock tune are omitted from the chorus sections of the song, with the exception of the introduction, which contains a truncated version of them.

Even though Presencer was used to provide live trumpet parts, there are several reasons to believe that the horn section figures during the chorus are likely being played on a synthesizer, rather than by live musicians: (1) Presencer is the only live horn player credited on this track, and he is not credited as saxophonist; a sax section responds to the call of the trumpets in this section; (2) the "cold" timbre of the horns in the chorus runs counter to the warmer, more vibrato-rich sound that a person playing an instrument would produce; and (3) the attack and decay of the horns—the beginning and ending of the sounds they produce—is more abrupt than would likely be possible with live musicians.

The guitar stabs in the chorus serve several purposes in the arrangement. They perform a call-and-response role with the horn sections, as they have a similar melodic contour and voicings. The guitar also gives an extra layer of "funk" that enhances the track's danceability through minimalistic funk voicings with short rhythmic gestures, as would be typical on a James Brown recording. These stabs may also cover up an imperfection with the chorus sample taken from the piano solo, as the portion of the solo that this sample was pulled from was only a partial iteration of the main vamp on the Hancock recording.

The complexity of the musical elements of hip hop and jazz interacting with one another in this example achieves the "funk and fusion . . . fly illusion" that the song's lyrics proclaim. By integrally fusing the elements of these two genres in the studio through multiple sampling and live in-studio processes, Us3 created a new product that is illusively homogenous and at times difficult to break into its component parts by ear. The integral combination of elements from classic Blue Note recordings and new musical elements added by Us3 provided an update for the Blue Note sound and aesthetic in the era of hip hop and an entry point to jazz for a younger generation.

Continued

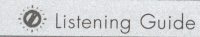

Listening Guide

Listening to Us3 Continued

0:01	"Ladies and gentlemen . . ."	Sample of Pee Wee Marquette introduction to Art Blakey's *A Night at Birdland, Vol. 1* (1951).
0:10		Snare crack, then introduction to "Cantaloupe Island" and superimposed drum machine enter.
0:18		Electric bass (not in Hancock recording) added, introduction section repeated.
0:26	Throughout: "Yeah, yeah . . . what's that" vocal samples from Lou Donaldson's "Everything I Do Gonna Be Funky (From Now On)"	Sample of melody from first eight bars of "Cantaloupe Island" form.
0:35		Guitar (not in original recording) enters in measure 5 of the "Cantaloupe Island" form.
0:44	"How about a big hand now"—continuation of Pee Wee Marquette sample "Wait, wait a minute"—unidentified (original?) sample	
0:47	"Groovy, groovy, jazzy, funky . . ."	Bass, left-hand piano, drum machine play "Cantaloupe Island" intro groove interspersed with Hancock introduction sample.
1:11	"Dip, Trip, Flip Fantasia"	Drum break.
1:13	"Yeah . . ." —continuation of Donaldson samples	Horn section shout chorus over first eight bars of "Cantaloupe Island" form.
1:21	"Biggity biggity bop" "Yeah . . . funky, funky"—continuation of Donaldson samples	Shout section trade between guitar and horns over second eight bars of "Cantaloupe Island" form.
1:29	"Feel the beat drop . . ."	The second verse enters, with the same musical texture as the first.
1:44	"You move your feet . . ."	The Hancock sample is removed; the drum machine and added bass continue.
1:46	"Back to the fact . . ."	The call-and-response horn section is added. These horns and the drum machine and bass pattern are all original to "Cantaloop."

1:54	"Many trip the tour . . ."	The more rhythmically active tambourine part enters, beginning a rhythmic and textural build-up towards the next chorus.
2:00	"Dip, trip, flip fantasia . . ."	The horn section plays together an octave higher than in previous iterations, building intensity before leading into the call-and-response chorus figure with the song's tagline. This continues, interspersed with the Donaldson and original samples, through two iterations of the "Cantaloupe Island" form.
2:35	"Jump to the jam . . ."	The musical texture is again pared down to drum machine, bass, and left-hand piano doubling the bass line. The Hancock sample is interspersed throughout this verse.
2:58	"Dip, trip, flip fantasia . . ."	The drum break returns with the song's tagline.
3:00	"Ya don't stop . . ."	Rashaan Kelly delivers typical MC "Ya don't stop," etc., lyrics. Gerard Presencer begins playing the "Cantaloupe Island" melody on trumpet. The samples continue to be interspersed throughout.
3:16		Presencer departs from the "Cantaloupe Island" melody and begins an improvised trumpet solo in the style of Freddie Hubbard. The samples can still be heard throughout this solo.
3:33		The horn shout section returns; Presencer continues his solo over the song's form as the song fades out.

The fusion of jazz and hip hop began when rappers such as Gang Starr, Digable Planets, and A Tribe Called Quest sampled jazz melodies and rhythms from recordings by Sonny Rollins, Art Blakey, and Roy Ayers, among others. Gang Starr was the first rap group to work directly with jazz musicians, recording "Jazz Music" with Branford Marsalis for Spike Lee's movie *Mo' Better Blues* (1990). Most jazz musicians did not recognize the potential of rap for musical experimentation until after 1990. Saxophonist Greg Osby was first to collaborate with rappers, producing a musical hybrid that he called "street jazz." De La Soul and the Jungle Brothers were other notable early jazz-rap artists.

A Tribe Called Quest favored jazz-infused tracks rather than recycling soul music samples employed by other Afrocentric and message rappers. They successfully combined intelligent lyrics, danceable beats, and party anthems on songs like "Excursions" (1991), which encouraged listeners to "Get in the zone of positivity, not negativity." It is included on their album *The Low End Theory*, which remains one of the masterpieces of jazz-rap fusion. Q-Tip addresses the continuum of African American music and its relation to generational connection:

> *You could find the abstract by listenin' to hip hop*
> *My pops used to say it reminded him of bebop*
> *I said well Daddy don't you know that things go in cycles?*

His comparing hip hop to bebop addresses their shared aesthetics and production sensibilities: expanding chord structures, range of tempi, and rhythmic displacement. In another connection with the past, the song's vocal interludes include samples from "Time Is Running Out," by the revolutionary 1960s group the Last Poets (see Chapter 4).

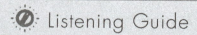

Listening Guide

Listening to A Tribe Called Quest

"EXCURSIONS"

COMPOSED BY Jonathan "Q-Tip" Davis

PERFORMED BY Q-Tip (vocals/co-producer), Phife Dawg (vocals/producer), Ali Shaheed (co-producer), Skeff Anselm (producer), and Bob Power (mixer)

Appears on *The Low End Theory*, 1991, Jive 1418-2-J.

Released in 1991, "Excursions" is a prime example of A Tribe Called Quest's mellow and esoteric jazz-rap fusion that offered an alternative to the funk-based gangsta and hardcore rap (which had dominated the rap market since the late 1980s) and separated it from the new jack swing (which blurred the jazz-R&B boundaries) playing regularly on pop radio stations.

One of the key elements of A Tribe Called Quest's sound is their approach to lyricism and vocal delivery. Q-Tip's voice is mellow, unstressed, and pleasant, and a few minimal interjections are added by his associate Phife Dawg. Q-Tip's alternate MC moniker, the Abstract, alludes to his thoughtful and eclectic rhymes that pervade "Excursions" and to the group's cerebral production techniques. The themes of these verses are varied, ranging from boasts about the group's musical prowess for a "hardcore" generation ("beats that are hard, beats that are funky"), to Afrocentrism ("all the way to Africa, a.k.a. the motherland"), to familial and intergenerational connections ("you could find the Abstract listening to hip-hop, my pops used to say, it reminded him of be-bop"), to the religious ("That's the right hand, Black Man," referring to the Muslim notion that the left is reserved for personal hygiene and not for greetings). The interludes between verses have spaced-out vocal sounds, consisting of reverb-laden overdubs of several versions of Q-Tip's voice on top of itself with vocalizations of "what," "come on," and "we gotta make moves." The two interludes continue with vocal samples from the Last Poets' "Time" (1971) punched in during the second half of each one; the Last Poets' Afrocentric revolutionary poetry figures prominently in the mix. These samples provide a further layer of racial and political consciousness that adds to the intellectual bent Q-Tip establishes for himself in his verses centered on gaining knowledge, complete with comparisons to Shakespeare, Edgar Allan Poe, and Langston Hughes.

Many themes in the lyrics are further accentuated by the group's use of samples. Some of this sampling serves to outline the song's Afrocentric themes. The two Last Poets samples that appear in the second half of each respective interlude are extended and brought forward in the mix in order to highlight their revolutionary poetry and West African drums. The song's main bass line, sampled from Art Blakey's "A Chant for Bu" (1973), makes intergenerational musical contact in a way that reinforces the song's lyrical connection of bebop and hip hop. The Blakey sample is also used twice: it provides both the main bass groove for "Excursions," with the bass line being the only accompaniment for nearly the first 30 seconds of the song, and the horn melody that is used as the song's instrumental interlude. The drum sample that enters at 0:29 is from the Shades of Brown's "The Soil I Tilled for You" (1970) and is mixed with an added drum machine that accentuates the bass, kick, and hi-hat patterns in this break. This drum groove continues in tandem with the Art Blakey bass line throughout the song, and it is remarkable how well the soul drums and hard bop bass line dovetail with one another in this context, a testament to A Tribe Called Quest's masterful production techniques. The samples' four generations of musical continuity—1950s hard bop, '60s revolutionary poetry, '70s soul, and '90s rap—can be heard simultaneously during the song's interludes. The MC's chill-styled raps fade into the background and are replaced by the Last Poets' Omar Ben Hassen frenziedly pleading that time is running out. Abruptly, the song ends.

A Tribe Called Quest's production techniques, which feature prominently in this song, are primarily based on their creative use of sampling. While other jazz-rap fusion artists, such as Miles Davis, Buckshot LeFonque, or Us3, combined samples from recordings with original musical materials created in the studio, A Tribe Called Quest typically focused their production on manipulating a number of samples in order to create their jazz-rap soundscapes, masterfully matching beats and grooves from older jazz and soul recordings in order to craft their grooves and then adding their vocals to these combinations. By using jazz samples and connecting their modern rhymes to a cultural lineage of black poetry, Tribe intentionally distanced themselves from pop trends (e.g., MC Hammer) and gangsta trends (e.g., N.W.A.) and took the opportunity to claim themselves as purveyors of "real" hip hop—a privileged authenticity because it connects their brand of rap with a legitimate classical black music and folk genuineness. "Excursions" exemplifies the group's lyrical and sonic brand of jazz-rap fusion; it offers a glimpse into their Afrocentric synthesis of musical and lyrical elements from a broad swath of 20th century African American music and illuminates the lyrical eclecticism that matches their musical variety.

Continued

Listening Guide

Listening to A Tribe Called Quest Continued

0:00		The introductory bass line begins. This sample is taken from the introduction to Art Blakey's "A Chant for Bu."
0:10	"Back in the days . . ."	Q-Tip raps the first verse over the bass line.
0:29	"Come on everybody . . ."	The song's drums enter, with the main drum break sampled from the Shades of Brown's "The Soil I Tilled." There is a drum machine added to this sample that accentuates the kick, snare, and hi-hat patterns.
0:49	"You need leverage to sever . . ."	There is a very short break in the song's groove timed with these lyrics. The groove returns immediately after.
0:51	"The unit, yes the unit . . ."	Phife Dawg can be heard interjecting vocalizations ("Uh," etc.) and highlighting significant lines and rhymes.
1:09	"If you dis . . ."	There is another break in the instrumentation timed with the lyrics. The groove immediately returns.
1:36	"If you botch up . . ."	There is another break in the instrumentation timed with the lyrics. The groove immediately returns.
1:41	"Come on we gotta make moves . . ."	A horn melody, also sampled from "A Chant for Bu," enters for the instrumental interlude. A number of overdubbed voices (Q-Tip and Phife Dawg added in the studio) can be heard interjecting "Huh," "What," and "We gotta make moves."
2:00	"Moooooove . . ."	The last "move" is held, transitioning into the coming vocal sample.
2:02	"Time, time is a ship . . ."	A vocal sample from the Last Poets' "Time" begins. "Word" and other extraneous vocal sounds can be heard in the background as the interlude music continues.
2:18	"Time is dancing, boogalooing . . ."	The main drum groove breaks to highlight the end of the Last Poets' sample, allowing the voices and drums from this sample to be heard more clearly.
2:20	"We gotta be a winner all the time . . ."	The verse texture and arrangement returns as Q-Tip begins the song's second verse.
2:39	"If you don't like it . . ."	There is another break in the instrumentation timed with the lyrics. The groove immediately returns.
3:19	"The Abstract poet . . ."	There is another break in the instrumentation timed with the lyrics.

3:20	". . . and Edgar Allan Poe . . ."	The interlude arrangement returns, as before.
3:40	"Moooooove . . ."	The last "move" is held, transitioning into the coming sample.
3:41	"Time is running out . . ."	Another sample from a different section of "Time" enters as the interlude music continues playing.
3:51	"Passing and running . . ."	The instrumental groove drops out and the Last Poets sample ends the song.

Women in Hip Hop and Rap

We (collectively speaking) have a history of viewing female participation in art as the object to be discussed, painted, sculpted, honored, or discredited. In hip hop culture, we (still speaking collectively) "include" women and study women as they have responded to this male-dominated genre. Female participation in hip hop remains both ignored and oftentimes not taken seriously. As in sports, women in hip hop are treated as a secondary or side topic. For example, if one were to ask, "Did you watch the basketball game last night?" most would assume one is referring to a men's basketball game—an unfair assumption, but probably true. If one were referring to the women's team, the phrasing would have to be more specific, as in, "Did you see the *women's* basketball game last night?" Why? Hip hop, like sports, is a treated like a masculine terrain. However, we cannot mistake the map for the territory.

Women participated in hip hop from the beginning. Recall our discussion of the roots of hip hop in African American folklore traditions, particularly the double dutch jump-rope traditions of young girls (see Chapter 4). Women played key roles in the earliest days of hip hop; recall it was Cindy Campbell who actually threw the earliest significant party where her brother Clive (Kool Herc) displayed his DJing skills (see Chapter 2). If not for her, maybe the South Bronx youth party culture would have never evolved the way it did. In the later '70s, if not for the vision of producer Sylvia Robinson, "rap music" or reality raps ("The Message") might not have broken through to the pop music scene. We must also remember that Debbie Harry and her group Blondie helped turn middle America on to this new musical genre with the only "rap single" to reach the number one spot on the *Billboard* pop charts during the entire decade of the 1980s. And we cannot forget Roxanne Shanté, who brought "battling"—already familiar to the local community—into the recording studio for the translocal community to consume. Had it not been for these important feats, we might not be dealing with one of the most powerful pop-cultural forces in the world today.

Women as Objects from a Male Rapper Perspective

In rap lyrics, women are often portrayed as lying and manipulative, more interested in fancy clothes and jewelry than in being faithful to their man. Women who fail to respond to the rapper's sexual advances are called "bitches," but they are labeled "hos" if they enjoy sex. In just one example of the misogynist content of rap lyrics, rapper Slick Rick advised his listeners to "Treat Her Like a Prostitute" (1988), because women are not to be trusted. 2 Live Crew's "Hoochie Mama" (1995) and Ice Cube's "Don't Trust 'Em" (1992) express similar sentiments.

However, there also are examples, even by hardcore rappers, that are female supportive or female empowering. 2Pac's "Dear Mama" (1995) is an open letter to the artist's mother, relating his troubled but loving relationship with her. It is both an honorific biography of Afeni Shakur and a "shout-out" to all mothers, especially single mothers raising children in the mad streets of the ghetto. Black Star's "Brown Skin Lady" (1995) celebrates women of color; it is a rap ballad directed at male listeners, asking men to stop being a "victim" to the beauty myths of Western European standards and to start celebrating the natural beauty of their darker-complexioned sisters. It masterfully and harmoniously integrates the R&B-rap fusion aesthetic with the high-pitch screeches and syncopated rhythms of the hardcore music scene.

Queen Latifah, 1991.
Source: *Photo © Ebet Roberts*

Women as Subject: Towards a Womanist Approach to Hip Hop

No other group of artists address better the violent, misogynistic lyrics of gangsta rap than women rap artists. Female rappers have grappled with a broad range of subjects through their songs, including Afrocentricity, justice and the female protagonist, sisterhood, social issues, sexuality from a female-pleasure perspective, relationships, and verbal skills. The women have been able to challenge the misogynistic and deprecating sentiments and images in gangsta rap through videos and lyrics that promote empowerment.

Queen Latifah's "U.N.I.T.Y. (Who You Calling a Bitch?)" (1993) denounces sexist attitudes and violence against women. She opens the discussion by suggesting that there are exceptions for the use of the term ("Now don't be getting mad, when we are playing, it's cool") but she explains it in a way that is very different from N.W.A.'s "A Bitch Iz a Bitch" (1988), which concludes that *every* female is one, with the broad definitive list at the end of the song. Latifah raised the key question herself:

Everybody's on this bandwagon mentality, now everybody wants to beat up a girl—everybody thinks a girl is a bitch. It's like don't you have sisters? Don't you have mothers?

Latifah is victorious in more ways than one. "U.N.I.T.Y." came off the album *Black Reign*, which was released on Motown Records after she was dropped from Tommy Boy Records—a bastion of male rappers. The album was also the first from a female rap artist to go gold. "U.N.I.T.Y." won the Best Rap Solo Grammy in 1994 and became another womanist anthem. Unlike with "Ladies First" (1989), which was written by a male rapper, Apache, no one could argue with Latifah's lyrical skills.

White Rappers in the 1990s

The 1990s were also bookended by the success-failure-success of white artists' acceptance into the dominantly African American male rap music preserve. The Beastie Boys were one of rap music's most enduring acts and are credited with helping rap music cross over to pop music radio and television in 1986 alongside Run-D.M.C. However, they never were fully accepted as rap musicians by rap fans or critics. By their second album, *Paul's Boutique* (1989), they had abandoned heavy-metal riffs and bad-boy, adolescent rhymes in favor of more sophisticated rhyme schemes given in their signature nasal delivery and accompanied by an incredible demonstration of sampling art by their producers, the Dust Brothers. The album sold fewer than one million copies and forever moved the Beastie Boys away from rap music fans and into the domain of indie rock and alternative college-radio scenes. It is understandable that record executives would take a different approach in marketing white rappers to the masses.

Despite the fact that Vanilla Ice came onto the rap music scene in 1990, four years after the Beastie Boys, he made the most lasting impression by a white performer of rap music until 1998. His single "Ice Ice Baby" (1990) sold quadruple-platinum in its first month and his face graced the cover of many teen-heartthrob magazines for the following year. His famous fade haircut and super baggy pants were borrowed from the biggest rap act of 1989, MC Hammer, and he tried to appeal to the emerging gangsta rap style by rapping about a drive-by shoot-up, featuring his famous catchphrase, "Word to ya Mutha!" In order to demonstrate street credibility, he or his publicist claimed that he was from Miami, Florida, attended the same high school as 2 Live Crew's Luther Campbell, and had been in several street brawls during his days as a member of a tough Miami street gang. However, his star lost its luster almost overnight when former friends from his middle-class Dallas, Texas, neighborhood exposed him as a fraud. Attempts at reinvention as stoner Rasta Vanilla Ice failed in the mid-1990s.

Other white rappers followed with a modicum of success (3rd Bass, Marky Mark, Young Black Teenagers, Kid Rock, and House of Pain), but rap audiences scrutinized white rappers' legitimacy after falling for Vanilla Ice's life story in an age when "keepin' it real" mattered. Artists such as Vanilla Ice took on a persona and an imitative delivery style that matched the African American, hardcore, gangsta rappers. The public that eagerly consumed it at first was also quick to dismiss them as posers or discredit their street sensibilities.

Eminem faces off with Naxshawn Ox Breedlove in the film
***8 Mile,* 2002.**

Source: © AF archive/Alamy

In 1998, Dr. Dre presented his protégé Eminem, who helped change the image of the white rapper and proved that a white rapper could master the rapping tradition. Eminem hit the charts just after the tragic shootings at Columbine High School and played the role of a disgruntled, bullied misfit who was mad at the world. He mixed his angry and violent lyrics with sick humor and trenchant wit, following the path made by the Beastie Boys but with a caustic vulgarity and the goal to offend everyone and anyone. There was no doubt that Eminem could deliver some clever rhymes, but Dr. Dre and he were smart enough not to market Eminem as a denizen of impoverished Detroit, an urbanite living between a poor black neighborhood and a poor white neighborhood. Instead, they suggested a more believable white poverty to match mainstream stereotypes, associating the rapper with a rural, trailer park, "white trash" aesthetic. The images in Eminem's video for "I Just Don't Give a Fuck" (1998) display a believable white poverty and play on every cliché with no regrets: images in the video include a trailer home in a rural setting, abandoned cars and school buses in the yard, alien visitors in the fashion of *Weekly World News* tabloid, a grandma figure in curlers and housecoat being beaten by her grandson, and a poor white family eating fast-food fried chicken and watermelon.

Eminem gave a voice to those misfits, outsider kids who felt like aliens in their home environments. His vocal delivery on his first album, especially noticeable on "My Name Is," remained nasal, and the rhymes were largely vile, misogynistic, and violent but definitely not gangsta. On "I Just Don't Give a Fuck," Eminem also participated in dis rapping against fellow white rappers who had acquired some fame in rap music:

> *I'm nicer than Pete [Nice of 3rd Bass]*
> *but I'm on a search to crush a milk bone [as in Miilkbone, his only potential white rapper rival at that time]*
> *I'm everlasting [Everlast of House of Pain], I melt Vanilla Ice like Silicone*
> *I'm ill enough to just straight up dis you for no reason.*

Eminem gained his initial fame as a comical, foul-mouthed sociopath whose bleached-blond, roman-style haircut and skater-punk dress revealed anything but an attempt to look like the gangsta rappers dominating the rap scene in the late 1990s.

CHAPTER SUMMARY

The 1990s saw the rise in popularity of hardcore rap that often featured themes of violence, misogyny, and anger at the continuing repression of African American youth. As hardcore became increasingly mainstream, mainstream American institutions reacted against it, culminating in the 1994 Senate hearings that addressed violence in rap lyrics. Issues of authenticity became increasingly important as more rap artists claimed to have been raised amid the gang life and drug use of the inner city. The quest for authenticity spilled over into the long battle between rappers 2Pac and the Notorious B.I.G (a.k.a. Biggie Smalls), culminating in their murders.

While hardcore rap was the dominant style, other forms grew in the '90s as well, including R&B-rap and jazz-rap fusions, and a new spirituality in Christian rap and the work of Lauryn Hill. Female rappers responded to the violent, misogynistic imagery of mainstream rap by bringing a feminist perspective. Similar to women rappers, white artists were viewed as adjectival by the fans and the industry, but by the year 2000, white rappers were no longer treated as novelty acts to the degree they once were. Eminem would remain an important figure in the recording industry well into the new millennium and help usher in a new generation of rappers. As rap music and hip hop culture changed and grew, "authenticity" in the new millennium would not remain the exclusive domain of the urban, poor, African American men; authenticity could be gained by middle-class African Americans, like Kanye West or Lupe Fiasco, or white rappers like Paul Wall and Aesop Rock, or non-gangsta-thug, non-cocaine-trade rappers like Rick Ross. In Chapter 9, we will explore these future talents and current trends in hip hop culture since the year 2000.

STUDY QUESTIONS

1. How might the lyrics in gangsta and X-rated rap reflect reality or an exaggerated version of reality?

2. To what extent have gangsta and X-rated rap successfully crossed over into the mainstream? What marketing strategies were employed?

3. Do the lyrics and images associated with songs by Lil' Kim like "Queen Bitch" or "Not Tonight" reflect a feminist/womanist ideology? Explain why or why not.

4. How are sexuality, power, masculinity, Afrocentrism, and feminism/womanism represented in the lyrics of "Brown Skin Lady" by Black Star (1995)?

5. Should certain songs and images be restricted to certain contexts for exposure? Explain your answer.

6. How were women positioned in hip hop during the early days of the old school?

7. Why is female sexuality a major theme in rap music? Compare N.W.A.'s "A Bitch Iz a Bitch" with Queen Latifah's "U.N.I.T.Y. (Who You Calling a Bitch?)". How are themes of female sexuality represented in current rap music? Has much changed?

8. Discuss the concept of fusing rap with other musical styles and the soundscapes that emerged. How are lyrical content and musical sounds different from the gangsta sound? Are any the same?

9. While Eminem might have had urban environmental experiences in his youth similar to some African American rappers, how was his "background" marketed differently in his debut album? Why would Dr. Dre introduce his protégé to rap music consumers this way?

KEY TERMS

Acid jazz

Christian rap

G-Funk

New jack swing

Parents Music Resource Center

R&B-rap fusion

Scratch art

Turntablism

Vamp

CHAPTER 9

HIP HOP CULTURE AND RAP MUSIC IN THE SECOND MILLENNIUM

Learning Objectives

When you have successfully completed this chapter, you will be able to discuss:

- Some of the issues that underscore and explain the current trends in post-2000 hip hop.
- The southern rap aesthetic and the new styles that grew out of the region.
- Underground hip hop's development and main practitioners.
- How technology and the DIY generation have restructured the recording industry.

Hip Hop: Into the New Millennium (1995–Today)

By the year 2010, not only had hip hop reaped the benefits of its 14-year cross-over successes, it had also influenced almost all facets of the *Billboard* chart-toppers. Among the many collaborators with hip hop artists were:

- Country collaborations: Nelly "Over and Over" with Tim McGraw in 2005
- Country fusionist DF Dub "Country Girl" (2003)
- Classical–hip hop fusion artist Miri Ben-Ari *Hip-Hop Violinist* (2005) and Nuttin' But Stringz *Struggle from the Subway to the Charts* (2006)

In addition, hip hop musicians and producers like Pharrell Williams, Missy Elliot, and Timbaland were in high demand to work with mainstream pop artists. The commercial and cultural dominance particularly of southern hip hop artists pushed the genre beyond its status as crossover music to become the aesthetic of mainstream pop music.

While mainstream hip hop flourished in the new millennium, gangsta rap did not entirely disappear. 50 Cent's gangsta pop song "In Da Club" (2003), a party song about a night of relaxation and revelry for the gangsta set, was single of the year; his bullet-ridden album cover for *Get Rich or Die Tryin'* from that same year offered fans the realness of a street hustler who survived gunshots wounds just as the martyred Tupac had done (see Chapter 8). Nevertheless, the digital age and self-publishing possibilities opened doors for the younger, hungrier, and alternatively "realer" MCs to challenge the played-out gangsta rap themes. At the opposite side of the commercial rap musical spectrum is Kanye West—a middle-class, college-dropout super-producer-turned-rapper. And all these trends in the second millennium were framed by the many subterranean, or underground, hip hop scenes that began emerging in the 1990s.

What Is Underground Hip Hop?

Underground hip hop is an umbrella term that refers to independently produced, alternative styles that intentionally shift away from the dominant tastes and directions of commercial rap. It is the product of subterranean music scenes that are under the radar of the mainstream rap music fan base in part because they are formulated and supported by local performers and audiences. As a result, there is no one "underground" style. During the mid-'90s, underground rap ranged from the aggressively leftist politics of Dead Prez, to the highly literate styles of Aceyalone, to the sociopathic nihilism of pre- [and post-] commercial Eminem, to the futuristic, trippy musicianship of Dr. Octagon (Kool Keith with Dan "The Automator" Nakamura and DJ Q-Bert), and even to commercial, conscious rap by the Grammy-nominated artists Common and Lauryn Hill.

Hip hop began as an underground youth music scene in the 1970s and remained relatively marginalized until Run-D.M.C. and second-generation superstars crossed their brand of rap music into the pop music markets (see Chapter 6). Since that time, independent rap scenes have continuously emerged, especially after gangsta rap's domination. Many of the scenes offered alternatives to commercial gangsta rap or thug hip hop, such as Los Angeles's Freestyle Fellowship and Project Blowed or Minneapolis's Rhymesayers Entertainment. These groups helped open the doors for the alternative rap artists of the post-2000s, from Lupe Fiasco to Drake, Kid Cudi, and Wale. Other regional scenes arose to change rap music's soundscape, not to challenge commercial rap's lyrical themes or content. These included the Bay Area's hyphy movement and the southern-state scenes that appealed to local fans until they achieved mainstream success in the first years of the second millennium.

The South

In 2006, iconic rapper Nas (Queens, New York) released his single "Hip Hop Is Dead," which echoed the grievances of many hip hop fans of the '80s and '90s, especially those who believed their only choices were between East Coast and West Coast rap. He asks at the end of the first verse, "So nigga, who's your top ten?/Is it MC Shan [Queens]? Is it MC Ren [Los Angeles]?" It turns out that it is neither. Hip hop, of course, is not dead. As Atlanta-raised rapper Ludacris proclaimed on the T-shirt he wore to the 2007 BET Hip Hop Awards, "Hip Hop Ain't Dead. . . . It Lives in the South." The new millennium was ushered in by ambitious, multiregional southern rappers whose territory has been humorously referred to as the third coast, while the two former coastal powerhouses have unwillingly had to deal with their status as underdogs.

Once the hip hop sound exploded out of the South Bronx in 1979 and onto radio airwaves and cable television, regionalization of hip hop was unstoppable; however, it was not until the late 1990s that the South truly emerged as a dominant commercial factor in the music scene. The term "**Dirty South**" was used to describe this new style, borrowed from the title of Goodie Mob's song from their 1995 debut album *Soul Food*. This term was used as a way of breaking the bicoastal orientation of the market, but it was less successful in terms of encapsulating a region as large as the South within a single production style. In fact, fans and critics alike identified distinct southern styles particularly centered in Atlanta (Ludacris, Goodie Mob, Outkast) and New Orleans (Master P, C-Murder, Silkk the Shocker).

As a regional contributor to the family of hip hop styles, the South has made its particular aesthetic sensibility known since the mid-'80s with the emergence of Miami's 2 Live Crew and the Miami Bass sound, but it can be argued that musical and verbal artistic elements from the South have been present since the subculture began in the 1970s.

The southern United States was ground zero for the African diaspora, and many key elements of southern African American folklife were derived from the old world's dance forms, musical sensibilities, and verbal artistry (see Chapter 4). Further, it was southern African Americans who brought this culture to the northern states in the early decades of the 20th century, especially after World War II. Some of the slurs, moans, shouts, melodic ornamentation, and, most importantly, the percussive qualities of text in the delivery of hip hop's rhymes are oratory and musical practices that have roots in the southern black church. The adaption of the preacher's call-and-response pattern placed the MC in continual dialogue with his partygoers, making his vocal performance simultaneously a distinct entity and one seemingly blended with those of his audience. Consider the preacher's final "Huhs" throughout his sermons as inspiration for East Coast MC Melle Mel's rhythmic vocables in the chorus of "The Message" (1982): "Don't push me cause I'm close to the edge/I'm trying not to lose my head, hah-huh, huh-huh." West Coast rapper Snoop Dogg has incorporated southern-inspired drawls and twangs in his music since the early days, audible in "Nuthin' but a 'G' Thang" (1992), "Pump Pump" (1993), and "Gin and Juice" (1993), in which his signature southern-accented Californian style made it easily translated into an underground cover hit for bluegrass artists the Gourds in 2001. Also consider the redemption-centered, twanging, melodic lyricism of midwestern rappers Bone Thugs-n-Harmony, in their single "Tha Crossroads" (1997), or the sermonic church style of underground rapper MF Doom on Madvillain's "Accordion" (2002):

> Is he still a fly guy clappin' if nobody ain't hear it
> And can they testify from inner spirit
> In living, the true gods
> Givin' y'all nothing but the lick like two broads

> *Got more lyrics than the church got 'Ooh Lords' [pronounced lAH-ds]*
> *And he hold the mic and your attention like two swords [pronounced sAH-ds]."*

Southern rap continued to embody stylistic features and performance practices indigenous to southern African American musical and verbal folk traditions. A southern-fried, ghetto-hustling-flavored boast can be heard in New Orleans rapper B.G.'s 1997 hit "Bling-Bling," which was the most popular and overused expression in hip hop. Dozens-inspired ritual duels continued to drive the competitive edge of the culture, as in the 2004–2007 battle for the title of King of the South between T.I. and Ludacris.

Although the term "Dirty South" began to be used nationwide in the late '90s to embrace a kind of unified musical movement, a singular Dirty South aesthetic is idealized rather than realized. A soundscape that includes fast, bouncy, non-G-funk beats and raunchy lyrics—which by Dirty South standards is not pejorative—illustrates some of the practices that many southern artists follow. Much of its inspiration likely came from Miami Bass and the X-rated raps of the mid-1980s (see Chapter 8). However, while the uptempo similarities might reflect a general, regional trend, there are exceptions; for example, Houston's syrupy-slow, chopped and screwed musical subculture and Memphis artists 8Ball & MJG's brilliant "Comin' Out Hard" (1993) provided listeners with a southern-mannered, gangsta style. These wild thug-protagonists rap over medium laid-back samples of Simply Red's soft-rock classic "Holding Back the Years" (1985) and smooth R&B classic "Stay" by Rufus featuring Chaka Khan. 8Ball & MJG along with DJ Screw in Houston created the underground music scene that Three 6 Mafia and Paul Wall would expand into the mainstream by 2007.

Southern Hip Hop Styles

The idea of southern hip hop is inherently diverse; that is, there is not one South and, unlike the East-West, the southern scene has not been reductively isolated to New York City and Los Angeles (ignoring other great cities, like Oakland and Philadelphia, that produced important rap acts). Several centers of activity have managed to transmit the southern ways of making hip hop beyond traditional boundaries of the South: predominantly Miami and Atlanta on the east, Houston and Memphis on the west, and New Orleans feeding off the two regions, while Virginians have made their own distinct mark. These extremes in musical styles and approaches are connected musically, especially by the deep driving bass. Oftentimes, the main selling point is regional pride.

Southern Message Rap

While southern hip hop did not follow the trajectory set forth by the earliest conscious southern rap act, Arrested Development, their African-centeredness survived in the rural orientation of Louisville's Nappy Roots and the soulful sounds of Atlanta's Outkast. Fronted by André "André 3000" Benjamin and Antwan "Big Boi" Patton,

Outkast took southern hip hop in an innovative new direction away from booming aggression and toward expanding musical arrangements, playing with melody, and offering more positive, elaborate lyrics. Outkast received a Grammy nomination for the single "Rosa Parks" (1998). However, their celebration was short-lived in that the estate of Rosa Parks was offended by the language used and brought a lawsuit against the duo for unlawful use of her name; subsequently, Outkast paid a cash settlement to the Parks estate. The group remained important into the new millennium, eventually releasing a joint solo-project album, *Speakerboxxx/The Love Below*, in 2003. Each member produced signature pop crossover singles—"The Way You Move" by Big Boi and "Hey Ya!" by André 3000—signaling the beginning of the end of the group's dominance on the popular music scene.

Southern Gangsta

In the era following N.W.A.'s *Straight Outta Compton* (1988), more rappers welcomed the gangsta classification and focused their narratives on the chaotic, rough, and seedy side of inner-city life expressed through rough language and choice expletives. The earliest incarnation of southern gangsta rap came out of Houston with dark, horrorcore-variety tales by the Geto Boys. Their stories about everyday street violence and drug-dealing depravity revealed how ghetto living inspired criminal behavior, depression, and suicidal thoughts. In "Mind of a Lunatic" (1990), critics aptly observed the verses describing rape, mutilation, and murder but ignored the statements underscoring the environmental roots of the senseless tolerance of criminal behavior.

In New Orleans, Master P—through his own recordings and those of other rappers on his label No Limit—shifted the attention away from the West Coast models to establish the South's dominance in the gangsta rap scene. His second release, *The Ghettos Tryin to Kill Me!* (1994), an album that includes references to drug dealing and murder, produced by the No Limit posse (C-Murder, Silkk the Shocker, Mystikal, Mia X), established the new gangsta rap model, eventually attracting West Coast superstar Snoop Dogg into their pack. No Limit produced subsequent hits by Silkk the Shocker (*Charge It 2 Da Game*, 1998) and C-Murder (*Life or Death*, 1998). Cash Money Records, also based out of New Orleans, had enormous commercial success with a very similar musical sensibility, but more aggressively promoted their young stars, like Juvenile and a 16-year-old Lil Wayne.

Bounce Music (New Orleans)

Bounce music incorporates New Orleans parade-strutting carnival beats and Mardi Gras chants into a bass-and-percussion-heavy hip hop aesthetic. The word "bounce" appears often in the lyrics of these songs and it also describes the energetic feel of the music. New Orleans's Cash Money Records brought bounce music to the mainstream. By 1993, gangsta lyrics were incorporated into the style, producing "gangsta bounce." Bounce is famous for its drumline progressions, fluttering hi-hats, snare trills, and trademark "Triggerman" sample, generated from the golden era single "Drag Rap" (1984), by Bronx group the Showboys. Juvenile's "Pimpinabitch" (1999) and David Banner's "Like a Pimp" (2003) both showcase this signature sample.

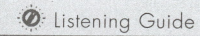

Listening Guide

Listening to David Banner, Featuring Lil' Flip

"LIKE A PIMP"

COMPOSED BY Lavell "David Banner" Crump, Chad Lamar "Pimp C" Butler, and W. Weston

PERFORMED BY David Banner (vocals/producer) and Lil' Flip (vocals)

Appears on *Mississippi: The Album*, 2003, Universal Records B0000312-02.

Though David Banner was born in Jackson, Mississippi, his "Like a Pimp" reflects the stylistic conventions of New Orleans bounce music. Bounce functions largely as club music. While it may vary in tempo, it is often very repetitive, with samples of repeated melodies of a few notes looped throughout the song, often without musical breaks, interludes, or bridges. Bounce music typically consists of a repeated chorus with intermittent verses often delivered in a semi-aggressive shouted manner or even in a full-blown, boisterous chant to match lyrics dealing with money-making, drug and alcohol use, sex, and partying. Bounce videos often show images of street parties, complete with the genre's characteristic "booty pop" (or "twerking"), a rhythmic gyrating dance typically performed by women that involves vigorously shaking one's rear end while the rest of the body remains relatively stationary.

Banner's vocal delivery on the chorus and second and third verses of this song is burly and raspy; his voice is strained and distorted, his consonants are explosive, and his vowels swallowed. Banner makes the song's lyrics about money, women, and partying sound threatening, which may be seen as a permutation of the aggressive vocal styles that hardcore and gangsta rappers of the 1990s traded in. While Banner's delivery is over the top with aggression, Lil' Flip's is more relaxed. Flip, from Houston, Texas, raps his verses with an even, much less agitated voice than Banner, and his flow is slow enough for his southern drawl to come through. The contrast can be heard on the song's repeated chorus with "real girls get down on the floor"—a line borrowed from UGK's "Take It Off"—delivered aggressively and deliberately by Banner, while Lil' Flip's syrupy delivery interjects "like a pimp" after Banner's line. The two rappers serve as foils to one another: Banner escalates the volume, energy, and intensity of the song and Lil' Flip smooths it out, giving "like a pimp" an ebb and flow that increases the song's interest in spite of its repetition that may otherwise seem monotonous.

The song's soundscape remains the same for its entirety, consisting of a repeated, four-bar loop. This loop is essentially a version of the "Triggerman" beat, extrapolated from the Showboys' "Drag Rap" (1986), which features a repeated melody played on a synthesizer programmed to sound like a xylophone. The original melody consists of a few notes of a limited range (in this case, within a few semitones of one another) that creates a hypnotic effect when looped indefinitely. The tempo of the original sample is significantly slowed down on "Like a Pimp," which simultaneously lowers the pitch of the original synthesized xylophone melody. A drum machine and additional synthesizers have been added to this sample in the studio. The drum machine highlights key rhythms in the melody with synthesized stabs inserted in a repeated pattern to add another sonic texture, while another warbling synthesized squeal can be heard at the end of each four-bar phrase, which serves as a kind of placeholder marking the end of each phrase.

"Like a Pimp" is firmly representative of the club-oriented bounce music that is a characteristic New Orleans style. The song's smooth yet bouncy groove, bawdy themes, aggressive delivery, repetitive beat, and chorus demonstrate the characteristics of early second-millennium southern club rap.

0:00		An electronic synthesizer line, sampled from the Showboys' "Drag Rap," enters, along with drum machines, synthesizer stabs, and a warbling synthesizer squeal, the latter three added to the sample in the studio. This comprises the song's main groove and continues throughout.
0:03	"Real girls get down on the floor . . ."	The chorus enters here, rapped by Banner, based primarily on a line borrowed from UGK's "Take It Off."
0:14	"Like a pimp . . ."	Lil' Flip enters, adding his interjection of "Like a pimp" to the song's chorus.
0:26	"By the time I hit the door . . ."	Lil' Flip enters with his first verse as the instrumental groove continues. To highlight important lyrical phrases and rhymes, Flip's vocal is often double-tracked with some well-applied delay in the studio: notably, the discrepancies in the way he articulates certain words and his intonation in "What is y'all sayin'?" (ca. 00:56) and "Choo-choo!" (ca. 01:03).
1:20	"Real girls get down on the floor . . ."	The chorus returns here and remains the same as in the song's intro.
1:47	"Step into the club . . ."	Banner begins his first verse. Just as with Flip's verse, Banner's voice is sometimes multitracked to emphasize key words.

Continued

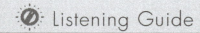
Listening Guide

Listening to David Banner Featuring Lil' Flip Continued

2:27	"Like a pimp . . ."	Flip anticipates the chorus with this line, and it continues immediately, as before.
2:53	"Now don't you hate them . . ."	Flip's multitracked vocal with delay returns, beginning the song's third verse. In this verse the two rappers trade four-measure phrases with one another.
3:06	"Oh you can catch us at . . ."	Banner enters here for his four-measure phrase.
3:20	"We make em . . ."	Flip returns for the next four-measure phrase.
3:34	"Go on touch your toes and . . ."	Banner picks up here for his final four-measure phrase.
3:46	"Lil' Flip, my N—a . . ."	Flip finishes Banner's rhyme here with his own name and continues to talk over the groove, saying, "Get your money" as the groove vamps.
4:07	"Get your money!"	This final line echoes as the groove drops out.
4:11		The synthesizer stabs that were present throughout serve as the song's final tag.

Lil Wayne Phenomenon

Lil Wayne (Dwayne Michael Carter Jr.) first gained notice in the late '90s as the youngest member of Cash Money Millionaires' Hot Boys, which also included Juvenile, Turk, and B.G. He became a solo act in 1999 and had a huge smash with the title track "Tha Block Is Hot" from his debut album. Over the following two to three years, Cash Money dropped every other Hot Boy but kept Wayne—in fact, between 2005 and 2007 he was president of Cash Money Records—and during that time he began to pop up more frequently on other rappers' tracks in the style of Puff Daddy during the early Bad Boy days. After years of giving his music away for free on a series of brilliant mixtapes, Wayne proved that his fans would still pay for his music, releasing *Tha Carter III* in 2008, which sold a million copies in its first week and included the pop-friendly, *Billboard* chart-topper "Lollipop." This tattooed, syrup-swigging, stoner superstar is probably also the oddest pop superstar since Michael Jackson. In his own words, "We are not the same—I'm a Martian" (from the 2007 single "Show Me What You Got").

In 2010, Lil Wayne was charged with gun possession stemming from a July 2007 arrest and eventually pled guilty to attempted gun possession. He was released from New York's Rikers Island prison facility on November 4, 2010, after serving eight months of his yearlong sentence. Weeks later, he released *I Am Not a Human Being* (2010), re-establishing his credentials as a rapper (after the experimental, rock music detour on *Rebirth* in February of the same year). At this time, the one-time mentee also became a mentor as he guided the careers of young hip hop stars Drake and Nicki Minaj. In 2011, Lil Wayne released *Tha Carter IV*. While this album was neither his wittiest nor most dexterous work to date, it sold huge numbers in its first week. Many of his fans' favorite songs were collaborations with younger artists like Bruno Mars, Drake, and Cory Gunz. However, Wayne's alien weirdness and boastful introspection also make appearances. In "She Will," Wayne boasts of his ability to bounce back from intense celebrity scrutiny and defy the psychological pressure to snap: "I've been at the top for a while/And I ain't jumped yet."

Lil Wayne onstage in New Orleans, 2008.
Source: © ZUMA Press, Inc./Alamy

Chopped and Screwed (Houston)

Screwed music—later **chopped and screwed**—took its name from the late DJ Screw (Robert Earl Davis Jr.), who pioneered this hazy, sleepy groove in the early 1990s. DJ Screw slowed down the tempo of two songs on his turntable's pitch-control knob to beat-match them. "Screwed" referred to this slow tempo, while "chopped" described the cuts, scratches, pauses, and rewinds that accompany his slowed-down mixes. Screwed fans likened the hypnotic pace of the music with the dulling effects of their choice drug codeine syrup—sometimes mixed with liquor, soda, or dissolved Jolly Rancher candy. In the second half of the 1990s, DJ Screw released several independently produced albums, rejecting offers from Priority Records in order to keep his music unadulterated by commercial objectives. In the late '90s, screwed music became an integral part of an entire subculture in Houston. DJ Screw died of an overdose in 2000 before seeing his brand of hip hop cross over. By 2000, Three 6 Mafia and UGK released a national hit, "Sippin' on Some Syrup," that truly introduced chopped and screwed to the mainstream. Paul Wall's 2005 release, *The Peoples Champ [Chopped and Screwed]*, continued the legacy of Screw's brand of hip hop.

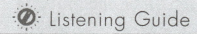 Listening Guide

Listening to Three 6 Mafia, Featuring UGK and Project Pat

"SIPPIN' ON SOME SYRUP"

COMPOSED BY Bun B, DJ Paul, Juicy J, and Pimp C

PERFORMED BY Darnell "Crunchy Black" Carlton (vocals), Lola "Gangsta Boo" Mitchell (vocals), Robert "Koopsta Knicca" Cooper Phillips (vocals), Ricky "Lord Infamous" Dunigan (vocals), Patrick "Project Pat" Houston (vocals), Chad "Pimp C" Butler (vocals), Bernard "Bun B" Freeman (vocals), Project Pat (vocals)

MIXED BY Lil' Pat

PRODUCED BY Paul "DJ Paul" Beauregard and Jordan "Juicy J" Houston

Appears on *When the Smoke Clears*, 2000, Loud Records 497506 2.

Houston native DJ Screw pioneered a style called screwed music or chopped and screwed in the early 1990s. It was characterized by the use of samples that have been slowed to a fraction of their original speed, affecting both their tempo and pitch, and then mixed with one another in ways that make them intentionally sound out of sync, similar to a drunken stammering or stuttering. Originally these samples were slowed down manually on a turntable, and the stuttering effect was created by using two copies of the same record played on two different turntables; the DJ manipulated a cross-fader to switch between them while the two records were playing slightly out of sync, one record starting a second or two before the other. Now the effect is produced electronically with computer software or a digital sampler that emulates this process and gives the producer more control over the exact metrics of time and pitch.

Three 6 Mafia's "Sippin' on Some Syrup" is a commercial example of chopped and screwed music combined with elements of more typical mainstream rap music production. As a result, it crossed over into non-southern markets easily. The stuttered (chopped) and slowed down (screwed) samples sound disorienting, and this disorientation creates a sonic experience that emulates the high one gets while ingesting codeine-based cough syrup, the drug of choice for many practitioners of screwed music. This codeine-based cough syrup is the "sizzurp" that the rappers refer to in this song, and it pervades many southern rap scenes in a variety of configurations, from straight out of the bottle to "Purple Drink," a concoction of the cough syrup mixed with soda and Jolly Ranchers candy.

"Sippin' on Some Syrup" is performed by a gathering of southern rap artists: Three 6 Mafia, from Memphis, and UGK, from Houston. The vocal sample that serves as the song's chorus and appears throughout the song is from former Three 6 Mafia member Project Pat, who re-recorded in the studio the "sippin' on some sizzurp" line he originally created on "Ballers" (1999), which appeared at about 00:34

on the original. This re-recorded sample has been recorded yet again and subjected to the processes of chopping and screwing using a digital sampler, slowing it down considerably from the original recording. This sample is on a constant loop during "Sippin'"; it can be heard featured in the foreground during the song's chorus and is mixed in the background during the rapped verses.

The live vocals on this track are delivered by the members of Three 6 Mafia and UGK. The song begins with an introduction spoken by UGK members Pimp C and Bun B, attacking "bitches" but referring to men who aren't fit to roll with their crew and extolling their virtues as competent drug users. Pimp C begins the song's first verse, rapping about tricked-out cars and cough syrup, with a slow flow that emphasizes his southern drawl. DJ Paul of Three 6 Mafia continues with the song's second verse, resuming the drug themes in a fuller-voiced and faster flow than Pimp C. The song's sampled chorus enters between this set of two verses and the next and plays several times. Juicy J, also of Three 6 Mafia, enters with the song's third verse, rapping about ecstasy and cocaine with a start-and-stop flow, busy at the beginning of lines and tapering to slower endings. Finally Bun B enters with the song's last verse, dealing with more eclectic themes than his predecessors, including references to famous mobsters, a Duke Ellington tune ("Perdido," 1941), and Zinger snack cakes, ultimately returning to the drug-based themes that pervade the rest of the song. Bun B's voice is deeper and faster than Juicy J's, and he has a more active flow as the song's final verse draws to a conclusion. This motion of the verses, from MCs with slower and softer flows to those with louder and busier ones, effectively gives the song a shape as it builds towards its repeated choruses.

In addition to the Project Pat sample, "Sippin' on Some Syrup" begins with a harsh and clear, buzzing keyboard synthesizer lead and hi-hat playing as a musical introduction during UGK's spoken vocal introduction, which soon gives way to the main instrumental groove that will continue throughout the song. When the Project Pat sample enters, so do the rest of the sounds that provide the backdrop for the group's lyrics. A second sample is used throughout and may be recognized by its distinctive crisp and deep synthesizer lead and electric piano sounds; this is borrowed from the introduction of Marvin Gaye's "Is That Enough" (1978). Interestingly, this sample is neither chopped nor screwed and, due to its lighter timbre and higher pitches, seems to float above the rest of the track. Underneath this sample, a drum machine and bass guitar, both added in the studio, can be heard playing a repetitive groove throughout. The opening harsh and clear synthesizer lead sounds at the beginning of each four-measure phrase and gradually tapers out through the second measure before disappearing for the final two bars of each phrase. Once this conglomerate of samples and original material enters, the soundscape remains consistent, with only some more hi-hat activity added to the drum machine's

Continued

Listening Guide

Listening to Three 6 Mafia, Featuring UGK and Project Pat Continued

part during the song's third verse. Much of the musical interest is created by moving the chopped and screwed Project Pat sample from the foreground to the background of the song's mix, for the choruses and verses, respectively.

"Sippin' on Some Syrup" mixes the chopped and screwed style with more conventional rap production elements in this celebration of the use of codeine-based cough syrup for its narcotic effects. This meeting of Memphis-based Three 6 Mafia, Project Pat, and Houston-based UGK is an important crossover of southern rap styles into non-southern markets and the unique drug culture associated with them.

0:00	"Triple six . . ."	A group vocal begins the song, announcing "Triple six." Bun B of UGK speaks an intro, "You old pussy ass . . . booty-ass . . . trill ass" with interjections of "Pourin' up and showin' up, bitch" from his bandmate Pimp C. This occurs over a low-pitched harsh and clear, buzzing synthesizer lead referred to as a "buzz saw" sound effect, which comes in the form of very fast streams of electrical pulses. Some hi-hat clicks are also introduced by a drum machine.
0:15	"Yeah, N——a, y'all know the m—— f——' score . . ."	Pimp C takes over the spoken introduction.
0:21	"N——a, It's some sippin' ass . . ."	Bun B continues. The two MCs continue alternating the spoken portion of the song's intro.
0:28	"And we ain't playin' with you . . ."	The synthesizer lead settles on one very low note as the MCs wrap up the song's spoken introduction.
0:32	"Sippin' on some sizzurp . . ."	The song's main groove and chorus enter. The chorus vocals consist of a sample from Project Pat that had originally appeared on "Ballers," which is chopped and screwed here to provide the slow tempo, low pitch, and characteristic stutter of this song's chorus. A second sample, from Marvin Gaye's "Is That Enough," enters here, featuring a crisp and deep synthesizer lead and electric piano sounds. These samples are overlaid on a drum machine pattern, with bass and snare drums added to the existing hi-hat pattern and a bass line added in-studio on a bass guitar or synthesizer. The low-pitched harsh and clear synthesizer lead continues here. This soundscape remains the same throughout the song, with the vocal sample fading back in the mix (but still audible) during the verses and coming forward during the song's choruses.

1:00	"I'm trill, working the wheel . . ."	The vocal sample is brought back in the mix as Pimp C begins the song's first verse.
1:42	"Some n——s scared to flaunt it . . ."	DJ Paul of Three 6 Mafia enters with his verse. The soundscape continues.
2:25	"Sippin' on some sizzurp . . ."	The vocal sample is brought forward in the mix as the chorus returns.
2:39	"People always askin' me . . ."	The vocal sample fades back in the mix as Juicy J of Three 6 Mafia begins his verse. Some extra hi-hat sounds programmed on the drum machine can be heard.
3:21	"N——a tell me what you know . . ."	Bun B enters with his verse. The soundscape remains the same.
4:04	"Sippin' on some sizzurp . . ."	The chorus sample is brought back to the front of the mix and repeats several times as the song fades out.

Crunk (Memphis and Atlanta)/Crunk & B

Crunk is high-energy club music that emerged in the late '90s. It is distinguished by gritty, hoarse chants and antiphonic, repetitive refrains. The term has had fluctuating meaning, probably combining the words "crazy" and "drunk" or "chronic" and "drunk" to refer to the state of being both drunk from alcohol and high on marijuana.

The pioneers of this style are primarily Atlanta-based rappers, such as Lil Jon, Ying Yang Twins, and Bone Crusher. Unlike the mainstream rap trend to overlay rap lyrics onto R&B hooks, crunk's sound relies on highly synthesized, bottom-heavy rhythms and looped drum machines repeated throughout a song to accompany shouted party chants. Lil Jon's "Get Crunk" (1997) is a tough party-chanting, electronic drum-corps-oriented tune designed to get the party going. According to David Banner, crunk is a party music, but "you're only partying to get away from the pain"—which echoes much of the South Bronx's original intention for the hip hop subculture.

Ice Cube (left), Lil Jon (center) and Xzibit (right) on the Third Annual VH1 Hip Hop Honors show, 2006.

Source: *Photo: Ray Tamarra,* © *Everett Collection Inc/Alamy*

By 2004, crunk had crossed over and Lil Jon was producing superstar R&B singers like Usher ("Yeah") and Ciara ("Goodies" or "Oh" with Ludacris), creating a fusion style referred to as **Crunk & B**. While Crunk was all about being wild and in-your-face, Ciara's Crunk & B was leisurely and seductive.

Snap Music (Atlanta)

The Atlanta quartet Dem Franchize Boys had hits in 2005 and 2006 with "I Think They Like Me" and "Lean Wit It, Rock Wit It," adding a mellowness to the crunk aesthetic by slowing down the tempo and replacing the snare beat with finger snaps; ergo, **snap music**. The style's lyrically spare, club-music orientation had major cross-over appeal: it is more relaxed than crunk, but not as sleepy as chopped and screwed. The definitive snap music hit, "Laffy Taffy," by another Atlanta quartet, D4L, reached number one in early 2006 with a bare-minimum tune accompanied by a single finger-snapping beat and deep bass.

Cocaine Rap

Cocaine rap is a drug-trade revival style that brings a new focus on the underworld perils of the cocaine trade. Some of the early credit for reviving this topic has to go to the Virginia-born brothers the Clipse (Malice and Pusha T), with their record "Grindin'" from 2002—a crisp and sparse drumline production put together by fellow Virginians the Neptunes (Pharrell Williams and Chad Hugo). The song begins with Pharrell introducing the listener to a new southern sound experience and himself, with a drawled interjection by Pusha T ("I'm your pusha") that recalls Ice-T's 1988 anti-drug-sale song—but unlike Ice-T, the duo are not playing with the narcotic-sale metaphor. In the third verse, Malice spits, "My grind's 'bout family, never been about fame/From days I wasn't able [Abel] there was always 'caine [Cain]"—alluding to the Bible, brotherhood, and his role in the drug trade in one quick run. Lyrically, this isn't the best, but it's easily the Neptunes' most sonically arresting song. The Clipse's Pusha would find his voice and perfect his serpentine-like flow in the years to follow in records like *Hell Hath No Fury* (2006).

By 2005, rapping about the drug trade was enjoying a full revival among southern artists, as exemplified in the work of Rick Ross. On his 2006 album *Port of Miami*, he celebrates his status as the biggest dealer in his hood and Miami's fame as port of entry for South American narcotics. Ross and other artists often claim real-life experience dealing coke and boast of their skills as salesmen, not as party people. Atlanta rapper Young Jeezy, nicknamed the "Snowman," tells us in "The Realest," "I'm the motherfucking realest; they liars, they phonies, they fakes; these niggas ain't ever touched the weight." Jeezy pays homage to the architects of southern gangsta rap, the Geto Boys, borrowing the title of one of their songs, "my mind's playing tricks on me," on this record.

South as Pop

Not only were southern rap artists guiding the rap music market, they were also dominating the pop music market in the first half of the 2000s, in particular Virginia artists such as Missy Elliot, Timbaland, and the Neptunes. The producers the

Neptunes first made it big in hip hop in 2000 with huge hits like Mystikal's "Shake Ya Ass" and Jay-Z's "I Just Wanna Love You (Give It 2 Me)." The team transitioned from rap to pop in 2001, producing Britney Spears ("I'm a Slave 4 U"), 'N Sync ("Girlfriend"), and Usher ("U Don't Have to Call"). Timbaland followed suit, crossing over from his hip hop productions to working with pop stars Nelly Furtado, Gwen Stefani, and Justin Timberlake in 2006. In that year alone, Timbaland produced seven singles receiving airplay worldwide by Nelly Furtado and Justin Timberlake, as well as his own single "Give It to Me" (2006) that featured both pop singers.

Underground Rap as Independent or Alternative Rap Music

In addition to the regional sounds of the South, alternative rap movements intent on anticommercialism were forming as early as 1989–1992 in places like Los Angeles and Minneapolis.

Rhymesayers Entertainment

Until the late 1990s, major-label investment in rap from cities other than L.A. and New York was largely nonexistent. It took independent record label owners in the 1990s to develop local artists that would provide an infrastructure for independent, non-gangsta rap. Among the first was Too $hort from East Oakland, California, who is honored as the progenitor of the Bay Area local scene. As a sophomore at Fremont High School, he began to sell the mixtapes that he made in his bedroom using a Radio Shack mixer and mismatched stereo equipment. His entrepreneurship, DIY spirit, and ability to build a strong, localized fan base landed him a record deal with Jive Zomba Records that launched his hugely successful "pimps and playas" commercial career.

In Minneapolis, Minnesota, an MC coalition known as Headshots—Phull Surkle, the Native Ones, Beyond (now known as Musab), Atmosphere, Anthony Davis (better known as Ant), and CEO Brent Sayers—adopted the do-it-yourself credo and formed the label Rhymesayers Entertainment, not only to be the owners of their own recordings but to have complete control of their artistic futures.

In 1996, they offered their first official release, Beyond's *Comparison*, which was followed by the now classic 1997 release *Overcast* by Atmosphere, featuring Sean Michael Daley (a.k.a. Slug). Working with producer Ant, Slug created songs like "Scapegoat" that wed Ant's dark, melodic musical collages with his boastful yet introspective lyrics. Slug argues that we do not own our problems or take responsibility for them but rather make excuses or blame other forces for the ills we endure:

> *It's the virus that takes the lives of the weak and the strong.*
> *It's the drama that keeps on between me and my seed's mom.*
> *It's that need to speak long. It's that hunger for attention.*
> *It's the wack, who attack songs of redemption.*
> *It's prevention. It's the first solution.*
> *It's loose. It's out for retribution.*

It's mental pollution . . . and public execution.
It's the nails that keep my hands and feet to these boards.
It's the part time job that governs what you can afford.
It's the fear. It's the fake.
It's clear it can make time stop,
and leave you stranded in the year of the snake.
It's the dollar, yen, pound. It's all denomination.
It's hourly wages for your professional observations.
It's on your face and it's in your eyes.
It's everything you be.
'Cause it ain't me, motherfucker, 'cause it ain't me, uh.

Rhymesayers Entertainment ultimately became a point of entry, a "gateway" label for rap fans searching for alternative music scenes, and even today maintains a niche market at the national and international level. Today, the roster has expanded considerably with underground rap strongholds such as MF Doom, Brother Ali, Psalm One, and Abstract Rude.

The Underground Scene in Los Angeles: The Good Life Café and Project Blowed

In the early 1990s, another counter-pop-cultural scene was developing in Los Angeles based in a small, black-owned, independent health food store on Crenshaw Boulevard in the Leimert Park neighborhood. The Leimert Park arts scene was born as a community-based effort to quell the volatile atmosphere born from gang warfare plaguing South Central Los Angeles since the 1980s and particularly since the Rodney King uprising in 1992. Fifth Street Dick's Coffee Company started the movement by placing communal tables outside its storefront. The shop revitalized the all-night chess slams and verbal duels that had disappeared as a result of the threat of gang violence. The Good Life Café followed suit and transformed street kids into MCs, poets, and writers.

The Good Life Café promoted healthy living and provided the infrastructure for the "unprocessed" hip hop of L.A.'s underground classical age. Beginning in December 1989, the café's co-founder B. Hall reserved Thursday night for the youth in the neighborhood to perform hip hop so long as they followed her four rules:

- No cursing on the mic.
- No leaning on the paintings.
- No gum on the floor.
- No "miggitty, miggitty, miggitty . . ." or other formulaic stalling devices.

B. Hall's rules established a set of codes for appropriate behavior in this environment that were reminiscent of the party-culture values established by Herc and Bam for their generation of partygoers (see Chapter 2). These rules also demanded that performers honor the word and put some thought behind their raps, because resorting to profanity, formulaic devices, or a "gangsta" posture (i.e., no leaning) would be reasons to cut the mic. Additionally, if a performer was not cutting muster, the audience would chant loudly, "Please, pass the mic!" Being told to "pass the mic" was the verbal equivalent to a hook dragging a performer off the stage for less-than-skillful lyrics or delivery style. A rapper who came out of this scene, Aceyalone, showed how these rules influenced his changing behavior in Marcyliena Moran's ethnography on the L.A. underground scene: "It wasn't like I chose to get out of trouble, it just happened that way. And I don't know . . . but it was more like, naturally, hanging out with these guys, doing hip hop, was a little more fun than hanging out with gang bangers" (2009: 17).

Furthermore, L.A. was still recovering from the uprising after the Rodney King verdict. The Good Life provided a place to heal through lyrics and music and learn what other young people were thinking about during that time besides thug life. The club also fostered new styles, such as **choppin' it up and stylin'**, which was crunching sentences together faster than normal to break up the rhythm. Myka 9 of the Freestyle Fellowship did some smooth choppin' for his song "Mary" (ca. 1993; heard more emphatically in the live performance than in the recorded version). Some of the important artists that came out of the Good Life include Aceyalone, Myka 9, P.E.A.C.E., Self Jupiter of the Freestyle Fellowship, Eve, Volume 10, Pigeon John, Figures of Speech, Abstract Rude, Medusa, and Chali 2na. The official open mic ran from 8 to 10 p.m.; after-hours battles ensued in the parking lot, where impromptu ciphers were created and stars from the Café and challengers could practice their "*CALI*-sthentics."

The Good Life Café ended its open-mic nights in 1995. However, the youth leaders took the initiative to keep the independent spirit born there and transport it a few blocks away to the corner of 43rd Place and Leimert, which became affectionately identified by L.A. African American youth of that era as the heart of the hip hop cultural and arts movement. Here, the Video 3333 and KAOS Network art center continued the momentum with Thursday night hip hop workshops called Project Blowed. At Project Blowed, the youth of L.A. could continue to hone their craft and testify that L.A. hip hop was not just "gangsta." KAOS Network has since expanded onto the Internet and still promotes local art and black consciousness through art.

The Millennials (or the Millennial Generation)

By the end of the first decade of the 21st century, the appeal of thugs and hustlers was beginning to wane, and a new style, drawing directly from those underground scenes in the late 1990s, was emerging. Instead of ghetto-life narratives laden with sales of narcotics, shoot-outs, and the sexual exploitation of young ladies, stories about family drama, troubled relationships, the aftermath of partying too hard, and the concerns of the black middle class all came to the fore. Many of this generation of fans and musicians couldn't care less about "keeping it real." When the truth was revealed about Rick Ross's embellished career as a cocaine dealer and that his time spent in the penitentiary was as a corrections officer, his fans did not desert him. When the thug-wannabe character Papa Doc in the film *8 Mile* (2002) was outed by B-Rabbit for being black, middle-class, and educated, it amounted to a major victory for the outsider; however, in the new order, such a revelation would hardly matter:

> *But I know something about you,*
> *You went to Cranbrook. That's a private school!*
> *What's the matter, Bub? You embarrassed?*
> *This guy ain't a gangster. His real name's Clarence.*
> *And Clarence lives at home with both parents.*
> *And Clarence parents have a real good marriage.*

Part of this new attitude came from a group of rap entrepreneurs known as **backpackers** because of their living-with-less philosophy, commitment to independent labels, DIY (do-it-yourself) approach to making music, and fashion style based on skinny jeans, hoodies, and retro sneakers rather than the high fashions of the gangsta rappers. "Backpacker" was a term used to identify young hip hop enthusiasts who were looking for an alternative expression that was not gangsta, not materialistic (in terms of lyrics perhaps more so than practice), and devoted to raising consciousness in the community. The earliest participants in the subculture were committed to anticommercialism and antimaterialism, so much so that it earned them a reputation for being complainers and nerds. The backpack itself symbolized a kind of hobo-chic along with their aversion to baggy pants and excessive bling. They would produce viable non-hustler rappers to a rap music audience more willing to embrace newer models. In fact, by 2011, two of hip hop's shining stars were neither born in the United States nor products of the ghetto: Drake and Nicki Minaj, both discussed later in this chapter.

Pharrell Williams and Kanye West

Arguably, the crossover began early in the new millennium in the work of two superstars: Pharrell Williams and Kanye West. Hip hop producer and artist Pharrell Williams, of the production duo the Neptunes and the hip hop group N.E.R.D., was highly influential in introducing this new attitude to rap music. N.E.R.D. was an appropriate title for Williams's group given their transcendence of the thug stereotype and their embrace of pop culture trends: making it acceptable to skateboard, wear neon colors and skinny jeans in an era of extremely oversized clothing, watch Japanese anime, and embrace geek lore. Backpackers were also the first to be connected with the term **nerdcore**, which has since become a musical scene in its own right, largely with white rappers on the Internet, such as MC Frontalot, who exploits his privileges, experiences at M.I.T., and love for sci-fi. Chicago-based producer-turned-rapper Kanye West has dominated the commercial pop and rap scenes since the release of his debut solo *College Dropout* in 2003. West proved that being the son of an English professor and professional photographer, growing up middle-class and midwestern, and looking college-preppy did not have to be a liability. His rise to stardom came soon after he dropped out of Chicago State University to produce beats for Bad Boy and Jay-Z's Roc-A-Fella Records. His early productions included creating the bass-heavy, hard-rock sounds for Jay-Z's dis rap "Take Over" (2001), in which West blends the Doors' "Five to One" with the guttural, horrorcore-imitation of David Bowie's "Fame" (1975):

> *I know you missin' all the—FAAAAAAAME!*
> *But along with celebrity comes bout seventy shots to your frame*
> *. . . That's why your—LAAAAAAAME!*
> *Career come to a end . . .*

After much prodding, a reluctant Jay-Z agreed to release West's non-hustler rap style on his label. As opposed to suppressing his origins, West laid it all out in the album's autobiographical title, *College Dropout.* From this album emerged an unlikely hit, "Through the Wire," in which he recounted the painful, life-changing car accident that almost killed him. West performed the rap literally through the constraining wire of the oral device keeping his mouth in a fixed position, and applying the slurring delivery popularized in chopped and screwed style:

Three 6 Mafia "Sippin' on Some Syrup"(feat. UGK) (2000)	Kanye West "Through the Wire" (2003)
Sippin' on some **siz-zurp**, sip, sippin' sippin' on some, sip	. . . I drink a Boost for breakfast, and Ensure for **dessert** Somebody ordered pancakes I just sip the **sizzurp** That right there could drive a sane man **bizzerk** Not to worry y'all Mr. H 2 the Izzo's back to **wizzerk** . . .

Following the lead of Wu-Tang Clan producer RZA, who sped up the tempo of the soul samples that he used in his backing tracks, West speeds up the vocals of Chaka Khan's "Through the Fire" (1985) to produce what would become his signature chipmunk sound effect.

West continued to produce hits for other artists as well as for himself on *Late Registration* (2005) and completed the college trilogy with *Graduation* in 2009. West also became famous for his polarizing antics that at times revealed a petulant, self-indulgent brat, as in his drunken rant during Taylor Swift's Grammy Award acceptance in 2010, but also an unlikely revolutionary who nervously critiqued President Bush's lax response to the 2005 Hurricane Katrina disaster—a most gangsta and politically radical act coming from a preppy rap artist.

Kanye West helped usher in a new commercial potential for non-hustlers in the rap game. While only occasionally tapping into socially conscious raps himself, he mentored a fellow Chicagoan, Lupe Fiasco, who never strayed from socially activist raps and has remained committed to this notion of the underground spirit. In 2006, Lupe Fiasco garnered an underground following among the backpacker scene and eventually crossed over into a mainstream fan base that had been wallowing in a murky pool of snap music, crunk, and G-unit gangsta rap. Lupe's first commercial

Kanye West, 2007.
Source: © steve black/Alamy

release *Food & Liquor* (2006) made underground themes palatable for the mainstream market. For example, in the self-reflexive piece "American Terrorist," Fiasco tackles issues of political, religious, and cultural "terrorism" at a time when federal anti-terrorism policies scared folks from challenging the authority of the state.

The following year, Fiasco released *The Cool* and expanded his narrative and character development. However, with his crossover success came the perennial problems of commodifying one's art while holding on to one's integrity. Four years passed before he released his third album, due to years of clashes with his record label, Atlantic Records, which considered his songs insufficiently commercial. In the tradition of his forefathers—like Public Enemy, Tribe, Common, Talib Kweli, and other conscious rappers—Fiasco wanted to produce popular music to incite hip hop fans into action. Finally, devoted fans organized on the Internet to demonstrate outside Atlantic's Manhattan headquarters on October 15, 2010—a numerically significant date as it alludes to Lupe Fiasco's independent label, 1st and 15th Entertainment. His grassroots, hip hop–empowered fans applied the pressure for Atlantic executives to set a release date for *Lasers* in 2011. On the cover, an "A" is spray-painted atop the "O" of the word "Losers," creating the symbol for anarchy.

Young Innovators

In this post-Kanye/Lupe rap planet that was born from both the middle-class, midwestern independent record ethos of Rhymesayers and what Marcyliena Morgan referred to as "the flight, fight and freedom" signifying of the L.A. underground came a throng of twenty-somethings talking about real-life issues reflecting their own experiences. Some standout artists since the mid-2000s:

- Wale is a witty lyricist and first-generation Nigerian American who offers a universalizing diagnosis of contemporary youth in *Attention Deficit* (2009). The deeply introspective lyrics of "Shades" expose a young man full of doubts and sadness who nonetheless has the resolve to deal with the "chip on his shoulder" about his skin tone and not being accepted by native-born African Americans. His message is that his listeners need to love themselves and the tones that they are born with.
- Kid Cudi, a Cleveland rapper of Mexican American and African American parentage, released two Afro-futuristic, nerdy-chic, stoner albums in 2009 and 2010. His work ranges from songs like "Trapped in My Mind" and

"Marijuana," which are stoner, mind-ecstasy favorites among the twenty-something set, to the haunting, aching, melancholic narrative of "Mr. Rager," which is accompanied by an electronica-flavored beat and French-soundtrack melodic line reminding listeners of his film-student past.

- Odd Future (short for Odd Future Wolf Gang Kill Them All, acronym OFWGKTA) combine the sardonic, sick humor of a young Eminem with the visually descriptive, vitriolic slasher films en vogue in the new millennium. The collective of 16- to 23-year-olds from Los Angeles are aggressively subversive and lyrically nihilistic, and packaged as middle-class, skateboarding punks in the tradition of MTV's *Jackass* series. By 2011, their 11 albums were available online for free download on their own website, plus their channel on YouTube allowed access to the entire crew's video interpretations, for the sophisticated A.V. Club set. They have managed to shock parents who were contemporaries of Marilyn Manson. Teenaged member Earl Sweatshirt and his rap "Earl" got him in enough trouble with his mom that she yanked him out of the group because of his graphic lyrics, such as:

    > Yo, I'm a hot and bothered astronaut crashing while
    > Jacking off to buffering vids of Asher Roth eating apple sauce
    > Sent to Earth to poke Catholics in the ass with saws
    > And knock blunt ashes into their caskets and laugh it off . . .

    Upon his return from boarding school in Samoa, Earl Sweatshirt released *Doris* in 2013. The album introduced listeners to a mature Earl, one who was willing to share a broader range of emotions with his fans and demonstrate am impactful lyrical complexity.
- Mixtape wunderkind Stalley is a self-described regular, good guy who is adamantly against signing with a major label, favoring releasing his own mixtapes that weave raps about small-town Ohio hardships atop whimsical beats and Tropicália samples.
- Politically conscious lyricist K'naan, a Somali-born Canadian rapper, describes problems with essentializing Islam and Africans, ignoring the large differences that exist among Muslim and African ethnic groups and nations. His own African [North] American experience defines much of his music making, as does his mission to raise awareness about Somalia. In the song "ABC's" (2009), K'Naan questions, if not challenges, the dangers of America's inner cities, comparing them to the levels of violence and poverty faced by Mogadishu youth. His rapping is supported by a sample of Chubb Rock's golden era classic "Treat 'Em Right" (1990), as well as a verse contributed by Rock that is blended with the Ethiopian jazz legend Mulatu Astatke's "Kasalefkut-Hulu" (1972).
- M.I.A. (Mathangi "Maya" Arulpragasam) is a British rapper-producer of Sri Lankan/Tamil descent whose work shows the influence of techno-garage-rap fusion styles. She has recorded dance-oriented, politically angst-ridden songs grounded in a feminine and feministic style, such as "Born Free" (2010), a song that addresses the oppression and extrajudicial killing of Tamil Tiger fighters, referencing article 1 from the United Nations Declaration on Human Rights.

Nicki Minaj performs on ABC's *Good Morning America*, 2011.
Source: © ZUMA Press, Inc./Alamy

Drake and Nicki Minaj

Among these young, up-and-coming artists at the end of the decade, two of the most ardently promoted and mentored newcomers led the pack, Drake and Nicki Minaj. Drake—a biracial, Canadian-born former child actor—successfully transformed himself into a platinum-selling, legitimate hip hop superstar with pop appeal in 2006. After three years of releasing mixtapes, he finally got a sleeper hit with the single "Replacement Girl" (featuring Trey Songz) and exposure on BET's popular *106th & Park* music television program. He continued to receive relentless hype and many make guest appearances on other rap artists' songs before releasing his much-anticipated album *Thank Me Later* (2010), re-establishing the cockiness that fans first encountered in his original, laid-back, boastful single.

In the 2009 single "Forever" (Kanye West, Lil Wayne, and Eminem), Drake begins by testifying to the DIY spirit and meritorious braggadocio, "Everybody gets a deal/I did it without one . . ./understand nothing was done for me. . . ." Each megastar added their story of being driven and self-sufficient "to the top . . . packin' stadiums" and including the young Drake in their ranks: "The passion and the flame's ignited/You can't put it out once we light it." In this song, the young rap protégé is symbolically "passed the mic" by Kanye West, his mentor Lil Wayne, and Eminem.

Nicki Minaj (Trinidadian by way of Queens, New York) also earned a strong reputation with her underground mixtapes available on her MySpace.com page and a trio—if not more—of colorful alter egos including Harajuku Barbie, Nicki, and Roman (a gay youth).While other sexy-female rappers stuck to the paradigm Lil' Kim and Foxxy Brown established in the 1990s (including Trina and Remy Ma), Nicki also tapped into the lyrical and delivery styles of Missy Elliot, shifting voices to suit the appropriate persona rapping the rhymes. Furthermore, her unique sound and cunning lyricism could overshadow veterans; she dominated the Kanye West single "Monster" in 2010 that also featured Jay-Z and Rick Ross. In the video for the song we see the pink-haired Harajuku Barbie character rapping clever lines in her high-pitched voice while being brutally interrogated by Vampire Nicki, who raps viciously in a deeply guttural, Jamaican-accented voice:

> *Vampire Nicki:*
> *Pull up in the monster*
> *Automobile gangster*

With a bad bitch that came from Sri Lanka [M.I.A.]Yeah I'm in that Tonka,
color of Willy Wonka
You could be the King but watch the Queen conquer
Ok first things first I'll eat your brains
Then I'mma start rocking gold teeth and fangs
Cause that's what a muthaf-cking monster do
Hairdresser from Milan, that's the monster do
Monster Giuseppe heel that's the monster shoe
Young Money [Entertainment] is the roster and the monster crew
And I'm all up all up all up in the bank with the funny face
And if I'm fake I ain't notice cause my money ain't

Harajuku Barbie:
Let me get this straight wait I'm the rookie
But my features and my shows ten times your pay?
50k for a verse, no album out! (shifts voice back to Vampire Nicki)
Yeah my money's so tall that my Barbies gotta climb it
Hotter than a Middle Eastern climate. Violent.
Tony Matterhorn, "Dutty Wine it, wine it!"
Nicki on them titties when I sign it
How these n-ggas so one-track minded?

Harajuku Barbie:
But really, really I don't give a F-U-C-K
Forget Barbie. Fuck Nicki. She's fake.
She's on a diet but my pockets eating cheese cake (shifts voice back to
Vampire Nicki)
And I'll say bride of Chucky is child's play [reference to the horror film
franchise]
Just killed another career it's a mild day
Besides 'Ye, they can't stand besides me
I think me, you and Am [Amber Rose] should ménage Friday

Vampire Nicki:
Pink wig thick ass give 'em whip lash
I think big get cash make 'em blink fast
Now look at what you just saw I think this is what you live forAaaahhh, I'm
a muthafucking monster!

The song refers to her rising career (the fact that she is a celebrity in demand after releasing a complete album). gives her the opportunity to commemorate her Giuseppe Zanotti shoes in the same way Run-D.M.C. honored Adidas, and, of course, demonstrates the command she has for the verbal art form. It also allows her to play with the rumors about her bisexuality: being both King and Queen via her alter egos and the sexual liaison with Kanye West's girlfriend at time, Amber Rose.

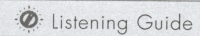 Listening Guide

Listening to Kanye West, Featuring Rick Ross, Jay-Z, Nicki Minaj, and Bon Iver

"MONSTER"

COMPOSED BY Jeff Bhasker, Kanye West, Onika Maraj, and William Roberts

PERFORMED BY Kanye West (vocals/producer), Rick Ross (vocals), Jay-Z (vocals), Nicki Minaj (vocals), Bon Iver (vocals), and Jeff Bhasker (piano)

PRODUCTION/MIXED BY Mike Dean

Appears on *My Beautiful Dark Twisted Fantasy*, 2010, Roc-A-Fella Records B0014695-02; peaked at no. 18 on *Billboard* Hot 100 and no. 15 on Rap Chart.

Kanye West's "Monster" is a summit of several of the biggest names in rap music of the 2000s: West, Rick Ross, and Jay-Z, along with an up-and-coming rapper who would go on to achieve superstardom, Nicki Minaj, and an alternative folk-rock artist, Bon Iver. The sonic and lyrical diversity of "Monster" reflect the variety of the talents of well-established, commercially successful artists present on the recording. It also introduced the mass rap market to Minaj, who steals the spotlight from the veterans. This track highlights the eclectic approaches that characterize West's output as a producer and MC.

The song is introduced by Bon Iver ghoulishly singing the opening lines, "I shoot the lights out," and continuing for the next 18 seconds entirely unaccompanied. Iver seems to be the most out-of-place artist in the "Monster" lineup, as he is predominantly known for alternative folk music that leans heavily on acoustic guitars, ambient soundscapes, and vocals that are higher-pitched, plaintive, and ethereal, rather than drum machines, samplers, and hardcore rap verses. Iver and West are mutual admirers, however, and share some similar approaches to production: the two artists both have a signature penchant for incorporating electronically altered sounds, particularly voices, into their music by using a variety of overdubbing and phase- and pitch-shifting techniques. This approach is apparent here as Iver's voice is overdubbed upon itself several times, with electronic distortion and pitch shifting added. These effects both give the timbre of his voice an electronic tinge and place it singing in unison with itself across a span of several octaves, some of which have an unnaturally full tone in what may otherwise be an uncomfortable singing range for a male voice. Bon Iver's heavily processed voice singing the introduction's winding minor-key melody also sets up the eerie feel that characterizes the rest of the song lyrically and musically.

The rapped portion of "Monster" begins with Rick Ross delivering a disproportionately short verse in his signature grisly, deep voice. Ross's short section is born from the lion's roar and the beginning of a busy, African-inspired, electronic tom drum pattern accentuated by his line, "As you run through my jungles all you hear is rumbles," which simultaneously references the toughness and greatness of Muhammad Ali (a revered rhyme master in his own right), his famous 1974 "Rumble in the Jungle" boxing match held in Zaire against George Foreman, and the 1990s electronic dance music genre called **jungle**. Ross discusses his prowess as an MC then quickly passes the mic to West after a mere 10 seconds. The first iteration of the song's chorus enters immediately after Ross finishes.

The chorus, rapped by West in an even-paced and vocally explosive manner, with strong consonants and emphatic enunciation, is heavily processed like the song's introduction. Distortion is added to his voice and its pitch is dramatically dropped on the lyric "I'm a m——f—— Monster," to create the effect of an unnaturally deep voice recalling a horror-film monster and resembling the sound of a record being manually slowed down.

Immediately after this chorus, West begins his first verse, his voice no longer electronically distorted but sounding with pristine studio clarity. West alters his flow to contrast with the chorus, boasting of his lyrical prowess in a sing-song, start-and-stop manner, accelerating at the beginning of lines and slowing in order to emphatically deliver his end-of-line rhymes, which he also leans into with vocal accents on the final words of phrases. West often delivers his boasts with surprising creativity—this verse contains an "interview" section in which he creates a conversation between a journalist (in a higher, more nasal voice) and himself (in his regular rap voice) as a commentary on his fame. West even manages to rhyme "sarcophagus" with "esophagus," before returning to the song's chorus.

Jay-Z enters during the second chorus, rapping a few key lines with West before launching into his own verse. Jay-Z, West's mentor, delivers his verse with his signature cool, quiet intensity. He touches on the themes implied by the song's title more frequently than anyone else on the track, mentioning a number of horror-movie monsters by name and drawing parallels between horror films and his trademark rhymes about hustling, fame, and fortune. Jay-Z describes those who try to take advantage of his success without achieving success in their own right as "vampires and bloodsuckers," complementing the song's title.

The song's final, and arguably strongest, verse is delivered by newcomer Nicki Minaj with the unparalleled viciousness of an unknown MC attempting to prove herself on an already star-studded track. While Minaj would soon become a pop-superstar rapper, her early-mixtape-era style surfaces periodically here. One of the key elements of Minaj's verse is her use of two different personas: a monstrous, vampiric persona with an explosive, deep guttural flow that often explodes into a curdled yell, and another "Harajuku Barbie"

Continued

Listening to Kanye West, Featuring Rick Ross, Jay-Z, Nicki Minaj, and Bon Iver **Continued**

persona that serves as a foil to "Vampire Nicki," complete with a high-pitched, sexy-baby voice. The first persona's sound is most often employed when she raps in Roman's voice, "Roman" being another recurrent character, a gay male youth she channels in her raps. Minaj's second persona, "Harajuku Barbie," is a character based on equal parts hyperfeminine, pop-culture style icons: the American Barbie doll and the Japanese sexy-schoolgirl anime character. Minaj tends to use this voice sarcastically in lines that reference her inexperience ("So let me get this straight—wait, I'm the rookie?"), and the listener can "hear" the stereotypical dumb blonde spitting clever rhymes. This Harajuku Barbie switches into Vampire Nicki seamlessly, without so much as a break in Minaj's voice. The implied Jekyll-and-Hyde-esque shift aurally highlights the song's horror-story themes and provides a snapshot of Minaj as two different rappers rolled into one—a creation of alter egos that became a trademark of her style. Minaj's creative rhymes and lyrical, acrobatic prowess make her stream-of-consciousness approach to this verse overwhelmingly convincing and arguably allow her to best the veteran MCs on the track.

Bon Iver returns after Minaj's verse, singing a new melody as the instrumental arrangement is slowly pared down toward the song's end. The lyrics that comprise this vocal **coda**, "I crossed the line and I'll let God decide . . .," are delivered with more gusto than Iver's introduction to "Monster" and have considerably more vocal ornamentation. Iver overdubs soul-influenced vocal runs to accentuate the lyrics, and a final, heavily ornamented "headed home" ends the song.

The soundscape of "Monster" is indicative of West's unique production approach, one that depends on his mastery of studio techniques and an unparalleled sensitivity to the ebb and flow of the various musicians' contributions to this track. The song also represents a trend emerging in the musical production of rap music and pop music at that time. "Monster" is not built around any musical samples from other source material. That is, every element of the song's groove and arrangement is original, created and programmed by West and Mike Dean in the studio. The only samples that are used are of screams: an individual voice and a roar that sounds like a crowd screaming. Both are likely "stock" sounds and cannot be easily traced to a single identifiable source. These samples are further obscured by the ways West chooses to utilize them. The crowd scream and single-voice samples are both played backwards when they appear. While this technique further obscures any connection they might have to an original commercial record or generic stock set of recordings, it also alludes to urban legend practices of youth in the 1970s and 1980s, called backmasking, in which listeners played vinyl records backward to hear hidden sinister messages allegedly connected to the occult. In addition to the backward-playback samples, West plays the Roland TR-808 kick drum backward during the song's coda, which creates a similar disorientation and further enhances the horror theme of the song.

The vast majority of the instrumental material on "Monster" was composed, performed, and arranged by West, with the exception of piano added by frequent collaborator Jeff Bhasker. Much of the instrumental arrangement incorporates two drum machines, one that is very forward in the mix and consists of kick, snare, and hi-hat sounds and a second, further back in the mix, that consists of a busy tom pattern reminiscent of jungle electronic dance music. This meta-genre draws on African musical and drumming influences but is also aligned to the rhythmic, exotic sound played as early as the 1920s by Duke Ellington's band, nicknamed the Jungle Band. Each of these patterns is manipulated intentionally to serve at times as the primary accompaniment and at others as punched-in accents. The rest of the arrangement consists of a number of programmed synthesizer sounds, including string stabs and a mellow, full, bouncing bass line. All of these elements appear periodically, although irregularly, throughout. At times the entire group of instruments plays simultaneously, while at other times only a single drum sound is heard. At times the instruments drop out to allow an MC to deliver a line unencumbered, while at others the instruments are gradually added to the arrangement, building a verse to a higher level of activity as the lyrics crescendo. The song's coda operates on the opposite principle: percussive elements leave as the song gradually becomes softer and less rhythmically active, and sustained synthesizer strings and piano enter with their gentler tones permeating the texture as the song gradually winds to a stop.

"Monster" is a meeting of several of 2010's best rappers at the top of their games and has a sonic eclecticism that matches its diverse roster. West pairs the talents of his various guests with a sensitive approach to production that highlights, line-by-line, his guests' strengths as rappers and serves to create the eerie, horror-influenced sonic atmosphere of "Monster."

| 0:00 | "I shoot the lights out . . ." | The song's introduction is sung by Bon Iver. His voice is processed with a number of electronic effects that create distortion and transpose his voice into several octaves. |
| 0:18 | | A human scream and lion's roar can be heard, transitioning into the song's main groove. |

Continued

☼ Listening Guide

Listening to Kanye West, Featuring Rick Ross, Jay-Z, Nicki Minaj, and Bon Iver Continued

0:21	"Bitch, I'm a monster . . ."	Rick Ross enters with his brief introductory verse. A full-sounding drum machine with kick, snare, and hi-hat sounds can be heard playing in the foreground, with an electronic tom drum sound programmed further back in the mix.
0:31	"Gossip, gossip, n——a just stop it . . ."	The song's chorus begins, rapped by Kanye West with studio-added effects distorting his voice. These vocals are altered further with a pitch-shifting effect on the line "I'm a m——f—— monster."
0:35	"I'ma need to see your . . ."	A disorienting, backward-played sample of what sounds like a crowd screaming enters.
0:41	"Drop it, drop it . . ."	The crowd-scream sample exits. Two synthesizers can be heard, both with mellow, round tones—one stabs rhythmically while the other plays a repeated, bouncing bass line. A distorted sample of a single voice enters, played backwards.
0:51	"Best livin' or dead . . ."	The chorus ends and West continues with his verse without vocal distortion. The soundscape otherwise remains the same.
1:01	"To another level, bitch . . ."	The crowd-scream sample is punched in. This occurs periodically throughout the rest of the song.
1:12	"I heard people sayin' . . ."	More layers are added to the drum machine part: the bass drum can be heard more clearly in the mix, and snare drum and hi-hat sounds are added.
1:29	"God damn, Yeezy . . ."	Kanye begins an "interview" with himself, alternating between a higher-pitched voice of an "interviewer" persona and his own medium-range rapping voice.
1:43	"Cause you will never . . ."	All the snare drum and hi-hat exit. Kick and tom rolls continue to be punched in at the ends of phrases.
1:53	"Now she claimin' that . . ."	The full drum machine arrangement returns.
2:01	"My presence is a present . . ."	Everything but the kick sound is absent when Kanye delivers this line.
2:03	"Gossip, gossip, n——a just stop it . . ."	The chorus returns.

2:23	"Sasquatch, Godzilla, King Kong . . ."	Jay-Z begins his verse, with only the electronic tom drum sounds present here.
2:31	"Everybody knows I'm a moth-erfuckin' monster . . ."	Jay-Z delivers this line a cappella (without instrumental accompaniment).
2:33	"Conquer, stomp ya . . ."	The verse soundscape returns, with full drum machine, synthe-sizers, and the backwards single-voice sample.
2:44	"Murder, murder, in black convertibles . . ."	Everything but the electronic tom drums and vocals drop out.
2:54	"Love . . . I don't get enough of it . . ."	Everything but Jay-Z's voice and the kick drum machine sound is absent.
3:02	"Millin' about, spillin' they feelin's . . ."	This phrase is entirely a cappella.
3:04	"All I see is these fake fucks . . ."	The full verse soundscape returns.
3:12	"Seems to be the only way . . ."	This line is a cappella. Immediately after, the roar sample is added again before the chorus.
3:15	"Gossip, gossip, n——a just stop it . . ."	The chorus returns.
3:35	"Pull up in a monster . . ."	Nicki Minaj begins the verse as her "Evil Nicki" persona. The electronic tom drum sounds and kick drum can be heard.
3:45	"First things first, I'll eat your brain . . ."	As Minaj continues, the snare drum and hi-hat sounds enter.
3:55	"Monster Giuseppe heel is the monster shoe . . ."	The snare and hi-hat exit, returning the drum machine pattern to the kick and electronic tom drum sounds.
4:05	"But my money ain't . . ."	This curdled yell signals the end of "Evil Nicki's" first section.
4:06	"So let me get this straight . . ."	Minaj's "Barbie" persona enters here; the kick drum and electronic tom drums continue.
4:12	"Fifty-K for a verse, no album out . . ."	Minaj switches personas mid-line, returning to her "Evil" voice.
4:16	"Hotter than a Middle Eastern climate . . ."	"Evil Nicki" continues as the bass, snare, and hi-hat groove returns.
4:26	"But really, really I don't give a F-U-C-K . . ."	"Barbie Nicki" returns and the soundscape continues.

Continued

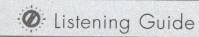

Listening Guide

Listening to Kanye West, Featuring Rick Ross, Jay-Z, Nicki Minaj, and Bon Iver **Continued**

4:31	"She on a diabolical . . ."	Minaj again switches personas mid-line. The synthesizer is now punched in at the beginning of each measure as she continues in her "Barbie Nicki" persona.
4:44	"Pink wig, dick, ass . . ."	Minaj switches back to "Evil Nicki." The entire soundscape is taken out except for the kick sound and echoed vocal phrases.
4:52	"I'm a motherfucking monster . . ."	Minaj screams, and delivers this line in a curdled voice; the roar sample can be heard again.
4:55		A musical interlude enters here; the drum machine kick, snare, and hi-hat, "electronic tom" drums, synthesizer, and backwards single-voice sample continue.
5:05		The interlude continues, and the synthesizer is taken out of the mix.
5:10		The bass, snare drums, and hi-hat exit; only the electronic tom drum sounds continue.
5:15	"I, I, cross the line . . ."	Bon Iver's distorted and pitch-altered vocals return with added soulful embellishments; electronic tom drums continue; kick, snare, and hi-hat sounds return.
5:35	"I, I, cross the line . . ."	Synthesized strings and a piano sound are added here.
5:41	"I let God decide . . ."	The bass, snare, and hi-hat sounds exit.
6:02	"I let God decide . . ."	Only a bass drum sound played backward, strings, and electric piano can be heard with these vocals as the song winds to a stop.

The range of rap acts that flourished in the new millennium represented a diversity and global representation not witnessed since the golden era in the latter days of the 1980s. Much of the thematic core—even to the present—of rap music has been a discourse of life in the "hood," in particular, stories about survival or empowerment entrenched in the concrete jungle of America's ghettos. Hip hop artists that strayed from or resisted this narrative structure were often regarded as fakes and, therefore, not "keepin' it real." However, with the work of the new-millennium rappers, "keepin' it real" could once again include experiences that were not exclusively urban, male, or even American. Furthermore, consumers were rummaging around the Internet for unsigned acts, especially targeting social networking sites like MySpace, Facebook, and YouTube. As a result, artists did not have to rely on major labels and corporate record executives to produce or distribute their music. In fact, the advent of the MP3, laptop-friendly music-production applications, and a username on a social networking website could make any wannabe rapper-producer into a *real* rapper and producer.

Hip Hop Futurism

Hip hop aficionados have always embraced advances in technology. While purists still yearn for the flexibility they had with vinyl (and with good reason), by the mid-'90s many DJ-producers were putting their turntables on the shelf and exploring the future possibilities that laptop technology offered. While CDs were easily duplicated, the advent of a universal compression file format, the MP3, allowed music fans to compress audio from CDs and share files on the Internet, both legally and illegally on peer-to-peer sites such as Napster. By the mid-2000s, CD sales were dropping in favor of MP3 sales. The rise of digital music files enabled users to store hundreds of songs and small videos while also giving them the option to organize and construct their own mixtapes on a device that was no larger than a couple of sticks of chewing gum.

Such portable players also revolutionized the way consumers listened to music. Inexpensive earplugs (or headphones, to a lesser degree) replaced boom box speakers so that listening became an intimate, personal act. Apple was definitely on the vanguard of this new technology when it created its iTunes store in 2003. Users could now purchase individual songs from an album as opposed to an entire album for as little as $0.99 per song, which returned music consumers to the bygone days of the 45 rpm single; however, it also deterred fans from listening to an artist's concept album from beginning to end (think Dr. Dre's *The Chronic* or Lauryn Hill's *The Miseducation of Lauryn Hill*). According to Reebee Garafalo, more than 95 percent of digital audio consumers downloaded individual tracks rather than complete albums in 2006 (Garafalo 367). By 2010, retail outlets like Tower Records had closed all their stores and the only genre of music still making profits in CD sales was country music.

Record companies had to change their operations in order to survive, in terms of music product distribution and music publishing and abandoning the old model of music manufacturing. They also had a new competitor in the market to contend with: the tech-savvy music consumer. Along with these emerging modes of purchasing music, owning digital audio files, a laptop computer, and good-quality music software could transform the casual music listener into a novice DJ-producer, mixing and remixing his or her own **mashups**. Furthermore, the Internet's free-of-charge, social networking websites allowed music fans to share their creations without having to register, pay for, and maintain a website domain. In the early 2000s, MySpace.com, for example, became the source for fans to learn about new artists and new trends; that is, they were not relying on the radio, music television, or industry magazines to direct their attention.

Free, interactive networking sites, which dominated the DIY music scene from 2003 to 2010, were used by millions for self-promotion and retail of homemade mixtapes and videos. Similar sites like Facebook and YouTube allowed users to create social environments with "virtual" friends, fans, and followers to share digital media, to blog, and to collect visitors' comments or critiques. Despite all the access to create and distribute music without the help of the major labels, digging through all of this material has become more difficult. Hip hop freestyle enthusiasts can release one or more tracks a day, but without the skill or effort to self-edit. So Internet fans hunt and hunt before hitting something memorable or pleasant to listen to all the way through, let alone repeatedly.

By the end of the decade record executives were trolling through these sites in pursuit of new artists and viral video entrepreneurs. For example, in 2004, 16-year-old DeAndre Way, better known as Soulja Boy Tell 'Em, self-published his song "Crank Dat (Soulja Boy)" along with a video teaching YouTube viewers to do his signature "Crank Dat" dance. The video went viral, partly as a result of the Crank Dat dance craze and a rumor about the true meaning behind the lyrics "Superman Dat (OH!)" (recast as "Superman dat ho"). The rapper denied any sexual subtext to the lyrics. Interscope Records signed the teen sensation to record a full-length album, *iSouljaBoyTellem*, in 2008, playing with Apple's domination of pop-cultural sensibilities in the title. The Interscope recording of "Crank Dat (Soulja Boy)" (2007) managed to reach number one on the *Billboard* charts and still make this major label lots of money despite the fact it could be downloaded for free on the Internet.

In a strikingly short period of time, the rules dictated by the music industry for years were rendered obsolete by tech-savvy younger music fans. The emergence of indie rappers, the Internet, and DIY ingenuity have transformed the ways we conceive of musicianship and music distribution.

CHAPTER SUMMARY

This chapter summarizes the changes in the rap world over the last two decades. It begins with the rise of underground hip hop as a reaction to the popularity of gangsta rap. New styles developed in different regions of the country, most notably the southern United States, that challenged the domination of ghetto-themed, misogynistic, and violent rappers who had topped the pop charts in the late '90s/early '00s. Out of these many scenes came a group of new rap stars known as the young millennials. They espoused a wider vision of authenticity, including the concerns of suburban and middle-class blacks along with people of color from around the world. While Kanye West came solidly out of a middle-class background, his music was accepted even by the inner-city core audience for rap. Young stars like Nicki Minaj represented a new generation of empowered female rappers who embraced their rich ethnic identities.

STUDY QUESTIONS

1. Which cities can be considered epicenters of southern hip hop style?

2. B. Hall, co-founder of the Good Life Café and the hip hop open mic, which ran from 1989 to 1992, had four basic rules that mirrored Kool Herc's strategies for social control, entertainment, and competition. What were those rules and how might they have guided the rappers' performances?

3. In this chapter, we discussed a couple of regional hip hop scenes that opposed the lyrical content and soundscape of gangsta rap and pop rap of the 1990s and provided new blueprint for fans and future artist to follow. Identify the sites and groups that provided us with the blueprints of "underground" rap styles and their roles in hip hop between 2000 and 2010.

4. What role does "keepin' it real" play in the music or in the lives of the artists after 2000?

KEY TERMS

Backpacker	Cocaine rap	Jungle
Bounce music	Coda	Mashup
Chopped and screwed	Crunk	Nerdcore
Choppin' it up and stylin'	Crunk & B	Snap music
	Dirty South	Underground hip hop

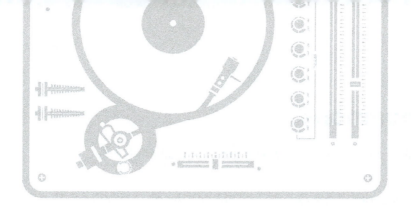

CONCLUSION

Learning Objectives

When you have successfully completed this chapter, you will be able to:

- Show how hip hop pioneers "branded" their styles to set their work apart from other creators.
- Understand processes of descent, dissent, and affinity in the development of hip hop.
- Describe how the term "hip hop" has been applied to different artistic expressions over the decades.
- Understand how hip hop has become a translocal and transnational phenomenon.

What Is Hip Hop? Round Two

Hip hop is approaching its half-century mark and has gripped American culture and spread throughout the world, influencing all types of expression well beyond just popular music. Therefore, let us begin this last chapter asking the same question that we posed in Chapter 1: What is hip hop?

Throughout this text, we mapped specific styles of rap music, largely rooted in a particular location and fostered by a community of young and creative artists. Originally, these artists worked in four distinct folk-art forms: graffiti, breakin', DJing, and MCing. The audience played a key role in the creation of this art: the interaction between artist and audience was central to hip hop's performance. We traced the roots of hip hop culture to the aesthetic values born from both the African and African American diasporas.

As music became hip hop's focal point, we examined the first "brands" of hip hop music created by a series of Bronx-based artists. We began with b-beat by Kool

Herc as it showcased his signature "merry-go-round technique" (see Chapter 3) of breakbeat juggling. We then looked at the turntablist artistry of Grandmaster Flash and his "clock theory," transforming the turntable into a multifaceted rhythmic and melody-making instrument. Then we moved to another brand of hip hop music, Afrika Bambaataa's electro-funk, which incorporated keyboards and drum machines into the sound collages he created with the turntables.

Branding one's own style became more complicated when the Bronx subculture was appropriated by other New Yorkers and then spread to almost every corner of the world after the commercial release of "Rapper's Delight." The brands became subordinated by an umbrella term, "rap music," created to neatly characterize this new recitative lyrical art form performed atop familiar, studio-recorded music. Almost immediately, the other three elements of this young subculture were separated from rap music, and musical elements such as mixing multiple beats, toasting, party chants, and sung elements became definitively not rap music. The community from the South Bronx where it all began got lost in the shuffle as the small, interactive audience transformed into a large, passive audience consuming the mass-produced commodities offered by the rap music industry. In the 30-plus years after the first commercial recordings, new rap communities formed all over the country and debates between those community members arose. Some made distinctions between rap music and hip hop that usually did not include dance, painting—or DJing, for that matter. Claims were made—and continue to be—that *real* hip hop is conscious, or *real* hip hop is not commercial, or *real* hip hop is gangsta, or *real* hip hop is African American . . . and so on. That bygone community's framework is re-established and revised as the hip hop community has grown to be not only translocal but transnational as well.

The ethnomusicologist Kay Kaufman Shelemay, in an article titled "Musical Communities: Rethinking the Collective in Music" (2011), described how the processes of descent, dissent, and affinity affect musical communities. Processes of **descent** dominate traditional ideas (if not ideals) about a musical community. Members are united in shared identities that may be based on historical or negotiated fact, or on a number of categories that often converge and overlap; for example, the earliest MCing descent community emerged from processes informed by African-diasporic heritage and the experiences of the urban poor in New York City. **Dissent** is the reaction of following generations of artists to earlier aesthetic rules (such as the underground rap movement of the late '90s reacting against gangsta rap, as we explored in Chapter 9). **Affinity** refers to the attraction of different listeners and performers to a musical style based on individual preferences and a strong desire for social association with others equally invested in and enamored of the music scene, regardless of ethnicity, age, or gender. Ultimately, every descent community will become re-established as a community of dissent; the aficionados of rap music and hip hop culture are no exception. The term "hip hop community" continues to be shaped by a multitude of musical cultures, and those collectivities perpetually unsettle the notion of it being a static sonic marker of social groupings. Hip hop of yore was never a singular music style, and the same applies to the contemporary world. Today's fans and creators often use the term "hip hop" to describe everything from the crooning pop ballads by Usher, Rihanna, or Frank Ocean to the thug raps of Rick Ross or Waka Flocka Flame.

In addition, we have to include the international, or transnational, hip hop productions and hybridized brands such as hiplife in Ghana, Nederhop in the Netherlands, or J-rap in Japan. Examples from across the globe swing along a continuum of contemporary American hip hop style performed in other languages to hybridized forms incorporating elements from other cultures to replace or to add to the American ones. The wide-ranging examples indicate the involvement of American—African American and African diasporic—cultural contributions in a variety of critical, stylistic, and often politically postcolonial discourses significant and relevant to their local audiences. Transnational considerations of hip hop culture's foundation push us to both refigure American music and reimagine the aesthetic geographies of the United States, as well as the nation-based intellectual and artistic geographies of the countries that are reproducing it. What can we learn from these newer artistic and intellectual formations in their attempt to stay within the parameters of the United States "hip hop tradition" while appealing to the particularities that make their hip hop graffiti, dance, and music their own?

Like the ever-expanding ripples across water when we drop a pebble into it, all things hip hop have grown out from its epicenter and disseminated from each emerging hip hop collective, broadening its impact and morphing into a plethora of soundscapes, dance styles, and expressive art forms. The intent of a survey book like this is to explore that growth, but it still has several limitations. Of course the chapters in this volume synthesize a great deal of information about the historical, cultural, and sociological meanings of many of the central figures, styles (or brands), events, and sources that structure the culture of hip hop. However, by no means is this book meant to be encyclopedic. Its primary purpose is to provide a broad overview as the culture came to be so that the student of hip hop can address the more challenging issues about hip hop culture, popular music, media studies, youth behavior, race and class, and politics. The next step is to critique culture.

Students of hip hop can address current issues and debates and go beyond formulating an opinion based on emotion or text only. Rather, they can draw on the hip hop culture's

Rick Rose, 2012.
Source: © Randy Miramontez/Alamy

history to analyze the latest artistic expressions and how they fit in contemporary society. For example, when confronted with a controversial song like Rocko's "U.O.E.N.O" (a euphemism to express "You ain't even know"), the informed listener can more fully analyze the 2013 hit with its musical production by Atlanta-based producer Childish Major. The listener can pick up on the southern style's minimalistic approach, which can be traced to the circuitous structure of Miami Bass of the 1980s, the dropped-tempo style of Houston's screwed music of the late 1990s/early 2000s, and the hypnotic, futuristic element, chillwave or cloud rap—two very similar dreamy, ambient directions hip hop music productions developed in the 2010s.

However, it was Rick Ross's lyrical contribution that made the recording controversial, reviving the controversial depiction of male domination of women, who are treated as passive sexual objects. In the lyric, Ross boasts of using a date-rape drug (Molly, a form of ecstasy) to bed an unsuspecting sexual partner: "Put Molly all in her champagne, she ain't even know it/I took her home and I enjoyed that, she ain't even know it." Lyrically, Ross draws on the signifying and ritual insult traditions in the canon of African American verbal lore. As we have seen, such bawdy street traditions were defended by Professor Henry Louis Gates Jr. in his First Amendment support for the off-color, overtly sexist rhymes of 2 Live Crew in 1990 (see Chapter 8). In a *New York Times* op-ed piece, "2 Live Crew Decoded," and in his testimony at 2 Live Crew's criminal trial, Gates articulated the brilliant ways in which 2 Live Crew and other rappers were engaged in "sexual carnivalesque"—reflecting the most exaggerated images and comically extravagant tales about black sexuality in racist America's consciousness.

Comparing the two situations, we could argue that Ross was similarly comically inflating a cliché about black sexuality. But what about the much broader currents of misogyny? In the 1990s, law professor Kimberlé Crenshaw was quick to remind Gates that minority women live at the intersection of racial and sexual subordination. She observed that in the song "Put Her in the Buck," male sexual satisfaction is aligned with pain and humiliation for the female partner. The rapper boasts that the male objective is "to abuse it . . . to bust the wall . . . to "break [her] backbone . . . slay you, rough and painful, . . ." make her "lick my ass up and down, Lick it till [her] tongue turns doodoo brown."

While another obscenity prosecution would be wrongheaded, it is important for the student to think critically about what he or she is listening to and how Ross's rhymes do, in fact, address a common date-rape argument; since rape has been defined as "forcible" (up until 2012 when the FBI changed its definition by removing that word), one cannot "rape" an unconscious person. Rick Ross proclaimed that he never used the word "rape," does not condone rape, and reached out to all his female fans to explain his meaning.

In the previous generation, a debate like this would have been largely left to the scholarly community. However, in this age of instantaneous, worldwide communication, hip hop fans and others can speak out, protest, and take action in ways that hold artists accountable. The results for Ross were immediate; having previously signed a promotion deal with the sneaker maker Reebok, Ross was quickly dropped by the firm as a result of the mobilization of protest groups like the online community UltraViolet, which collected about 100,000 signatures on an online document that threatened to boycott Reebok and protest at the company's Boston headquarters. In less than a month, on April 4, 2013, Reebok dropped its advertisements with Rick Ross and any further support of the artist. The lyrics have also been removed from the song but remain in circulation in rap lyric and video-archiving websites.

How is this different than the censorship of Ice-T's "Cop Killer" in 1992 by his record label, Warner Bros.? In the earlier case, a commercial corporation was responding to the misunderstanding of a lyric coming from conservative forces in the country. In trying to avoid controversy and bolster its profits, the label blocked an artist's ability to express himself. In this case, the outrage came from within the audience for the music itself. The music was not censored entirely; as we've noted, you can still find versions of this song on the web containing the offensive material. Ross's loss of a commercial endorsement deal with Reebok did not silence the rapper in the same way as if his commercial record label had dropped him or removed the song from circulation.

A similar outcry occurred when Lil Wayne appeared on Future's "Karate Chop" remix in 2013. Wayne recited lyrics comparing his treatment of the sex organ of his partner to the beaten teenaged body of Emmett Till, who purportedly flirted with a white woman in 1950s Mississippi: "Beat that pussy up like Emmett Till." Representatives of Lil Wayne claimed that those lyrics were never meant to appear on the final cut, and that an overanxious director prereleased the video on Vimeo.com before that line was removed. The backlash, in any case, was impressive; Epic Records removed the lyric from the commercially released version of the song, and PepsiCo withdrew Wayne's endorsement deal with Mountain Dew.

These two examples of modern rap music's relation to the hip hop community could be compared to a phenomenon called **participatory culture** in the early 1990s by media scholar Henry Jenkins. Participatory culture promotes the ways fans can be actively engaged beyond the consumption of popular culture: they can participate, perhaps by way of "textual poaching," in creating or inventing anew the work of an original author, democratizing something that might be perceived as corporate owned as opposed to owned by the people. While, in these particular examples, "the community" did not help in the composition of either song, it was integral to the editing process of a final draft. Media fans, Jenkins tells us, are "popular critics," the "true experts," whose close attention to the particularity of their collective's art forms can match academic critics (1992: 86).

Participatory culture didn't begin or end with the Internet; in fact, it has been a part of hip hop culture since day one: in the early days of the flourishing folk culture when DJs began juggling beats to create sound collages to match the ways the dancers were responding to the music or the MCs called out to the audience or put together clever rhymes and only succeeded based on the responses of the audience members. This exchange constructed an art form that conformed to the values and tastes of the community. The digital age reinvigorates that access to the performers (and corporations), encouraging the powers that produce hip hop to listen to the hip hop "community." Community members' blogging, tweets, and online protest have in some ways helped the artist "refine" the work or, at a minimum, address the concerns and values of the community. Yes, hip hop is a mass-cultural phenomenon that has indeed lost its sense of intimacy, irreproducible in the way it existed in its original community in the

South Bronx. However, the ethic that influenced artists back in the day holds them responsible in this reformed method of communicability.

Will participatory culture and listeners' reactions to rap lyrics, in effect, change the attitudes of hardcore rappers to resist the urge to write misogynistic, homophobic, or other offensive rhymes? That is yet to be seen. However, attitudinal changes are apparent with both established and up-and-coming rap artists. For example, Jay-Z (*Rolling Stone*, May 15, 2012) and T.I. (*RapFix Live*, May 16, 2012) publicly denounced homophobia, and T.I. came out in support of President Obama's stance on gay marriage in 2012. On the same day the Supreme Court ruled against California's ban on same-sex marriage and struck down the federal Defense of Marriage Act, Macklemore and Ryan Lewis's song "Same Love"—a song that promotes gay marriage—rose to number 28 on the *Billboard* Hot 100 chart and number 5 on the Rap Songs chart. Even the outlandishly offensive rhyme tricksters of Odd Future, a hip hop collective, who had previously kept their R&B colleague Frank Ocean's sexuality to themselves, supported him when he revealed his same-sex love experience in a Tumblr message and also suggested it on several songs on his album *Channel Orange*. Prior to Ocean's revelation, Odd Future had an openly lesbian producer and DJ, Syd tha Kyd. Odd Future member Tyler, the Creator offered support on Twitter: "My Big Brother Finally Fucking Did That. Proud Of That Nigga Cause I Know That Shit Is Difficult Or Whatever. Anyway. I'm A Toilet" (July 4, 2012). Of course, that has not stopped Tyler, the Creator from dropping homophobic epithets in his rhymes.

As we close this chapter and hip hop has already celebrated its 40th anniversary, Amiri Baraka's notion of tradition as the changing same remains especially relevant. The millennial youth creating hip hop music and culture have flipped the script, self-publishing their work on the web (see Chapter 9). No longer do the artists have to submit demos or pander to the commercial exploits of the major recording companies. Up-and-coming as well as established artists release their new sounds on digital mixtapes to the fans at will. Internet fandom has built a community that is international; a "space" for hip hop matters more than a "place" of hip hop. For example, A$AP Rocky, New York born and raised, has completely appropriated Houston's brand of hip hop music and the corresponding purple-drink drug culture as his own. Representing one's own place matters little; Drake's Canadian heritage or Nicki Minaj's Trinidadian origins rarely if ever are mentioned. It has not been the objective for these

A$AP Rocky, 2013.
Source: © Igor Vidyashev/ZUMAPRESS.Com/Alamy

Azealia Banks onstage at the Coachella Music & Arts Festival, 2012.

Source: © Jason Moo/ZUMA Press, Inc./Alamy

younger artists to put their 'hood on the hip hop map. Sites of hip hop culture, like virtual space, are becoming post-place-centric—perhaps even post-race-centered—or, at least, it is trying to be.

By the age of 40, Eminem has become a granddaddy of the rap tradition and a mentor to the current generation of rappers, legitimizing white participation in rap while neutralizing the memory of Vanilla Ice. His earlier sociopathic persona serves as a reference point for the sardonically absurd and outrageous rhymes of Earl Sweatshirt or Tyler, the Creator. Furthermore, his acknowledgement of his status—receiving privilege for performing a black music form—opened the doors for white rappers adopting this music as belonging to a new generation, across race, class, and ethnic lines. Examples include indie rapper Mac Miller, whose first album, *Blue Slide Park* (2011), debuted at number one on the *Billboard* 200; and Macklemore and Ryan Lewis, whose 2013 hit "Thrift Shop" reached number one on the *Billboard* chart.

While the consumer of hip hop music embraced these artists, the ebb and flow of this changing same has given us even younger, fresher artists contesting this displacement of hip hop's hood origin tales. Take for instance the Chicago-based controversial, extremely violent and despondent stories of Chief Keef, whose viral videos landed him a rumored multi-million-dollar recording contract at the age of 16. While he may have garnered a global audience with the Internet, his popularity was fueled by a committed, local fan base in the Chicago Public Schools. As frightening as his narratives might be, Keef reminds us of the current hyperviolence that Chicago's black and Latino youth encounter in their teen years. We also have the conscious writing of Kendrick Lamar, who in the fall of 2012 released his homage to Compton, made famous by N.W.A., revealing that its nightmarish living conditions of the 1980s have not changed. The gritty, visceral reality raps on "Compton" (featuring Compton legend Dr. Dre) and "m.A.A.d city" (featuring Compton's MC Eiht)—richly self-reflexive and ardently critical of the culture around him—are balanced with musical accompaniment and sonic collages that produce eerie images of living in the same ghettos, but 24 years later. Finally, we should also take Azealia Banks into consideration for putting New York City proper back on the hip hop map by commemorating her celebrated Manhattan area code in 2012 with her song "212." Perhaps in the 2020s, in our post-post world, hip hop will once again remind us of the importance of the local—that place and race still matter.

CHAPTER SUMMARY

In these last few pages, we revisited our first question, how do we define hip hop? It is a term that continues to be used so pervasively that it sometimes appears to mean everything and be applied to anything, and as a result is almost rendered meaningless. Not everything is hip hop; but at the same time, we cannot ignore that this very vibrant culture has grown over several generations since its inception in the early 1970s. Affinity with the hip hop arts has proven to be a catalyst to give its members worldwide a sense of belonging to something very real. That is, it connects an individual to others engaged with hip hop musical styles and other artistic expressions so that the individual feels part of a family of like-minded lovers of hip hop, in a way that rock-and-roll has not in a very long time. The 10 chapters in this book are hopefully a gateway for the reader to investigate further, to ask questions, to feel anything but sated, and to think critically about hip hop culture in all its facets.

KEY TERMS

Affinity (process of)

Descent (process of)

Dissent (process of)

Participatory culture

GLOSSARY

acid jazz: Around 1987, in the United Kingdom, club **DJ**s began playing jazz as well as funk and hip hop and called it "aceed" or acid jazz.

affinity: Affinity describes how a community of performers and fans are attracted to the same style of music. Individuals are drawn to a musical style as a way of participating in a larger community that does not necessarily correspond to their national or ethnic identities. This term was developed by the ethnomusicologist Kay Kaufman Shelemay in her attempt to clarify musical collectivities through processes of **descent**, **dissent**, and affinity.

Afrocentric: In hip hop, a style and philosophy centered on or derived from the idea of African heritage. Afrocentric artists identify Africa as the source for black aesthetics, ideals, practices, and social order. They express their African heritage through beats, lyrics, dress, and images. Artists in this style include Jungle Brothers, A Tribe Called Quest, Queen Latifah, De La Soul, and X Clan.

antiphony: *See* **call and response**.

arpeggiate: To play (a chord) as a series of ascending or descending notes.

b-beat music: Musical style created by DJ Kool Herc and his crew. The music was designed to accompany **breakin'**, or b-boying/b-girling dance styles.

b-boys and b-girls: The first generation of hip hop; dancers (breakers), graffiti artists, local kids from the neighborhood; sometimes used synonymously with "breakers."

b-boying or **b-girling:** *See* **breaking**.

baadman/baadwoman: An "outlaw" figure in folk narrative. A bad man might resort to acts of violence, but he could also be understood as a character who is getting things accomplished within an unjust social system; that is, in the case of African American toasts, he overcomes obstacles in an America that observes institutionalized racism and supports discrimination and segregation. Arguably, there are "baad woman" characters as well, such as Annie Christmas, Hurricane Annie, and Wicked Nell.

baby scratch: The basic DJ scratch form; moving the record back and forth continuously while the **cross-fader** is in the open position.

backpacker: A hip hop fan connected with the post-'90s, new-millennium alternative or underground rap scene. "Backpacker" was a term used to identify young hip hop enthusiasts who were looking for an alternative expression that was not gangsta, not materialistic (in terms of lyrics perhaps more so than practice), and devoted to raising consciousness in the community. The earliest participants in the subculture were committed to anticommercialism and antimaterialism, so much so that it earned them a reputation for being complainers and nerds. The backpack itself symbolized a kind of hobo-chic along with their aversion to baggy pants and excessive bling.

backspin/backspinning: A **DJ** technique credited to Grandmaster Flash, who originally called it **quick mix theory**. The DJ stops the record with his or her hand and reverses its direction to replay that portion of the record. The more you backspin, the more you destroy that part of the record; slick slipmats were added later to help soften and smooth the transition and preserve the records longer. DJs also redefined the uses of two different kinds of styluses: an elliptical stylus that stayed on the groove of the record, and a conical stylus that was shaped more like a nail and worked best for scratching.

bad man/bad woman: *See* **baadman/baadwoman**.

beatbox: A programmable drum machine that plays digital samples. *See also* **human beatbox**.

beatboxing: A vocal percussion; rhythmic phrasing and imitation of rhythm instruments, especially the drum machine; also called the human beatbox. Doug E. Fresh was a pioneer of this style. **The human beatbox** also became the trademark of the comic hip hop group the Fat Boys.

beat-juggling: Creating a new rhythmical composition by using two records and manipulating the arrangement of the elements (drum sounds, headnotes, etc.).

black: Refers to people of the African diaspora (e.g., African Americans, Jamaicans, Cubans), who share a heritage dominantly from the western, central, or southern regions of Africa.

black feminism: White middle-class, feminist activists had racial and class blind spots and would or could not address the social inequality experienced by African American women. Black feminism makes an effort to address racial identity in conjunction with gender inequality and responds to a feminism that is read by black women to mean "white feminism." *See also* **womanism**.

Black Power movement: The Black Power movement was inspired by the philosophy of black nationalism, which advocated self-sufficiency, self-control, and full participation in the decision-making process on issues affecting the lives of black people. These issues include political participation, economic empowerment, local school governance, and community control. The Black Power movement was spearheaded by the teachings of the Nation of Islam, Malcolm X, and Stokely Carmichael (of the Black Panthers), all of whom promoted the concepts of black pride, self-awareness, self-control, and national black unity. The Black Power movement sought to unify all blacks from southern and northern regions through a shared philosophy.

blaxploitation: A film genre popular in the early 1970s, made with black performers and aimed at a black audience. These low-budget films typically glorify black criminals and portray blacks as pimps, pushers, prostitutes, and gangsters. The films and their stock characters achieved cult status in the black community. Films include *Shaft*, *Foxy Brown*, *Super Fly*, and *Dolemite*.

bomb: A term used by graffiti writers: to write on or cover as many subway lines as possible.

boasting: An African American verbal art genre in which the performer praises or brags about personal attributes, material possessions, and verbal and technical skills. Boasting is a subcategory of storytelling and is related to **toasting**.

bounce music: A southern style of rap music that incorporates New Orleans parade-strutting beats with the hip hop aesthetic. The word "bounce" appears often in the lyrics and describes the energetic feel of the music.

break (breakdown): The most percussive or rhythmically complex section of a song. Popular with the dancers at Kool Herc's early parties and the inspiration for the development of **b-beat music** and b-boying, or **breaking**.

breakdancing: An industry term that came into use when West Coast funk dance styles blurred into the New York dance traditions and became popularized in theatrical film and music video productions in the mid-'80s, especially through the films *Breakin'* (1984) and *Breakin' 2: Electric Boogaloo* (1984). Many **b-boys** and **b-girls** reject the term and prefer **breaking** or b-boying.

breaking (breakin', b-boying or b-girling): A hip hop dance style developed by Caribbean, African American, and Latino youth dancing to Kool Herc's b-beat music. Much of the dance was adapted from James Brown's slides and good-footin', spins, Brooklyn uprocking, the Lindy Hop, tap dance, funk dance moves from the West Coast, etc., and linked together into a medley labeled "breaking" or "b-boying." Crews emerged (many from the urban gang culture), challenging other dancers to meet on the school ground, subway platform, or street corner, armed only with cardboard. It is a stylized form of combat through dance. **Breakdancing** is an industry term often rejected by the kids who invented the form. Kool Herc coined the term.

call and response: The verbal or nonverbal alternation between a leader and participatory audience. Also known as call-response and antiphony.

capoeira: A fight-like dance or dance-like fight created by enslaved Africans in Brazil that mixes elements of martial arts, dance, folklore, sport, ritual, and training for unarmed fighting.

chirp: An advanced **scratch** technique. Unlike other scratch techniques, this one begins with the cross-fader in the open position. As soon as the music begins, the record is pushed forward with the scratching hand by the **DJ**, who simultaneously closes the cross-fader with the other hand, then **backspins** with the scratch hand while quickly opening the cross-fader. The symmetrical pattern produces bird-like chirps.

chopped and screwed: A southern style of rap music from Houston, Texas. Originally, screwed music was named in honor of the late **DJ** Screw, who pioneered this hazy, sleepy groove in the early 1990s. The slower tempo defines the "screwed" portion, while the cuts, scratches, pauses, and rewinds that accompany these slowed-down mixes make up the "chopped."

choppin' up and stylin': An MCing term coined by the underground scenesters at the Good Life Café in Los Angeles in the 1990s. Choppin' it up is when the MC crunches sentences together faster than normal to break up the rhythm.

cipha (cipher): The ring formed by players of the dozens, **MCs** and **b-boys**. Oftentimes, combat takes place inside the ring.

clock theory: Developed by Grandmaster Flash to find the break of a recorded song quickly by eye on a vinyl record. The **DJ** makes a mark on the label with Magic Marker, sticky tape, or crayon so he or she knows exactly where the sound begins (the markings resemble the minute marks on clock). The DJ places the needles of two turntables down on the same break sections on two copies of a vinyl record. While one break is ending, the DJ pushes up the fade on the other, then spins the other record on the first turntable back one or two revolutions to the top of that break. When the second record's break is over, the DJ pushes on the first record's break section without pulling the needle off the record. Repeat. *See* **punch-phrasing**.

cocaine rap: A southern neo-gangsta rap style that focused on the drug trade in the 2000s, in particular cocaine and Miami as the port of entry for South American narcotics.

coda: The concluding section of a piece or movement in a song that often includes an embellishment or addition to the basic structure.

crew (posse): The entire group (**MC**/rappers, **DJ**, **b-boys**) creating a hip hop performance. Originally grouped around the DJ, the crew/posse later became associated with the MC/rapper, who took over the leadership position.

cross-fader: A transitional slide control on a **DJ** mixer for fading in one input channel while fading out another.

crossover hip hop: A broadening of the popular appeal of an artist (as a musician) or an artist's work that is often the result of a change in the artist's style.

crunk: A southern rap music style from Memphis and Atlanta. It is a high-energy club music characterized by gritty, hoarse chants and antiphonic, repetitive refrains that emerged in the late '90s. The term has been said to combine the words "crazy" and "drunk" or "chronic" and "drunk."

Crunk & B: A southern rap music style from Memphis and Atlanta in the mid-2000s that married **crunk** with **R&B**.

dancehall music: A Jamaican dance music with a hard-driving beat played through heavy bass speakers.

descent: Common cultural or historical background shared by members of a musical community. A term developed by the ethnomusicologist Kay Kaufman Shelemay in her attempt to clarify musical collectivities through processes of descent, **dissent**, and **affinity**.

diaspora: The breaking up and scattering of a people who had to settle far from their ancestral homeland.

digging the crates: Before the age of CDs and MP3s, the **DJ** relied on vinyl records to create a danceable sound collage. The records were often stored in wooden or plastic milk crates. To "dig the crates" refers to party DJs' pursuit of perfect beats on vinyl records in their own crates or new records in the crates at record vending establishments.

Dirty South: This term was used as a way of breaking the bicoastal orientation of the market, but it was less successful in encapsulating a region as large as the South within a single production style. A soundscape that includes fast, bouncy, non-**G-funk** beats and harsh lyrics illustrates some of the practices that many southern artists follow. The term was drawn from Goodie Mob's song "Dirty South," from their 1995 debut album *Soul Food*.

dis (diss): The act of showing disrespect to rival gang members or, in rap music, to a rival or established artist.

disco: A popular dance music during the late 1970s named after *discothèques*, which were dance clubs that played prerecorded music. Sound features include orchestral instruments, a heavy rhythm section, Latin percussion, synthesizers, and lyrics centered on dancing, romance, and partying.

dis rap (answer rap, response rap, diss rap)**:** A style of rap music that has its roots in battle culture and ritual dueling. Dis rap created a new model for unknown rappers to lyrically challenge established rap musicians or artists, discrediting their work in an **MC**-type battle in the recording studio. *See also* **gender duels**.

dissent: **Dissent** is the reaction of new artists to earlier aesthetic rules, such as the underground rap movement of the late '90s reacting against gangsta rap; for example, the Freestyle Fellowship and the MCs that participated in open mic night at the Good Life Café. This term was developed by the ethnomusicologist Kay Kaufman Shelemay in her attempt to clarify musical collectivities through processes of **descent, dissent,** and **affinity.**

distortion: The electronic manipulation of a sound source to change its tonality, usually by adding noise to a signal. Sly Stone was the first to employ devices to alter the spoken and sung voices and guitars in funk music; see, for example, Sly Stone's "Sex Machine."

DJ: Literally, disc jockey. However, the DJ tradition in hip hop began at live sound system dances in the South Bronx, New York, following the Jamaican tradition (thanks in part to native Jamaican Kool Herc). Eventually it led to toasts being recited while a disc or discs played. Major innovations by Grand Wizard Theodore, Grandmaster Flash, and Afrika Bambaataa led to **turntablism**, which is the art of manipulating sounds with a turntable and a mixer.

domestication process: This process more specifically refers to a *slave-domestication process* practiced in the colonial Americas up until emancipation. Veteran slaves or white overseers trained the new arrivals from Africa to adapt to their new circumstances. Despite the severe repression and violent enforcement to assimilate European cultural traditions, slaves maintained and creatively transformed their African heritage in these new territories. Their cultural values and traditions sustained them in their struggle against slavery.

double dutch: Typically, a jump-rope game played by girls in which two long jump ropes are simultaneously turned in opposite directions and one or more players jump inside the space made by the two ropes.

dozens, the (playing the dozens, doin' the dozens)**:** An African American form of verbal dueling; a game of ritualized insults. A competitive exchange of insults often addressing women special in the lives of the male combatants. Also known as capping, cracking, dissing, joning, ranking, ribbing, serving, signifying, sounding, snapping, and yo mama.

drum 'n' bass: *See* **jungle**.

dub: Instrumental-track version of a popular vocal track, often placed on the flip side (or B-side) of the single, consisting of bass and drum. Dub versions were initially recorded in response to the growing practice of DJs toasting on microphones at public dances.

dub poetry: Poetry imperfectly described as "reggae poetry." Recited over or inserted on instrumental tracks.

feminism: The theory of the political, economic, and social equality of the sexes; organized activity on behalf of women's rights and interests. *See* **black feminism; womanism**.

feminist hip hop: A style that introduced feminist perspectives to the hip hop tradition. Female rappers address a range of topics, including their verbal skills, relationships, and social and political issues; often includes a black feminist ideology to empower black women. Some artists include MC Lyte, Salt-n-Pepa, and Queen Latifah.

filtering: A mixing technique that is used to compress high-end and mid-range sounds while boosting the bass.

first-wave old school: The **old school** of hip hop culture is distinguished by two periods of development. First-wave old-school hip hop refers to the precommercial era (ca. 1973–1981) and includes the development of the foundational elements and live performances of the art forms at a local level. *See also* **old school** and **second-wave old school**.

Five Percent Nation (5% Nation; the Nation of Gods and Earths)**:** An offshoot of the Nation of Islam and guided by the teachings of Clarence 13X. The Five Percenters, or Five Percent rappers, included artists such as Brand Nubian, C. L. Smooth, Poor Righteous Teachers, and Wu-Tang Clan.

folktale: A characteristically anonymous and timeless tale circulated orally among a people.

footwork (floor rockin'): The fancy leg movements performed on the ground by a **b-boy** and supported by the arms.

four elements of hip hop: The four related artistic movements that originally formed hip hop culture: **graffiti** artists, mobile **DJs**, **breakers** (b-boys, b-girls, breakdancers), and MCs (later known as rappers). *See also* **hip hop**.

freestyle: a. The ability to improvise; for example, making up a verse or a series of dance moves on the spot. b. A brand of hip hop favored by Latino youth in the mid-1980s, also referred to as **Latino freestyle** or Latino hip hop.

freeze: A still pose within the dance sequence performed by **b-boys**.

funk: A musical genre characterized by group singing, complex polyrhythmic structures, percussive instrumental and vocal timbres, and a featured horn section. James Brown and Sly Stone were the godfathers of funk.

fusion: A merging of diverse, distinct, or separate elements into a unified whole; in popular music, combining different styles (as rap and rock were combined to create **rock-rap fusion**).

gang/gang culture: A loosely organized group of individuals who collaborate for social, and sometimes antisocial, reasons. Gangs provide protection to members and help give them status in a larger society that has often denied them a seat at the table. A key element is often engagement in a pattern of conflict with other gangs or society as a whole. Street gangs in urban communities are problematic, but they also provide structure and organization in the chaos of ghetto life. The "Three R's"—reputation, respect, and retaliation—are the glue that holds gangs together.

gangsta rap: A style of rap music distinguished by a raw, edgy, raucous sound and gritty tales about urban life. The lyrics were at times an accurate reflection of reality and at times exaggerated stories of debauchery and outlaw behavior. The most commercially successful form of hip hop music in the late '80s and early '90s, gangsta rap also caused considerable controversy.

gating reverb: Gating reverb is when the audio engineer limits the number of reverberations on a sound and cuts them off abruptly at a certain point as opposed to allowing a natural fadeout of the sound. Phil Collins popularized this technique with his 1981 hit "In the Air Tonight," but the sound faded in popularity by the end of the decade.

gender duels: The tradition of dissing and ritualized insult games between men and women during the golden era of commercial rap music (ca. 1984–1986). UTFO's "Roxanne, Roxanne," Roxanne Shanté's "Roxanne's Revenge," and The Real Roxanne's "The Real Roxanne" popularized ritual verbal dueling between genders (similar to playing the **dozens**) that established the model for the **dis rap**.

genre: A category of artistic, musical, or literary composition characterized by a particular style, form, or content. Rap music as a genre developed numerous styles and themes.

G-Funk: A brand of hip hop music created by Dr. Dre, Warren G, and Above the Law with a sound that is marked by piercing synthesizers, slow grooves, deep bass, and, occasionally, generic backing deep-vocals. Lyrics are typically **gangsta**.

glissando: A sliding movement from one pitch to another.

golden era rap: *See* **new school**.

gospel rap (Christian rap; gospel, Christian, or holy hip hop**):** The fusion of contemporary gospel and hip hop elements. Integrates gospel lyrics and Christian religious themes with hip hop lyrical rhymes and beats to create inspirational songs of faith. Artists include Gospel Gangstaz and DC Talk.

gospel style: Improvised and melismatic vocal style characterized by a strained, full-throated sound, often pushed to guttural shrieks and rasps suited to the extremes of emotion-laden lyrics. Vocal timbres extend from lyrical to percussive, and syncopated polyrhythms are accentuated with heavy, often hand-clapped accents on beats 2 and 4.

graffiti: An inscription or drawing made on some public surface (as a subway car or wall); a way to pass on unconventional views, mark turf, or make an artful expression. Among hip hop enthusiasts, it has two dominant forms: tagging, a scrawl of someone's name or nickname with a Magic Marker or spray paint; and writing, which is the sophisticated outlaw art form that follows a highly stylized lettering aesthetic, dramatic use of color, and large public surfaces.

griot: An African storyteller-musician. The griot (the more common colonialist French term) or jeli (the indigenous Mande term) is an itinerant poet-musician who is the custodian of his society's historical and cultural knowledge.

groove: The polyrhythmic foundation built on a syncopated bass line that locks with the bass drum pattern and is accompanied by a heavy backbeat (i.e., beats 2 and 4 in 4/4 time).

hardcore: A style of hip hop music marked by confrontation and aggression, whether in the lyrical subject matter, the hard, driving beats, the grating samples, or the production. The musical style of hardcore hip hop is aggressive, polytextured, polyrhythmic, and polysonic. Hardcore rap is tough, streetwise, and intense. Hardcore comprises conscious or nationalist hip hop style as well as **gangsta** and X-rated.

Herculoids/Herculords: The name of Kool Herc's crew (toasters and dancers), sometimes attributed to all his followers. At times, Herc's speakers were referred to as the Herculords and his crew as the Herculoids.

hip hop: Competitive cultural expressions of urban youth, consisting of **graffiti** artists, mobile **DJ**s, **breakers** (b-boys, b-girls, breakdancers), and **MCs** (later known as rappers). Hip hop provided both entertainment for inner-city youth and a new forum for competitive, nonviolent gang warfare. In the 1990s, "hip hop" began to be used conterminously with "rap music," or to separate commercial rap from underground or conscious rap, or to mean any **R&B** and pop music that incorporated rapping or DJing production.

hip hop ballad (rap ballad)**:** A song that features softer beats and lyrical themes of love and romance. Some artists that exemplify this style are LL Cool J ("I Need Love," 1987) and Snoop Dogg with Pharrell Williams ("Beautiful," 2003).

human beatbox: *See* **beatboxing**.

hustler: Initially associated with the stock characters in the toasting tradition and foundational to the characters of gangsta rap. There are two types of hustlers: (1) the **trickster** who lives by his wits, constantly scheming and manipulating others; (2) the badman (also, the **baadman**/baaadman) who rules by force and intimidation and feels justified in "beating" the system, making ends meet illegally or outside conventional paths, which often are not available to him (sometimes her, as in the case of Annie Christmas).

inner city: The usually older, economically impoverished, and more densely populated central section of a city.

jazz-rap (jazz–hip hop)**:** A fusion of jazz and hip hop. The rhythms of this style come almost entirely from hip hop, and the samples and sonic textures are drawn mainly from cool jazz, soul-jazz, and hard bop. Many of the artists that popularized this style saw jazz-rap as a more positive alternative to the **hardcore/gangsta** movement taking over rap's mainstream at the dawn of the '90s. Groups like A Tribe Called Quest, the Jungle Brothers, Digable Planets, and Gang Starr were notable early artists.

jeli: *See* **griot**.

jungle: A genre of electronic dance music that came out of London and Bristol, England, in early 1990s. It is marked by massive bass buildups and breakdowns that draw on British rave-scene, breakbeat hardcore techno, and reggae and dancehall. It is sometimes referred to as drum 'n' bass, but some turntablists argue that they are two separate genres.

Latino freestyle (Latin freestyle): A brand of hip hop favored by Latino youth in the mid-1980s; also referred to as Latino hip hop or **freestyle**.

locked-hands: A style of playing piano where both hands play the same rhythms, as though they are locked together.

locking: A West Coast dance created in the 1970s by Los Angeles native Don Campbell—also known as Don Campbellock. The movements incorporate an effect of locking the joints of the arms and body. The term "popping and locking" is often used as an umbrella term for a variety of West Coast dance styles. *See also* **popping**.

mashup (mash-up)**:** A kind of beat-juggling in which a **DJ** creates a piece of music by digitally overlaying instrumental segments with vocal segments from two or more recordings to create a new music collage.

MC (emcee, **rapper**): The percussive lyricist of hip hop. "Rapper's Delight" gave the MC a new name, "rapper," a label that continues to trouble old-schoolers. Also, master of ceremonies or mic controller.

melisma/melismatic: A vocal style that features stretching a single syllable of text over a string of notes.

merry-go-round: Kool Herc's **DJ** technique to put various breakbeats together using two turntables.

message rap (conscious/nationalist rap)**:** In the latter half of the 1980s, message hip hop became a viable form for addressing the problems faced by the black community and suggesting possible ways to solve those problems. The voices of message hip hop in the late 1980s–early 1990s express concern for forging a positive black identity, encouraging unity among African Americans, and liberating African Americans from a long history of oppression. Some examples are Kurtis Blow and KRS-One. *See also* **nationalist hip hop**, **Five Percent Nation**, and **Afrocentric**.

mixtape: A compilation of songs originally recorded onto a cassette tape and sold on the streets to showcase a **DJ**'s skills. The term continues to be used in reference to any compilation of **freestyles**, remixes, instrumentals, or other type of original songs usually released on CD or other digital format.

montuno: An Afro-Cuban rhythm; refers to the fastest and most improvisatory two- or four-bar phrase of repeating loops and interlocking sounds played throughout a piece.

nationalist hip hop (conscious hip hop)**:** Nationalist hip hop is rooted in the ideology of black nationalism and guided by the teachings of Malcolm X and the political activism of the Black Panthers. Nationalist hip hop artists encourage African Americans to be self-sufficient, to learn their history, and to acknowledge their past. Artists include Public Enemy, Paris, Boogie Down Productions, KRS-One, Sister Souljah, the Roots, Mos Def, and Dead Prez.

needle drop/needle dropping: The ability to place the needle in the same spot on the record at will by sight only. Grand Wizard Theodore was recognized as a master at this technique.

neo-soul: An **R&B** style that gained currency in the 1990s with a sound and musical stylings referencing the soul sounds of the 1960s.

nerdcore: The term "nerdcore" was once used for **backpacker** hip hop music before backpacker caught on. It currently refers to a musical scene in its own right, largely surrounding white rappers on the Internet, such as MC Frontalot, who exploit their privileges, expensive schooling, and love for sci-fi.

new jack swing: Teddy Riley was a jazz trumpet player but is perhaps best remembered as producer/songwriter for the new jack swing scene in the 1980s and 1990s. New jack swing artists began incorporating hip hop rhythms, samples, and production techniques into their soulful or funk R&B sound.

new school: Marking the period of rap music's transition from the inner city into mainstream popular culture, becoming more musically and culturally diverse. New-school rappers, such as Run-D.M.C. and Boogie Down Productions, kept the beats minimal, expanded lyric themes, and varied traditional rhyming patterns. They occasionally added hard-rock guitars or harder-sounding samples, and replaced live instruments with a battery of synthesized instruments and later samples. They paved the way for Public Enemy, whose edgy, political rhymes and dense, sample-heavy beats were the trailblazing sound of the late '80s and early '90s. Some rap groups, such as N.W.A., responded with **gangsta rap**. N.W.A. adopted Public Enemy's hard aggressive sound but concentrated on tales of violence, crime, and sex. Also known as golden era rap.

old school: Old-school rap is the style of the very first rap artists who emerged from New York City in the late '70s and early '80s. Old school is easily identified by its emphasis on simply having a good time (**party rap**). Aside from the socially conscious material of Grandmaster Flash and Kurtis Blow, which greatly expanded rap's horizons, most old-school rap had the fun, playful flavor of the block parties and dances where it was born. Old-school rap's recorded history begins with two 1979 singles, Fatback's "King Tim III" and the Sugarhill Gang's "Rapper's Delight," although the movement had been taking shape for almost a decade prior. Sugarhill Records quickly became the center for old-school rap, dominating the market until Run-D.M.C. upped the ante in 1983–1984. Their sound and style soon took over the rap world, making old school's party orientation and '70s funk, Latin, and 1960s–1970s **R&B** influences seem outdated. *See also* first-wave and second-wave old school.

Parents Music Resource Center (PMRC): An American organization founded in 1985 whose main concern was to denounce the obscenity and violence of rock and rap music on the grounds of child protection. They encouraged record labels to produce a labeling sticker to warn parents and prevent sales of "obscene" music to minors.

parody: A literary or musical work in which the style of an author or work is closely imitated for comic effect or in ridicule.

participatory culture: A term coined by media scholar Henry Jenkins in the early 1990s. Participatory culture promotes the ways fans can be actively engaged beyond the consumption of popular culture. Fans can participate, perhaps by way of "textual poaching," to co-create or to invent anew the work of an original author, democratizing something that might be perceived as corporate owned as opposed to owned by the folk. In the case of hip hop, "the community" did not help in the composition of songs, but it was integral to the process.

party rap: One of the early forms of commercial/**old-school** rap. Rap music designed to encourage partying, with often comical or upbeat lyrics.

playing the dozens: *See* **dozens, the**.

polyrhythms: The layering of different rhythmic patterns performed simultaneously.

polytextured: The layering of different sound qualities.

popping: A dance term used to describe a stop-start muscle contraction executed with the triceps, forearms, neck, chest, and legs. The dancer tenses and relaxes the muscles in an instant. Originated and developed on the West Coast in the early 1970s. The term "popping and locking" is often used as an umbrella term for a variety of West Coast dance styles. *See also* **locking**.

posse: *See* **crew**.

punch-phrasing: A **DJ** technique in which the DJ rhythmically inserts or "punches" very short segments of sound, such as horn hits or shouts, over another record playing on the other turntable. Born from Grandmaster Flash's **clock theory**.

punk: A mid-1970s genre that returned rock and roll to the basics: three chords and a simple melody, but played louder, faster, and more abrasively. Punk remained as part of the underground music scene in the United States, spawning the hardcore and indie-music scene of the 1980s–1990s (including grunge and rap-metal). Punk bands include artists such as the Ramones, Television, and the Sex Pistols.

quick mix theory: A method attributed to Grandmaster Flash, involving dexterously working one break seamlessly into another; originally, between duplicates of the records.

R&B (rhythm and blues): A name originally used in the late '40s/early '50s to describe African American popular music in general; more specifically, the soul or **funk** recordings of the '60s and '70s.

R&B hip hop: In the 1990s, rap artists began to team up with R&B and **funk** artists and producers and employ the R&B verse-chorus and funk song structure. It evolved in the late '80s, when urban contemporary soul artists began incorporating hip hop rhythms, samples, and production techniques into their sound. Some songs simply had hip hop beats, others had rapped sections and sung choruses. Artists include Bobby Brown, TLC, Heavy D and the Boyz, and Montell Jordan.

rap (rap music): The musical product of inner-city Caribbean, African American, and Latino communities, which were plagued by poverty, community decay, and the proliferation of drugs and gang violence during the late 1960s and early 1970s. A kind of street poetry, rhythmic chanting, or discursive singing that is sometimes improvised and accompanied by a montage of well-known recordings or new music. "Rap" was originally used to describe the art of verbal engagement designed to attract listeners. Rhyming schemes were not necessarily employed. It has become a music industry term used to describe a variety of musical styles usually involving some type of semi-spoken/rhymed lyrics.

rap ballad: *See* **hip hop ballad.**

rap-metal (also, nu-metal or rapcore): Fuses the most aggressive elements of hardcore rap and heavy metal. It became an extremely popular variation of alternative metal during the late '90s and was typically the domain of white musicians and white audiences. Much of rap-metal is performed with cathartic intensity by shout-rapping the lyrics instead of applying the linguistic and rhythmic complexity of traditional rap. Rap-metal always features a rapper as frontman. Limp Bizkit became rap-metal's most popular band during the late '90s, while Rage Against the Machine became its most political.

rock-rap fusion: Golden era artists fused rock with rap music. The production is built on DJ elements like scratching and sampling, minimalistic drum machine beats, hard-hitting rock-guitar solos, and an aggressive, staccato rapping style. Pioneers Run and D.M.C. changed the delivery style from the melodic rapping of the old school to a shout-like rapping style. The Beastie Boys followed and helped rap music cross over into the mainstream markets.

raptivist: A term coined by Harry Allen, a publicist for Public Enemy and music journalist, to describe politically active rappers and their fans.

reputation (rep): One of the **"Three R's" of gang culture.** Refers to the good opinion others hold of a gang member, specifically as a loyal, brave, and dependable warrior.

Reputation is of critical concern to individual gang members, as it reflects on the reputation of the entire gang. This component of gang culture translates, significantly, into the battle-culture ethic of hip hop culture.

respect: One of the **"Three R's" of gang culture**. A gang member must maintain high or special regard in his or her neighborhood, and this respect is sought not only for the individual but for his or her gang, family, and territory. This concept is reflected in the battle culture of **b-boys** and **MCs** in particular.

retaliation: One of the **"Three R's" of gang culture**. Retaliation, or revenge, is not only warranted, it is expected to keep the reputation of the insulted member and gang intact. The retaliatory strike can take a variety of forms, usually some kind of beatdown or rumble.

riff: A short recurrent melodic or rhythmic phrase.

rock the house (rockin'): An expression that denoted the **DJ** and **MC**'s power and control of crowds; also, to generate positive audible reaction and kinetic response from listeners.

rubato: In a performance, the practice of disregarding strict time in favor of expressive gradations by making small changes to the rhythmic values of individual notes. Italian for "robbed"—meaning some musical time has been stolen.

satire: Involves the use of humor and irony to make a point that is often critical of real situations. Most often used in humorous rap, novelty rap, comic rap, or comedy rap, it is designed to amuse and entertain. Frequently, it is the raps themselves that are humorous, but the music itself—particularly in the case of Biz Markie, arguably the greatest comedy rapper to date—can be clever and funny, as well. Comedy rap flourished in the '80s, when hip hop itself was lighter than it was in the '90s (when **gangsta** rap kept the music somber).

scat/scat singing: Jazz vocal improvisation; singing in which the singer substitutes improvised vocalized syllables for words in a song, imitating a musical instrument.

scratch art: A piece of beat-juggling music created by layering multiple **scratching** sound effects dominating the melodic moments in a sound collage.

scratch/scratching: Rotating and applying pressure to a record back and forth against the needle to create a rhythmic pattern.

second-wave old school: The **old school** of hip hop culture is distinguished by two periods of development. Second-wave old-school hip hop refers to the commercial era (ca. 1979–1983), which focused on rapping over disco beats and was driven by the record industry. At first, live studio musicians replaced records as accompaniment to the rappers, but this changed over time as new technologies were introduced. In the second wave, rap music overshadowed the other elements of hip hop. *See also* **old school** and **first-wave old school**.

signifyin': An African American verbal art genre. Signifyin' refers to a form of commentary that employs double meaning and hidden references, indirect insults exchanged during verbal dueling, or a way of subtly implying indirect messages intended as insults.

snap: An insult.

social clubs: Not all youth commingling self-identified as **gangs**. Many groups, such as the Ghetto Brothers or the Zulus, referred to their organizations as clubs. The social clubs sought alternatives to gang life. While they often designed their organizations after the gangs, they encouraged constructive rather than violent forms of competition through the **four elements of hip hop**. The **Black Power movement** and the ideology of the Black Panther Party influenced many of these early clubs.

social commentary: Rap styles that are sociopolitical, expounding aggressively on the social ills and political issues that adversely affect the critical mass of African Americans and other minorities living in inner-city communities. Themes include critiques of drug abuse, urban decay/neglect, sexism, and racial disharmony.

soul: Soul is a concept, aesthetic, and sensibility that embodies the ideology of the **Black Power movement**. It echoes the voices of college-aged students who rejected the integrationist philosophy of the 1950s civil rights leaders for the nationalist ideology of black nationalism. Soul came to describe a number of R&B-based music styles in the 1960s and is rooted in the musical aesthetic of the **gospel** tradition: gospel vocal and instrumental stylings, emotional intensity, and rhythmic complexity. Different regions of America produced different kinds of soul. In urban centers like New York, Philadelphia, and Chicago, the music concentrated on vocal interplay and smooth productions. In Detroit, Motown concentrated on creating a pop-oriented sound that was informed equally by gospel and 1960s **R&B**. In the South, the music became harder and tougher, relying on syncopated rhythms, raw vocals, and blaring horns. All of these styles formed soul, which ruled the black music charts throughout the '60s and also frequently crossed over into the pop charts. At the end of the '60s, soul began to splinter apart, as artists like James Brown and Sly Stone developed funk. Other examples are James Brown, the Isley Brothers, and Marvin Gaye.

speech as performance: A heightened speech experience; artful communication.

speech as practice: Everyday life communication; getting business done.

spirituality: A sensitivity or attachment to religious values often involving a life of prayer and devotion.

spoken word performance: Contains poems, stories, historical documents and speeches, or sketches as recited by authors and actors. Frequently, performances are enhanced with musical backdrops, but through it all, the emphasis remains on the spoken word.

stop time: An interruption of a rhythmic pattern punctuated with strongly accented rhythms and rests; the effect draws attention to key moments in a guitar solo or sets up an instrumental breakdown.

storytelling: The art of narrative performance.

tag: A guerrilla signature; the flamboyantly written or painted nicknames graffitists used to protect their identity that gave their work an air of personalized mystery.

telegraph/telegraphing (funk guitar technique): Telegraphing resembles the electronic beeping of a telegraph machine; produced by playing a single note or chord in repeated rapid-fire phrases of short, disconnected rhythms to make the instrument perform percussively. The technique can be applied to other pitch instruments and is most common in **funk**.

"Three R's" of gang culture: Term developed by gang scholar Steve Nawojczyk, referring to the three driving factors in gangs: **reputation**, **respect**, and **retaliation**.

toasts/toasting (African American): An African American verbal art genre; praises about an antiauthority, heroic figure; toasts can be an enactment, recasting, or exaggeration of an actual event.

toasts/toasting (Jamaican): A Jamaican verbal art and musical genre; especially, a mobile **DJ**'s rap over an instrumental track. Toasters chanted rhymes that praised dancers and addressed topical concerns. Toasting in the Jamaican tradition draws heavily on African American radio DJs of the 1950–1960s doing African American toasts during their shows.

top rockin': **B-boying** or breaking technique that is performed standing upright. The structure and form of top rockin' came from a variety of sources, including Brooklyn uprocking, tap, the Lindy Hop, salsa, and upright moves from Afro-Cuban, African, and Native American dances. Later in its development, moves from the West Coast, such as boogalooing and **locking**, and martial art films were incorporated into it.

tradition: Tradition is a temporal concept that entangles the past with the present and affects or creates the future. Tradition involves practicing lore and passing it from one generation to the next, from one environment to another. As Amiri Baraka (1966) observed, tradition is the "changing same." Tradition is dynamic, not static, and can adapt to new situations.

transformer scratch: A scratching technique created by tapping a cross-fader to chop up a long scratch sound into smaller scratch pieces, creating a rhythmic stuttering effect. Attributed to DJ Jazzy Jeff and DJ Cash Money of Philadelphia in the 1980s. The name is derived from the sound made by the iconic robots on the popular 1980s television cartoon show *Transformers*.

trickster: A clever character (human or animal in a folk narrative tradition) who is able to manipulate others to get what he or she wants.

turntablism: A musical art form developed by hip hop **DJs** and **scratch** artists. The turntablist transforms the turntable, stylus, mixer, cross-fader, vinyl records, and other DJ tools into an instrument.

underground rap: Underground rap is not a genre. It typically refers to rap music that (1) pushes musical boundaries and has lyrics that are more inventive than **gangsta** clichés, or (2) represents new soundscapes and themes not evident in commercial rap music. The two styles share little regard for mainstream conventions, and they celebrate their independent status.

vamp: Short chord progression that is repeated multiple times in sequence.

verbal competition: Refers to a rapper's boasts about verbal skills, physical attributes, and material possessions, the technological skills of the **DJ**, and their ability to **rock the house** while trading insults among members of the same group (known as posse or crew) or directing insults at other groups.

verbal riddims: Jamaican patois for verbal rhythms.

wah-wah (effect): An electronic musical sound, activated by a pedal, usually on electric guitars, that produces a crying sound.

wigger (wigga): A spiteful slurring of the epithet "white nigger"; the phenomenon of whites identifying with an idea of being black. Like "nigger lover" during the civil rights era, whites who objected to other whites embracing black culture first used the term. In the 1990s it was used by whites who embraced black culture to call out other whites who defamed black culture.

wild style: The complicated multicolored, interlocking letters, connectors, and other ornamentation developed by hip hop graffiti writers of the late 1970s/mid-1980s. Considered the most difficult style of graffiti writing to master.

womanism: Coined by the author and activist Alice Walker to give visibility to the experience of African American and other women of color who are part of the feminist movement but also face other obstacles as a result of race or ethnicity; advocacy of the rights of women, based on a theory of equality. *See* **black feminism** and **feminism**.

writing: The term used by graffitists to describe the style of aerosol graffiti art produced by the hip hop community.

X-rated rap (dirty rap): Hip hop that is focused solely on sex. The fathers of the genre, 2 Live Crew, were one of the leading groups of the groove-heavy Miami bass sound, and that bass-driven groove remained at the foundation of dirty rap. Most dirty rap was simply raunchy **party rap**, designed to keep the party rolling.

REFERENCES

Adorno, Theodore W. 1973/2004. *Philosophy of Modern Music.* Translated by Anne G. Mitchell and Wesley V. Blomster. New York: The Continuum International Publishing Group, Inc.

Alim, H. Samy. 2006. *Roc the Mic Right: The Language of Hip Hop Culture.* New York: Routledge.

Alim, H. Samy, Awad Ibrahim, and Alastair Pennycook, eds. 2009. *Global Linguistic Flows: Hip Hop Cultures, Youth Identities, and the Politics of Language.* New York: Routledge.

Almeida, Bira. 1986. *Capoeira: A Brazilian Art Form: History, Philosophy, and Practice.* Berkeley, CA: North Atlantic Books.

Arnason, H. H. 2003. *History of Modern Art.* Upper Saddle River, NJ: Prentice Hall.

Asante, M. K. Jr. 2008. *It's Bigger Than Hip-Hop: The Rise of the Post-Hip-Hop Generation.* New York: St. Martin's Press.

Atwood, Jane. *Capoeira: A Martial Art and a Cultural Tradition.* New York: Rosen Publishing Group.

@149st website (At149St.com).

Baines, Sally. "Physical Graffiti: Breaking Is Hard to Do." *Village Voice,* April 22, 1981.

Baraka, Amiri. 1968. "1966: The Changing Same (R&B and New Black Music)." In *Black Music,* 180–211. New York: William Morrow & Company, Inc.

Barlow, William. 1998. *Voice Over: The Making of Black Radio.* Philadelphia: Temple University Press.

Bartlett, Andrew. 1994/2004. "Air Shafts, Loudspeakers, and the Hip Hop Sample: Context and the African American Musical Aesthetic." Originally in *African American Review* 28 (4): 639–52. Reprinted in *That's the Joint: The Hip Hop Studies Reader,* edited by Murray Forman and Mark Anthony Neal. Routledge, 393–406.

Bennett, Dina. 1998. "Lauryn Hill." Unpublished paper in *Hip-Hop Music and Culture 1974–2000,* by Portia K. Maultsby and Fernando Orejuela. https://www.indiana.edu/~hiphop/

Berman, Eric. "The Godfathers of Rap: The rise and fall of the first heroes of hip-hop." *Rolling Stone Magazine* Issue 672/3 December 23, 1993–January 6, 1994.

Bogdanov, Vladimir, Chris Woodstra, Stephen Thomas Erlewine, and John Bush. 2003. *All Music Guide: The Definitive Guide to Rap and Hip-Hop.* San Francisco: Backbeat Books.

Bozza, Anthony. 2003. *Whatever You Say I Am: The Life and Times of Eminem.* London: Bantam Press.

Brewer, J. Mason. 1968. "A Harlem Jive Spiel [by Dan Burley]." In *American Negro Folklore,* 284. Chicago: Quadrangle Books.

Brown, Adrienne. 2012. "Drive Slow: Rehearing Hip Hop Automotivity." *Journal of Popular Music Studies* 24 (3): 265–75.

Bryant, Jerry H. 2003. *"Born in a Mighty Bad Land": The Violent Man in African American Folklore and Fiction.* Bloomington, IN: Indiana University Press.

Budman, Richard. "Interview with Nile Rodgers During Canadian Music Week in 2007." Uploaded by POPBOXTV on March 2, 2008. Produced by Richard Budman and John Bortolotti and archived in Budman's YouTube page, POPBOXTV (and www .shot7.com).

Burbach, Elizabeth A. 2013. "Hittin' the Streets with the NYC Transformerz." *Voices: The Journal of New York Folklore*, 39 (1–2): 32–35.

Butterfield, Fox. "On New York Walls, the Fading of Graffiti." *New York Times*, May 6, 1988.

Carson, E. Ann, and William J. Sabol. 2012. "Prisoners in 2011." *BJS [Bureau of Justice Statistics] Bulletin.* U.S. Department of Justice, Office of Justice Programs, Bureau of Justice Statistics. December 2012, NCJ 239808. Accessed on August 30, 2013. http:// www.bjs.gov/content/pub/pdf/p11.pdf

Castleman, Craig. 1999. *Getting Up: Subway Graffiti.* Cambridge, MA: MIT Press.

Chang, Jeff. 2005. *Can't Stop, Won't Stop: A History of the Hip-Hop Generation.* New York: Picador Press.

———, ed. 2006. *Total Chaos: The Art and Aesthetics of Hip-Hop.* New York: Basic Books. **Charles, Don Hogan.** "'Taki 183' Spawns Pen Pals." *New York Times*, July 21, 1971.

Charry, Eric, ed. 2012. *Hip Hop Africa: New African Music in a Globalizing World.* Bloomington, IN: Indiana University Press. **Checkoway, Laura.** 2008. "Inside 'The Miseducation of Lauryn Hill': Lawsuits, Grammys, and a Tiny Attic Studio in New Jersey; An Oral History of the Hip-Hop Classic on its Tenth Anniversary." *Rolling Stone Magazine Online*, August 26, 2008. http://www.rollingstone.com/music/news/ inside-the-miseducation-of-lauryn-hill-20080826. Accessed on July 25, 2013.

Cobb, William Jelani. 2007. *To the Break of Dawn: A Freestyle on the Hip-Hop Aesthetic.* New York: New York University Press.

Coker, Hodari Cheo. 1999. "N.W.A." In *The "Vibe" History of Hip Hop* edited by Alan Light. 251–253, 257–263. New York: Three Rivers Press.

Coleman, Brian. 2007. *Check the Technique: Liner Notes for Hip-Hop Junkies.* Foreword by Ahmir "?uestlove" Thompson. New York: Villard Books.

Coleridge, Samuel. 1898. *The Rime of the Ancient Mariner.* Edited, with introduction and notes, by Lincoln R. Gibbs. Boston: Ginn & Company Publishers.

Collins, Patricia Hill. 2006. *From Black Power to Hip-Hop: Racism, Nationalism, and Feminism.* Philadelphia: Temple University Press.

Condry, Ian. 2006. *Hip-Hop Japan: Rap and the Paths of Cultural Globalization.* Durham, NC: Duke University Press.

Conyers, James L. 2001. *African American Jazz and Rap: Social and Philosophical Examinations of Black Expressive Behavior.* Jefferson, NC: McFarland.

Coughlin, Brenda C., and Sudhir Alladi Venkatesh. 2003. "The Urban Street Gang After 1970." *Annual Review of Sociology* 29: 41–64

Coughtry, Jay. 1981. *The Notorious Triangle: Rhode Island and the African Slave Trade 1700–1807*. Philadelphia: Temple University Press.

Crenshaw, Kimberle. 1991. "Beyond Racism and Misogyny: Black Feminism and 2 Live Crew." *Boston Review* 16 (6): 6, 30–33.

DeFrantz, Thomas F. 2004. "The Black Beat Made Visible: Hip Hop Dance and Body Power. In *Of the Presence of the Body: Essays on Dance and Performance*, edited by Andre Lepecki, 64–81. Middletown, CT: Wesleyan University Press.

Demers, Joanna. 2003. "Sampling the 1970s in Hip-Hop." *Popular Music* 22 (1): 41–56.

Desch-Obi, T. J. 2002. "Combat and the Crossing of the *Kalunga*." In *Central Africans and the Cultural Transformations in the American Diaspora*, edited by Linda M. Heywood, 353–70. Cambridge: Cambridge University Press.

Dimitriadis, Greg. 2001. *Performing Identity/Performing Culture: Hip-Hop as Text, Pedagogy, and Lived Practice*. Oxford: Peter Lang.

Durden, Moncell, dir. 2009. *History and Concept of Hip-Hop Dance: The Street Culture that Became a Global Expression*. DVD. Dancetime Publications.

DXT. "The Hip-Hop DJ." From the Rock and Roll Hall of Fame website. https://web.archive.org/web/20100112231847/http://www.rockhall.com/exhibitpast/hip-hop-dj/. Accessed on November 28, 2007.

Dyson, Michael Eric. 1996. *Between God and Gangsta Rap: Bearing Witness to Black Culture*. New York: Oxford University Press.

_____. 2001. *Holler If You Hear Me: Searching for Tupac Shakur*. New York: Basic Civitas Books.

Edwards, Paul. 2009. *How to Rap: The Art and Science of the Hip-Hop MC*. Chicago: Chicago Review Press.

Entel, Nicolas, dir. 2001. *Hip Hop Shop*. DVD. Producers: Jellybean Benítez, Laurie Friedman, and Shelagh Saunders. Koch Vision.

Eure, Joseph D. 1991. *Nation Conscious Rap*. New York: PC International Press.

Fernando, S. H. Jr. 1994. *The New Beats: Exploring the Music, Culture, and Attitudes of Hip Hop*. New York: Anchor Books Doubleday.

_____. 1999. "Back in the Day: 1975–1979." In *The "Vibe" History of Hip Hop*, edited by Alan Light, 3–15, 18–21. New York: Three Rivers Press.

Finlayson, Angus. 2010. "The History of Sugar Hill Records: Keith Leblanc Interviewed." *Quietus*, July 21, 2010. http://thequietus.com/articles/04669-keith-leblanc-interview-sugar-hill. Accessed on March 4, 2014.

Flores, Juan. 2000. *From Bomba to Hip Hop: Puerto Rican Culture and Latino Identity*. New York: Columbia University Press.

Ford, Robert J. 1979. "B-Beats Bombarding Bronx: Mobile DJ Starts Something with Oldie R&B Disks." *Billboard* 41(2): 65.

Forman, Murray. 2002. *The 'Hood Comes First: Race, Space, and Place in Rap and Hip Hop*. Middletown, CT: Wesleyan University Press.

Fricke, Jim, and Charlie Ahearn, eds. 2002. *Yes Yes Y'all: The Experience Music Project Oral History of Hip Hop's First Decade*. Introduction by Nelson George. Cambridge, MA: Da Capo Press.

Fried, Carrie B. 1999. "Who'd Afraid of Rap: Differential Reactions to Music Lyrics." *Journal of Applied Social Psychology*. 29 (4): 705–21.

Fu-Kiau, Kimbwandènde Kia Bunseki. 2001. *African Cosmology of the Bantu-Kongo*. 2nd ed. New York: Athelia Henrietta Press.

Garofalo, Reebee. 2008. *Rockin' Out: Popular Music in the U.S.A.* 4th ed. Upper Saddle River, NJ: Pearson–Prentice Hall.

Gastman, Roger, and Caleb Neelon. 2010. *The History of American Graffiti*. New York: Harper Design.

Gates, Henry Louis Jr. 1988. *The Signifying Monkey: A Theory of African-American Literary Criticism*. New York: Oxford University Press.

––––––. 1990. "Op-Ed: 2 Live Crew, Decoded." *New York Times*, Tuesday, June 19.

Gaunt, Kyra. 2006. *The Games Black Girls Play: From Double-Dutch to Hip-Hop*. New York: New York University Press.

George, Nelson. 1993/2004. "Hip-Hop's Founding Fathers Speak the Truth." Originally printed in *The Source* 50 (November 1993): 44–50. Reprinted in *That's the Joint: The Hip-Hop Studies Reader*, edited by Murray Forman and Mark Anthony Neal, 45–55. New York: Routledge.

––––––. 1998. *Hip Hop America*. New York: Penguin.

Giddens, Anthony. 1994. *Beyond Left and Right: The Future of Radical Politics*. Cambridge: Polity.

Gilroy, Paul. 1993. *The Black Atlantic: Modernity and Double-Consciousness*. London: Verso.

Goldstein, Richard. 1980. "In Praise of Graffiti." *Village Voice*, December 24, 1980.

Gonzales, Evelyn. 2003. *The Bronx*. New York: Columbia University Press.

Gonzales, Michael A. 2008. "The Holy House of Hip-Hop." *New York Magazine*, September 28, 2008. http://nymag.com/anniversary/40th/50665/. Accessed on December 2, 2010.

––––––. 2012. "Coke La Rock: The Bronx's Unsung Hero Has the Distinction of Being Hip-Hop's First Rapper." *Wax Poetics* 51: 116–18.

Gosa, Travis L. 2009. "Hip-Hop Politics, Activism, and the Future of Hip-Hop." *Journal of Popular Music Studies*. 22 (2): 240–46.

Gottschild, Brenda Dixon. 1999. "Pure Spirit and Sheer Joy." *Dance Magazine* 73 (August): 60–63.

Grandmaster Caz. "The MC." From the Rock and Roll Hall of Fame website. https://web.archive.org/web/20100112232947/http://www.rockhall.com/exhibitpast/the-mc/ Accessed on November 28, 2007.

Grandmaster Flash and David Ritz. 2008. *The Adventures of Grandmaster Flash: My Life, My Beats.* New York: Random House.

Gross, Terry. 2002. "DJ and Hip-Hop Forefather Grandmaster Flash." Interview with Grandmaster Flash on *Fresh Air from WHYY.* Philadelphia, PA. Originally aired July 8, 2002.

_____. 2005. "Kool Herc: A Founding Father of Hip Hop." Interview with Kool Herc on *Fresh Air from WHYY.* Philadelphia, PA. Originally aired March 30, 2005.

Hager, Steven. "Afrika Bambaataa's Hip Hop." *Village Voice,* September 21, 1982.

_____. 1984. *Hip Hop: The Illustrated History of Break Dancing, Rap Music and Graffiti.* New York: St. Martin's Press.

_____. 2010. "Hip Hop Interviews: Coke La Rock, Hip Hop's First MC." http://www.youtube.com/watch?v=Hqi-_g894ss&list=PLFBA03C007B40AC42. Accessed on August 8, 2012.

_____. 2010. "Hip Hop Interviews: Birth of Scratch with Grand Wizard Theodore (at the 23rd Cannabis Cup)." http://www.youtube.com/watch?v=4-JBa6w0OHI&list=PLFBA03C007B40AC42. Accessed on August 8, 2012.

_____. 2010. "Hip Hop Interviews: Origins of Hip hop with Busy Bee Starski (at the 23rd Cannabis Cup)." http://www.youtube.com/watch?v=a8RXefG0Pbc&list=PLFBA03C007B40AC42. Accessed on August 8, 2012.

_____. 2010. "Hip Hop Interviews: Stay High 49." http://www.youtube.com/watch?v=6zFg1BABSkY&list=PLFBA03C007B40AC42. Accessed on August 8, 2012.

_____. 2010. "Hip Hop Interviews: A Master of Wild Style Named Dome (at the 23rd Cannabis Cup)." http://www.youtube.com/watch?v=sB4Jg3y1tSI&list=PLFBA03C007B40AC42. Accessed on August 8, 2012.

_____. 2010. "Hip Hop Interviews: Grandmaster Flash and the Wheels of Steel (at the 23rd Cannabis Cup)." http://www.youtube.com/watch?v=bho3-YsRYaM&list=PLFBA03C007B40AC42. Accessed on August 8, 2012.

Hale, Thomas A. 1999. *Griots and Griottes: Masters of Words and Music.* Bloomington, IN: Indiana University Press.

Hampton, Dream. 1999. "Bad Boy." In *The "Vibe" History of Hip Hop,* edited by Alan Light, 339–50. New York: Three Rivers Press.

Harrison, Anthony Kwame. 2009. *Hip Hop Underground: The Integrity and Ethics of Racial Identification.* Philadelphia: Temple University Press.

Haskins, James. 1974. *Street Gangs: Yesterday and Today.* New York: Hastings House.

Haugen, Jason D. 2003. "'Unladylike Divas': Language, Gender, and Female Gangsta Rappers." *Popular Music and Society* 26 (4): 429–44.

Hearne, John and Rex M. Nettleford. 1963. *Our Heritage.* Mona, Jamaica: University of West Indies.

Henderson, Errol A. 1996. "Black Nationalism and Rap Music." *Journal of Black Studies* 26 (3): 308–39.

Hermes, Will. "All Rise for the National Anthem of Hip Hop." *New York Times*. October 29, 2006. http://www.nytimes.com/2006/10/29/arts/music/29herm.html?pagewanted=1&_r=0

Herzog, Kenny. 2010. "The Latin Implosion: Freestyle's Mix of Rap and Dance Hit Hard Then Fell into Obscurity." *Waxpoetics* 41 (May/June): 56–62.

The History of Rock and Roll. 1995/2004. Time-Life Video. DVD.

Holloway, Joseph E. 2005. "The Origins of African American Culture." In *Africanisms in American Culture*, edited by Joseph E. Holloway, 18–38. Bloomington, IN: Indiana University Press.

Hughes, Langston, and Arna Bontemps, eds. 1958. *The Book of Negro Folklore*. New York: Dodd, Mead & Company.

Israel, dir. 2002. *The Freshest Kids: A History of the B-Boy*. DVD. Producers: Casey Suchan, Eric Brenner, and Quincy Jones III. Image Entertainment.

Jackson, Bruce. 1974. *"Get Your Ass in the Water and Swim Like Me": African-American Narrative Poetry from the Oral Tradition*. Cambridge: Harvard University Press.

Jamison, Laura. 1999. "Ladies First." In *The "Vibe" History of Hip Hop*, edited by Alan Light, 177–86. New York: Three Rivers Press.

Jenkins, Henry. 1992. *Textual Poachers: Television Fans and Participatory Culture*. New York: Routledge.

Jonnes, Jill. 2002. *South Bronx Rising: The Rise, Fall, and Resurrection of an American City*. New York: Fordham University Press.

Katz, Mark. 2012. *Groove Music: The Art and Culture of the Hip-Hop DJ*. New York: Oxford University Press.

Keyes, Cheryl. 2004. *Rap Music and Street Consciousness*. Champaign, IL: University of Illinois Press.

Kitwana, Bakari. 1994. *The Rap on Gangsta Rap: Who Run It? Gangsta Rap and Visions of Black Violence*. Chicago: Third World Press.

———. 2002. *The Hip Hop Generation: Young Blacks and the Crisis in African American Culture*. New York: Basic Civitas Books.

———. 2005. *Why White Kids Love Hip-Hop: Wankstas, Wiggers, Wannabes, and the Reality of Race in America*. New York: Basic Civitas Books.

Krims, Adam. 2000. *Rap Music and the Poetics of Identity*. Cambridge: Cambridge University Press.

LaBoskey, Sara. 2001. "Getting Off: Portrayals of Masculinity in Hip Hop Dance in Film." *Dance Research Journal* 33 (2): 112–20.

Laó-Montes, Agustín, and Arlene Dávila. 2001. *Mambo Montage: The Latinization of New York*. New York: Columbia University Press.

Leland, John, and Steve Stein. 1988. "What It Is." *Village Voice* (Hip Hop Nation Special Section, 26–30), January 19, 1988.

Levine, Richard. 1987. "M.T.A. Won't Charge 10 in Michael Stewart Case." *New York Times*, March 28, 1987.

Lévi-Strauss, Claude. 1978. *Myth and Meaning.* New York: Schocken Books.

Lomax, Alan. 1993. *The Land Where the Blues Began.* New York: Pantheon Books.

Lowe, Richard, dir. 2004. *And You Don't Stop: 30 Years of Hip Hop.* Film. Producer/director: Dana Heinz Perry. Director of photography: Hart Perry. Bring the Noise LLC.

Mao, Jeff. "Mythic Crates: DJ Kool Herc." *Wax Poetics.* Fall 2013 (56): 60–68.

Mao, Jeff. 2013. "Mythic Crates." *Wax Poetics.* 56: 60–68.

Maultsby, Portia K. 1979. "West African Influences and Retentions in U.S. Black Music: A Sociocultural Study." *Western Journal of Black Studies* 3 (3): 197–215.

_____. 2005. "Africanisms in African American Music." In *Africanisms in American Culture,* edited by Joseph Holloway. 2nd ed. Bloomington, IN: Indiana University Press.

Maultsby, Portia K., and Mellonee V. Burnim, eds. 2006. *African American Music: An Introduction.* New York: Routledge.

Mitchell, Tony. 2001. *Global Noise: Rap and Hip Hop Outside the USA.* Middletown, CT: Wesleyan University Press.

Miyakawa, Felicia. 2005. *Five Percenter Rap: God Hop's Music, Message, and Black Muslim Mission.* Bloomington, IN: Indiana University Press.

Morgan, Marcyliena. 2009. *The Real Hip Hop: Battling for Knowledge, Power, and Respect in the LA Underground.* Durham, NC: Duke University Press.

Nawojczyk, Steve. 1997. "Street Gang Dynamic." www.gangwar.com/dynamics.htm. Accessed in summer 2002.

Neal, Mark Anthony, and Murray Forman, eds. *That's the Joint! The Hip-Hop Studies Reader.* New York: Routledge, 2004.

Nelson, Havelock, and Michael A. Gonzalez. 1991. *Bring the Noise: A Guide to Hip-Hop Culture.* New York: Harmony Books.

Nielson, Erik. 2010. "Can't C Me": Surveillance and Rap Music." *Journal of Black Studies.* 40 (6): 1254–74.

Ntarangwi, Mwenda. 2009. *East African Hip Hop: Youth Culture and Globalization.* Champaign, IL: University of Illinois Press.

Ogbar, Jeffrey Ogbonna Green. 2007. *Hip-Hop Revolution: The Politics of Rap.* Lawrence, KS: University Press of Kansas.

Ogg, Alex, and David Upshal. 1999/2001. *The Hip Hop Years: A History of Rap.* New York: Fromm International.

Osumare, Halifu. 2008. *The Africanist Aesthetic in Global Hip-Hop: Power Moves.* New York: Palgrave Macmillan.

_____. 2012. *The Hiplife in Ghana: West African Indigenization of Hip-Hop.* New York: Palgrave Macmillan.

Oxford Music Online. *Oxford Dictionary of Music Online.* http://www
.oxfordmusiconline.com.

Pabon, Jorge. "Popmaster Fabel." 2006. "Physical Graffiti: The History of Hip-Hop
Dance." In *Total Chaos: The Art and Aesthetics of Hip-Hop*, edited by Jeff Chang. New
York: Basic Books.

Pardue, Derek. 2008. *Ideologies of Marginality in Brazilian Hip Hop.* New York:
Palgrave Macmillan.

Pennycook, Alastair. 2007. "Language, Localization, and the Real: Hip-Hop and
the Global Spread of Authenticity." *Journal of Language, Identity, and Education*
6 (2): 101–15.

Perkins, William Eric. 1996. *Droppin' Science: Critical Essays on Rap Music and Hip
Hop Culture.* Philadelphia: Temple University Press.

Pinn, Anthony B. 2003. *Noise and Spirit: The Religious and Spiritual Sensibilities of
Rap Music.* New York: New York University Press.

Potter, Russell A. 1995. *Spectacular Vernaculars: Hip Hop and the Politics of
Postmodernism.* Albany: State University of New York Press.

Quinn, Eithne. 2005. *Nuthin' but a "G" Thang: The Culture and Commerce of Gangsta
Rap.* New York: Columbia University Press.

Rajakumar, Mohanalakshmi. 2012. *Hip Hop Dance.* Santa Barbara, CA: Greenwood.

Rivera, Raquel Z. 2003. *New York Ricans from the Hip Hop Zone.* New York: Palgrave
Macmillan.

Ro, Ronin. 1996. *Gangsta: Merchandizing the Rhymes of Violence.* New York:
St. Martin's Press.

Roberts, John W. 1995. *From Hucklebuck to Hip Hop: Social Dance in the
African-American Community in Philadelphia.* Philadelphia: Odunde.

Rose, Tricia. 1994. "A Style Nobody Can Deal With: Politics, Style and the Postindus-
trial City in Hip-Hop." In *Microphone Fiends: Youth Music and Youth Culture*, edited
by Andrew Ross and Tricia Rose, 71–88. London: Routledge.

———. 1994. *Black Noise: Rap Music and Black Culture in Contemporary America.*
Hanover, NH: Wesleyan University Press, published by University Press of New England.

———. 2008. *The Hip Hop Wars: What We Talk About When We Talk About Hip-
Hop—and Why It Matters.* New York: Basic Civitas Books.

Roth, Molly. 2006. "*Ma Parole S'achète*: Money and Meaning in Malian *Jeliya*." In *Wari
Matters: Ethnographic Explorations of Money in the Mande World*, edited by Stephen
Wooten, 116–34. London: Global.

Sanchez, Ivan, and Luis Cedeño. 2009. *It's Just Begun: The Epic Journey of DJ Disco
Wiz, Hip Hop's First Latino DJ.* New York: Miss Rosen Editions.

Sanneh, Kelefa. "Rapping About Rappin': The Rise and Fall of Hip-Hop Tradition."
In *This Is Pop*, edited by Eric Weisbard, 223–34. Cambridge: Harvard University Press.

Schloss, Joseph G. 2004. *Making Beats: The Art of Sample-Based Hip-Hop.* Middletown,
CT: Wesleyan University Press.

_____. 2006. "'Like Old Folk Songs Handed Down from Generation to Generation': History, Canon, and Community in B-Boy Culture." *Ethnomusicology* 50 (3): 411–32.

_____. 2009. *Foundation.* New York: Oxford University Press.

Schneider, Eric C. 1999. *Vampires, Dragons, and Egyptian Kings: Youth Gangs in Postwar New York.* Princeton, NJ: Princeton University Press.

Sexton, Adam, ed. 1995. *Rap on Rap: Straight-Up Talk on Hip-Hop Culture.* New York: Delta.

Sharma, Nitasha Tamar. 2010. *Hip Hop Desis: South Asian Americans, Blackness, and a Global Race Consciousness.* Durham, NC: Duke University Press.

Shelemay, Kay Kaufman. 2011. "Musical Communities: Rethinking the Collective in Music." Journal of the American Musicological Society 64 (2): 349–90.

Sher, Sheri. 2008. *Mercedes Ladies.* New York: Dafina Publishing.

Silver, Tony, dir. 1984/2003. *Style Wars.* Documentary film. Plexifilm Group.

Smith, William E. 2005. *Hip Hop as Performance and Ritual: Biography and Ethnography in Underground Hip Hop.* Washington, DC: CLS Publications.

Solt, Andrew. 1995. *The History of Rock 'n' Roll: Up from the Underground.* Time-Life Video and Television/Warner Home Video.

Stewart, Jack. 2009. *Graffiti Kings: New York Mass Transit Art of the 1970s.* New York: Abrams.

stic.man. 2005. *The Art of Emcee-ing.* Atlanta, GA: Boss Up, Inc.

Sullivan, Randall. 2002. *LAbyrinth: A Detective Investigates the Murders of Tupac Shakur and Notorious B.I.G., the Implications of Death Row Records' Suge Knight, and the Origins of the Los Angeles Police Scandal.* New York: Atlantic Monthly Press.

Szwed, John F. 1995. "All That Beef, and Symbolic Action, Too! Notes on the Occasion of the Banning of 2 Live Crew's 'As Nasty as They Wanna Be'." In *Field of Folklore: Essays in Honor of Kenneth S. Goldstein*, edited by Roger D. Abrahams, 279–86. Bloomington, IN: Trickster Press.

Tanz, Jason. 2007. *Other People's Property: A Shadow History of Hip-Hop in White America.* New York: Bloomsbury.

Terkourafi, Marina. 2012. *The Languages of Global Hip Hop.* New York: Bloomsbury Academic.

Terrell, Tom. 1999. "The Second Wave: 1980–1983." In *The 'Vibe' History of Hip Hop*, edited by Alan Light, 43–52. New York: Three Rivers Press.

Tompkins, Dave. 2010. *How to Wreck a Nice Beach: The Vocoder from World War II to Hip-Hop; The Machine Speaks.* Brooklyn, NY: Melville House.

Toop, David. 2000. *Rap Attack 3.* London: Serpent's Tail.

Ultan, Lloyd. 1993. *The Bronx in the Frontier Era.* Dubuque, IA: Kendall/Hunt Publishing Company.

Walker, Sheila S. 2001. *African Roots/American Cultures: Africa in the Creation of the Americas.* Lanham, MD: Rowman & Littlefield Publishers.

Watkins, S. Craig. 2005. *Hip-Hop Matters: Politics, Popular Culture, and the Struggle for the Soul Movement.* Boston: Beacon Press.

Weis, Gary, dir. 1979. *80 Blocks from Tiffany's.* Documentary film. Pacific Arts.

Weiss, Brad. 2009. *Dreams and Hip Hop Barbershops: Global Fantasy in Urban Tanzania.* Bloomington, IN: Indiana University Press.

White, Armond. 2002. *Rebel for the Hell of It: The Life of Tupac Shakur.* Foreword by S. H. Fernando. Cambridge, MA: Da Capo Press.

Williams, Justin A. 2010. "The Construction of Jazz Rap as High Art in Hip-Hop Music." *Journal of Musicology* 27 (4): 435–59.

———. 2013. *Rhymin' and Stealin': Musical Borrowing in Hip-Hop.* Ann Arbor, MI: University of Michigan Press.

Wilson, D. Mark. 2007. "Post-Pomo Hip-Hop Homos: Hip-Hop Art, Gay Rappers, and Social Change." *Social Justice* 34 (1): 117–40.

Wilson, Olly. 1983. "Black Music as an Art Form." *Black Music Research Journal* 3: 1–22.

Wood, Joe. 1999. "Native Tongues: A Family Affair." In *The "Vibe" History of Hip Hop,* edited by Alan Light, 187–200. New York: Three Rivers Press.

INDEX

Italicized page numbers indicate a photograph on the designated page.

Printed in the USA/Agawam, MA
January 15, 2020

748217.025